School-Based Audiology

Brad A. Stach, PhD
Editor-in-Chief for Audiology

School-Based Audiology

Edited by
Cynthia McCormick Richburg
Donna Fisher Smiley

PLURAL
PUBLISHING
INC.

SAN DIEGO
OXFORD
BRISBANE

5521 Ruffin Road
San Diego, CA 92123

e-mail: info@pluralpublishing.com
Web site: http://www.pluralpublishing.com

49 Bath Street
Abingdon, Oxfordshire OX14 1EA
United Kingdom

FSC
www.fsc.org

MIX

Paper from
responsible sources

FSC® C011935

Typeset in 10½/13 Garamond by Flanagan's Publishing Services, Inc.
Printed in the United States of America by McNaughton and Gunn

Library of Congress Cataloging-in-Publication Data

Richburg, Cynthia McCormick, 1966-
  School-based audiology / Cynthia McCormick Richburg and Donna Fisher Smiley.
     p. ; cm.
  Includes bibliographical references and index.
  ISBN-13: 978-1-59756-385-7 (alk. paper)
  ISBN-10: 1-59756-385-4 (alk. paper)
  I. Smiley, Donna Fisher, 1966- II. Title.
  [DNLM: 1. Hearing Disorders—diagnosis. 2. Adolescent. 3. Audiology—organization
& administration. 4. Child. 5. Mass Screening--methods. 6. Rehabilitation of Hearing
Impaired--methods. 7. School Health Services--organization & administration. WV 271]
  LC-classification not assigned
  617.80071—dc23
                              2011028502

Contents

Foreword

The growth of school-based audiology practice is evident on many fronts, including the increase in the number of AuD programs that are offering coursework in this specialty area. In response to the growing need for textbook options, Cynthia Richburg and Donna Smiley, along with an impressive cast of supporting authors, have captured the essence of school-based audiology, focusing on the useful and real-world aspects of the practice as they are applied to the school setting. As the work of school-based audiologists expands, it is critical that all students in audiology graduate programs have a general understanding of the roles and responsibilities of audiologists in the education setting.

Each chapter of *School-Based Audiology* is designed to provide the necessary content to enable students to grasp basic concepts in school-based audiology practice. The chapters are enhanced with vignettes, which are contributed by practicing educational audiologists. These vignettes describe real-world situations and problems encountered in the audiologists' practices, and they provide the AuD student an "inside" look at what school-based audiologists do every day. The book addresses the educational and audiologic foundations that influenced the development of school-based practices, services such as hearing screening and hearing loss prevention, management of the classroom and the audiol-ogy program, and special topics including cochlear implants, the practice of audiology in schools for the deaf, and auditory processing disorders.

Children and youth with hearing loss need support from both their school-based and personal audiologists. This collaboration is necessary to ensure the best diagnosis and intervention for each student and to promote a successful transition from school to adulthood. As more children are supported with 504 plans (in lieu of Individual Education Programs [IEPs] under special education), all audiologists and other support providers (for example, speech-language pathologists and counselors) must work together. The goal is for these children to be supported fully to participate in their classrooms with their peers and to achieve passing grades. Accommodations that level the playing field appropriately and consistently have to be implemented so that students have this opportunity. Hearing and hearing assistance technology is a critical component of access to communication and instruction for students. Coursework in the application of audiology practice to the education setting assists all AuD students, regardless of future employment preferences, to understand and support the unique needs of children and youth. All audiologists share the responsibility of providing for children and youth with hearing disorders, so that they may achieve their future education and

employment goals and become productive members of their communities.

Cheryl DeConde Johnson
Educational Audiologist, Deaf
Education Consultant, and
Adjunct Faculty Lecturer
ADEvantage Consulting
Leadville, CO

Contributors

Natalie J. Benafield, AuD, CCC-A
Audiologist
Arkansas Children's Hospital
Little Rock, Arkansas
Chapter 8

Brenda L. Beverly, PhD, CCC-SLP
Associate Professor
Department of Speech Pathology and
    Audiology
University of South Alabama
Mobile, Alabama
Chapter 3

Susan J. Brannen, AuD, CCC-A
Chair of Department of Audiology
Monroe 2 Orleans Board of
    Cooperative Services
Spencerport, New York
Chapter 9

Jackie M. Davie, PhD, CCC-A
Associate Professor
Audiology Department
Nova Southeastern University
Fort Lauderdale, Florida
Chapter 5

Dee M. Lance, PhD, CCC-SLP
Associate Professor
Department of Speech-Language
    Pathology
University of Central Arkansas
Conway, Arkansas
Chapter 3

Frank E. Musiek, PhD, CCC-A
Professor, Director of Auditory
    Research
Department of Communication
    Sciences
University of Connecticut
Storrs, Connecticut
Chapter 13

**Cynthia McCormick Richburg, PhD,
CCC-A**
Associate Professor
Indiana University of Pennsylvania
Indiana, Pennsylvania
Chapters 1–2, 4–7, 9–11, 14

Erin C. Schafer, PhD, CCC-A
Associate Professor
Department of Speech and Hearing
    Sciences
University of North Texas
Denton, Texas
Chapter 12

Donna Fisher Smiley, PhD, CCC-A
Audiologist/Coordinator, EARS
    Program
Arkansas Children's Hospital
Little Rock, Arkansas
Chapters 1–2, 4–11, 14

Kathryn Tonkovich, MS, CCC-A
Audiologist
Primary Children's Medical Center
Salt Lake City, Utah
Chapter 11

Jeffrey Weihing, PhD, CCC-A
Assistant Professor
Department of Surgery—Division of
 Communicative Disorders
University of Louisville
Louisville, Kentucky
Chapter 13

Jace Wolfe, PhD, CCC-A
Director of Audiology
Hearts for Hearing Foundation
Oklahoma City, Oklahoma
Chapter 12

To Jim, James, and my parents for their constant support.

CMR

To Henry and Cade for their support and patience.

DFS

SECTION I

Foundations

1

The History of Audiology in the Schools

Cynthia M. Richburg and Donna F. Smiley

OBJECTIVES

By the end of this chapter, the reader will be able to:

1. Identify legislation that provides mandates and assistance for educating children with physical and mental disabilities.
2. Determine how the practice of school-based audiology has evolved from the 1960s to the present.
3. Identify and define terminology brought about by federal legislation and used in school-based audiology.

INTRODUCTION

One cannot enter the world of educational, or school-based, audiology without some knowledge about how this specialty area has evolved into the form we know today. It may be hard to believe that children born with hearing impairments once were treated as if they were mentally deficient and were either not educated, or educated separately from children with no hearing impairment. This negative treatment of children with hearing impairment might continue to exist today had it not been for progressive legislation and policies being established by governmental agencies, and the hard work and perseverance of many individuals. Knowing where we once stood and what it took to get where we currently are should make us better appreciate the responsibilities and job descriptions of audiologists working in school settings today.

Legislative Terminology

Audiologists who plan to work in an educational environment need to understand legislation that mandates audiological services provided in schools. Having a basic knowledge of governmental operations and terminology is useful for reading and understanding this legislation. In the United States, Congress passes laws. Each law is then given to an appropriate federal agency, which is assigned the task of developing regulations. Regulations are meant to provide instructions for how to go about enforcing the laws. Therefore, when a law passed by Congress pertains to education, the federal agency that develops regulations for enforcing that law is the federal Department of Education. These regulations are public record, and they are published daily in the *Federal Register* (http://www.whitehouse.gov/omb/fedreg/). The purpose of publishing regulations is to obtain reactions and concerns from the general public. Once the Department of Education has obtained public input regarding a regulation, the final ruling is published in the *Code of Federal Regulations* (CFR). All regulations, not just those pertaining to education, are contained within the CFR and divided into 50 titles. Each title is divided into chapters, and each chapter is divided into parts and sections. The title that pertains to educational regulations is known as *Title 34*.

With this knowledge, one is able to read citations or locate regulations mentioned in articles and textbooks. For example, 34 CFR 300.6[b] would be read as "Title 34, Chapter 300, Part 6, Section b," and pertains to educational assistive technology services (Adapted from English, 1995, pp. 2–3).

AUDIOLOGY SERVICES IN THE SCHOOLS BEFORE PUBLIC LAW 94-142

Early federal legislation supporting improved educational programming and services for school children with disabilities was essentially nonexistent until the 1950s and 1960s. The Teachers of the Deaf Act of 1961 (PL 87-276) was one of the first acts focused on persons with hearing impairments. This act funded training for instructional personnel working with children who were deaf or hard of hearing. Two additional acts, both enacted in 1965, provided states with direct grant assistance to help educate children with disabilities (the Elementary and Secondary Education Act of 1965 [PL 89-10] and the Elementary and Secondary Education Amendments of 1966 [PL 89-313]). These acts, along with several others, were crucial in providing opportunities for children with disabilities and their families.

The beginnings of audiology practices in the schools can be traced back to the mid-1960s, when the Joint Committee on Audiology and Education of the Deaf, chaired by Edgar Lowell, sponsored a research project and wrote a training manual entitled, "Audiology and Education of the Deaf" (1965). The two-year research project, which sent five different questionnaires to audiologists, teachers of the deaf, schools for the deaf, and speech and hearing centers, was intended to change the behaviors of audiologists and teachers of the deaf to "improve services to deaf people through fuller utilization of the skills that both professions can potentially bring to bear on that task" (p. i). The questionnaires were sent out to determine what audiological services were being provided in educational programs for the deaf and in speech and hearing centers throughout the country. The questionnaires were designed to assess the amount of audiology subject matter that was being provided in teacher of the deaf training programs and the amount of education subject matter that was being provided in audiology training programs. Finally, the questionnaires were written to examine the attitudes of audiologists and teachers toward their training and toward each other.

The joint committee members concluded that there should be more emphasis on cross-education and training, so that audiologists would know more about education and teachers of the deaf would know more about audiology. They also determined that cooperation between these two professional groups was needed to improve audiological services in all facilities. The committee formulated 29 recommendations for improving training and interprofessional relationships, which ultimately were meant to improve services provided to children and adults.

Another important document aimed at improving services for children with hearing impairments was the Babbidge

Report, also published in 1965. This report was the result of work from an advisory committee, led by Homer Babbidge. The U.S. Department of Health, Education, and Welfare commissioned this committee to report on the status of services to students who are deaf and hard of hearing in the United States. The committee determined that there was a dearth of services provided to these children, and it concluded that the general education and preparation for success in life was less than satisfactory, due to basic problems that children who are deaf/hard of hearing have with learning language.

In 1966, with the help of special grant funding from the United States Office of Education, Utah State University (USU) developed a curriculum that spanned 10 quarters of undergraduate and graduate coursework. The curriculum included courses in acoustics, phonetics, anatomy, clinical processes, communication and information theory, counseling, educational technology, electroacoustics, human growth, learning, and linguistics. Graduates of the USU program were expected to exhibit verbal and performance competencies derived from the areas of audiology and speech pathology, education of the hearing impaired, and general professional education. These early graduates typically completed a Master of Science degree in one year.

CHANGES OF THE 1970S

The 1970s were a very productive period in which federal legislation provided the means for better educating children with disabilities. The three laws most discussed in the literature describing school-based audiology in the 1970s include Section 504 of the Rehabilitation Act of 1973, the Education of the Handicapped Amendments of 1974 (Public Law 93-380), and the Education for All Handicapped Children Act of 1975 (Public Law 94-142). These legislative documents are considered to provide the foundation for educational audiology as it is practiced today.

Defining School-Based Audiology: Then and Now

Shortly after developing the Utah State University curriculum and initiating this specialty area, Frederick Berg and Samuel Fletcher (1970) made the first attempt to define educational audiology:

> Educational audiology conceptualizes the characteristics and needs of the hard of hearing child. It seeks for each such child to isolate the educational and audiological parameters of hearing impairment, to identify the communicative deficiencies arising from hearing disability and lack of educational adjustments, and to design and implement an individualized and ongoing program of facilitative support. (p. 41)

That definition by no means describes the depth and breadth to which the specialization of school-based audiology has grown. It is the Educational Audiology Association's position (EAA; 2009) that:

> Educational audiologists are uniquely qualified to facilitate support for students with hearing difficulties in the educational system. In addition to identification of a student's hearing loss, the educational audiologist has knowledge and skills regarding the impact of hearing loss on learning, relevant educational goals and benchmarks, and experience with strategies and technology for support within the classroom for both the student and the teacher. Educational audiology services should be comprehensive, collaborative, and designed to address the student's individual communication, academic, and psychosocial needs. (p. 1)

Find out more about the practice of educational audiology online at http://www.edaud.org. Documents such as *School-Based Audiology Services* (2009), *Recommended Professional Practices of Educational Audiologists* (2009), *Educational Audiology Services Under IDEA* (2010), *Audiology Services Under 504* (2010), and *The Educational Audiologist's Role in EHDI and On-Going Hearing Loss Surveillance in Young Children* (2010) provide detailed information about where the field of educational audiology currently stands.

Section 504 of the Rehabilitation Act of 1973

Section 504 of the Rehabilitation Act of 1973 (PL 93-112) defined "handicapped" individuals, but originated as a civil rights law directed at employing people with disabilities. Through the passing of several amendments, Section 504 now protects the rights of individuals with disabilities in academic and nonacademic (extracurricular) programs that receive federal funding, such as public school districts, institutions of higher education, hospitals, nursing homes, and human service programs. The Act is said to protect the rights of individuals exhibiting visible disabilities, as well as individuals with disabilities that are not apparent. The United States Department of Education maintains an Office for Civil Rights (OCR) with 12 enforcement offices to ensure that the recipients of the federal funds are adhering to the civil rights established in Section 504.

For employment purposes, the Act mandates that qualified persons with disabilities receive "reasonable accommodations" to allow them to perform the essential functions of a job for which they have applied or been hired to perform. "Reasonable accommodations" means that an employer must take reasonable actions to accommodate a person's disability, unless it would cause the employer undue hardship.

That same idea of reasonable accommodations is applied to the classroom with Subpart D of Section 504. A student is eligible for protection under Section 504 if he or she is determined to: (1) have a physical or mental impairment that substantially limits one or more major life activities; or (2) have a record of such an impairment; or (3) be regarded as having such an impairment. A nonexhaustive list of major life activities as defined in Section 504 regulation [34 CFR 104.3(j) (2)(ii)] includes caring for one's self, performing manual tasks, walking, seeing, hearing, speaking, breathing, learning, and working. Section 504 requires that schools (that receive federal funding) provide students with disabilities appropriate educational services designed to meet the student's individual educational needs as adequately as the needs of nondisabled students are met. This includes providing assessments (e.g., hearing evaluations) to determine if a disability is present, providing regular and/or special education programs to students needing them, and supplying related aids and services. It is important to note that, once a student is determined to be eligible for services under IDEA (i.e., needs specially designed instruction), then he or she must have an IEP and will no longer need a Section 504 plan because appropriate accommodations will be listed and carried out under the IEP (Office of Civil Rights, 2009).

Some potentially appropriate accommodations for a student who is deaf/hard of hearing might include preferential seating, a notetaker, and/or captioning for video materials. More information about accommodations is provided in Chapter 8. The OCR's Web page on the US Department of Education's Web site (http://www2 .ed.gov/about/offices/list/ocr/504faq .html) clearly explains the disabilities and services covered under Section 504 for preschool, elementary, secondary, and postsecondary students.

For children whose disability is not adversely affecting their education, but who need accommodations to access their education (the same as their peers), the impact of Section 504 is far reaching. As stated by Johnson, Benson, and Seaton (1997), two groups who benefit from Section 504 include children with mild hearing impairments and children with (central) auditory processing disorders. Children with these milder, less evident, conditions also require services and/or instrumentation to allow them to benefit from and access their education in the same way that their hearing peers do. It also is possible that, as children are identified and receive appropriate intervention earlier, then children with more severe degrees of hearing loss may not require special education services but only accommodations in the regular classroom, provided to them under Section 504.

The Education of the Handicapped Amendments of 1974 (PL 93-380)

Although PL 94-142 is commonly thought of as "the law" by which school-based audiology services were established and mandated, we would be remiss if we did not mention the contributions of the Education of the Handicapped Act of 1970 (PL 91-230), and the more focused contributions of the Education of the Handicapped Act Amendments of 1974 (PL 93-380), signed by then-President, Gerald Ford. PL 93-380 directed the states to develop individual state plans, which were to include time lines for implementation of full educational opportunities for children with disabilities. This law also required that procedural safeguards be used to protect children during identification, assessment, and placement procedures. Those protections included wording stating that testing and evaluation materials could not be discriminatory

in nature (i.e., the materials could not have cultural, racial, or linguistic biases, and tests should be validated on appropriate populations). It was said that Ford cleared the way for "increased Federal spending for the education of handicapped children" with a revised formula for distributing monies (Title I funding), equalizing per capita federal aid among states and local school districts, incorporating a fairer poverty standard, and accounting for population shifts noted since the 1960 Census (Gettings, 1974). Southern states and rural areas of the country were to have received more benefit from this law than large cities and relatively wealthy states. Therefore, federal funding was increased to help states meet the mandates placed on them for educating students with special needs.

The Education for All Handicapped Children Act of 1975 (PL 94-142)

The Education of All Handicapped Children Act (PL 94-142) mandated that all students with handicapping conditions between the ages of 3 and 21 years be afforded a free, appropriate public education (FAPE). It should be noted that under PL 94-142, local school systems were mandated to serve children ages 6 through 17. However, if they also educated nondisabled children in other age groups (i.e., 3 to 5 and 18- to 21-year-olds), then they would need to provide FAPE to children with disabilities in these extended age groups.

Along with FAPE, this piece of legislation provided other very important concepts and terms currently used in educational settings. For example, PL 94-142 (1975) provided for Individualized Education Programs (IEPs) and education in the least restrictive environment (LRE). In addition, the concepts of zero reject, nondiscriminatory assessment, procedural due process, and parental participation were introduced as basic principles in the subchapters of this law. These six basic principles continue today with the Individuals with Disabilities Education Act, or IDEA (PL 101-476, 1990 and subsequent reauthorizations). Therefore, it can be said that PL 94-142 was the precursor to IDEA.

Six Basic Principles of PL 94-142

- Zero Reject/Free Appropriate Public Education
- Nondiscriminatory Assessment
- Procedural Due Process
- Parental Participation
- Least Restrictive Environment
- Individualized Education Programs

Public Law 94-142 (1975) made the first reference to audiology, describing it as a "related service" for special education. A related service, as defined by PL 94-142, is a supportive service designed to enable a child with a disability to receive a free, appropriate public education as described in the individualized education program of the child. In summary, the services provided per the definition of audiology included:

(1) identification of children with hearing loss;

(2) determination of the range, nature, and degree of hearing loss, including referral for medical or other professional attention for the habilitation of hearing;

(3) provision of habilitation activities, such as language habilitation, auditory training, speech reading, (lipreading), hearing evaluation, and speech conservation;

(4) creation and administration of programs for prevention of hearing loss;

(5) counseling and guidance of pupils, parents, and teachers regarding hearing loss; and

(6) determination of the child's need for group and individual amplification, selecting and fitting an appropriate aid, and evaluating the effectiveness of amplification. (CFR 300.12[b])

The definition of audiology has remained essentially the same across the years. The only change in wording has occurred in the last part of the definition (6) where the term "the child's need" has been rephrased to "children's need."

THE INCLUSION OF INFANTS, TODDLERS, AND FAMILIES IN THE 1980S

The 1980s was a period of time in which local and state education agencies, parent groups, and advocacy groups worked together to interpret, amend, and expand previous legislation. The Education of the Handicapped Act Amendments of 1986, or PL 99-457, amended PL 94-142 and mandated services for children from 3 to 5 years of age and established services for infants and toddlers from birth through 2 years of age. (Note: PL 94-142 mandated these only if a state was already providing them to children without disabilities; under PL 99-457 services would be required for children with disabilities *regardless* of whether or not a state was providing them for children without disabilities.) The addition of services for children birth through 2 years was the result of mounting evidence that early intervention services for children with handicapping conditions and developmental delays worked to reduce further delays and eventually higher costs for state and local education agencies. In fact, in Section 671 of this document (i.e., PL 99-457), it states:

The Congress finds that there is an urgent and substantial need:

(1) to enhance the development of handicapped infants and toddlers and to minimize their potential for developmental delay;

(2) to reduce the educational costs to our society, including our Nation's schools, by minimizing the need for special education and related services after handicapped infants and toddlers reach school age;

(3) to minimize the likelihood of institutionalization of handicapped individuals and maximize the potential for their independent living in society; and

(4) to enhance the capacity of families to meet the special needs of their infants and toddlers with handicaps. (p. 2)

Early intervention services were described in this document as developmental services designed to meet a handicapped infant's or toddler's developmental needs in one or more of the following areas: physical development, cognitive development, language and speech development, psychosocial development, or self-help skills. The services were to be provided by "qualified personnel," of which audiologists were listed along with special educators, speech-language pathologists, psychologists, occupational and physical therapists, social workers, nurses, and nutritionists.

These personnel were to work together to develop an individualized family service plan, or IFSP. In Section 677 of this document, it was stated that each infant and toddler with a handicapping condition, along with the child's family, would receive "a multidisciplinary assessment of unique needs and the identification of services appropriate to meet such needs," and "a written individualized family service plan developed by a multidisciplinary team, including the parent or guardian . . . " The IFSP was to be developed and written within a reasonable time after the child's assessment, it was to undergo periodic review, and a detailed description of what the IFSP needed to contain was laid out in Section 677 (d) 1–7 (i.e., the child's present level of development and self-help skills, the family's strengths and weaknesses, the major outcomes expected to be achieved, specific intervention services needed to meet those outcomes, etc.).

THE PROLIFERATION OF LEGISLATION IN THE 1990s

The nineties began with the enactment of the Americans with Disabilities Act of 1990, or ADA. It was viewed by many as the most expansive and comprehensive piece of legislation enacted since PL 94-142. This document replaced the previously used term of "handicapped" with "disability." In its five titles, the ADA defined those covered by its protections and prohibited discrimination in all public and private employment, education, and recreational services, not just those receiving federal funding. It is said that the ADA has more power than Section 504 because it prohibits discrimination on the basis of disability by private entities, as well as by state and local governments. That is, the ADA made it possible for state and local governments, as well as Congress, to be subject to legal action.

Title II, a term commonly heard in the education arena, relates to the operations of elementary and secondary public schools and postsecondary institutions. The ADA mandated that reasonable accommodations were to be provided within the public and work environments for individuals with disabilities, as well as within schools. Although many of us take for granted the accessibilities afforded by the ADA and cannot remember what life was like before these mandates existed, we are reminded that effective communication and accessibility to communication are requirements of the ADA. As professionals in communication sciences and disorders, we should be assisting employers and school districts with taking the steps necessary to ensure that people with hearing loss have access to services and facilities in the same manner as those without hearing loss. We can do that by providing, for example, assistive listening devices (ALDs), qualified interpreters, real-time captioning, hearing aid compatible telephones, telecommunication devices for the deaf (TDD), alerting or warning systems that amplify signals or employ visual or vibrotactile devices, and/or prewritten materials in alternative formats (e.g., symbols or pictures). We also can instruct others to remove visual or acoustic barriers (e.g., poor lighting, unreadable signage, high noise levels, or high reverberation levels), modify policies or practices that are discriminatory in nature, and simply ask those with hearing loss about their needs and what works best for them.

After several amendments to federal legislation, the Individuals with Disabilities Education Act (IDEA) was enacted in 1990. IDEA, or PL 101-476, was the new name given to the Education of the Handicapped Act via the 1990 amendments, and it brought about the idea that children with hearing impairments could be educated in their local schools and not boarded in residential schools, which often were hundreds of miles from their homes. As mentioned earlier, IDEA stated that children with disabilities were to be allowed a free, appropriate public education (FAPE). In addition, it brought about the usage of "people first" language, meaning that "hearing impaired students" were to be referred to as "students with hearing impairment." Part B of this law expanded services to include students with disabilities from ages 18 to 21 years. Under special education services, the law added the concepts of "transition services" and assistive technology. Also, under related services, the law added rehabilitation counseling and social work services. Finally, services and rights were given to children with autism and traumatic brain injury, two groups not previously specified in legislation.

It is important to understand that IDEA is a funding statute. That means that, in order for states to receive funding from the federal government, each state must develop a plan to ensure that the requirements set forth by IDEA are being met. In addition, states have to set up standards for special education personnel, and those standards can be different in each state.

Special education law has been amended six times since the original enactment of PL 94-142. One such amendment was introduced in October of 1991 when Congress passed the Individuals with Disabilities Education Act Amendments, which then was known as PL 102-119. This amendment's primary purpose was reauthorizing the Part H program (which covered infants and toddlers, birth through 2 years of age) and renaming it The Early Intervention Program for Infants and Toddlers with Disabilities (and now it is Part C). This act required an IFSP, instead of an IEP, for children between birth and 3 years of age.

In 1997, amendments to IDEA were made (known as the "Reauthorization of IDEA" or PL 105-17), which challenged educators to improve results for children with disabilities and their families. It also addressed changes needed for increasing parental participation and decreasing the oppositional parent-school relationship seen in the late 1980s and early 1990s.

Although not a legislative act written specifically with children with hearing loss in mind, the Goals 2000: Educate America Act (1994; PL 103-227) developed eight National Education Goals to ensure that children with disabilities were educated to the maximum extent of their capabilities. These eight educational goals can be seen in the box below. Likewise, the Improving America's Schools Act (IASA) of 1994 provided for professional development and listed the skills and proficiencies for service providers,

---

The Eight National Education Goals set forth by *Goals 2000: Educate America Act of 1993* (PL 103-227)

By the year 2000:

1. All children in America will start school ready to learn.
2. The high school graduation rate will increase to at least 90%.
3. All students will leave grades 4, 8, and 12 having demonstrated competency over challenging subject matter including English, mathematics, science, foreign languages, civics and government, economics, the arts, history, and geography. Every school in America will ensure that all students learn to use their minds well, so they may be prepared for responsible citizenship, further learning, and productive employment in our nation's modern economy.
4. Students in the United States will be first in the world in mathematics and science achievement.
5. Every adult American will be literate and will possess the knowledge and skills necessary to compete in a global economy and exercise the rights and responsibilities of citizenship.
6. Every school in the United States will be free of drugs, violence, and the unauthorized presence of firearms and alcohol and will offer a disciplined environment conducive to learning.
7. The nation's teaching force will have access to programs for the continued improvement of their professional skills and the opportunity to acquire the knowledge and skills needed to instruct and prepare all American students for the next century.
8. Every school will promote partnerships that will increase parental involvement and participation in promoting the social, emotional, and academic growth of children.

including those listed as related service providers. Although not explicitly stated in the literature, "Goals 2000" and IASA were probably the driving forces behind the No Child Left Behind Act of 2001, which is discussed in more detail later in this chapter.

Before leaving the 1990s, we would be remiss if we did not mention the "transition movement" and the "inclusion movement." The transition movement came about during reauthorizations of IDEA. It refers to the transitioning of a student with disabilities from high school into the real world, and plans for this process are to be included in the student's IEP. Transitioning includes the idea that functional skills (e.g., shopping, cooking, managing finances, using public transportation, and knowing safety concerns both at home and in the community) need to be learned prior to graduating from high school and living independently away from family members and home.

The inclusion movement came about when advocacy groups, parents, and many professionals became concerned that students with disabilities were being segregated into specialized, self-contained classrooms. The "call for 'inclusion'" of disabled students into general education classrooms was a powerful movement that swept the nation in the 1990s and came about as a result of the IDEA provision that students with disabilities should be educated alongside students without disabilities in their neighborhood schools (Roeser & Downs, 2004, p. 11). See the box below for more information.

THE CONTINUATION OF LEGISLATION AFTER 2000

In January of 2002, President George W. Bush signed into law the No Child Left Behind Act (NCLB) of 2001. This act represents four key principles: (1) stronger accountability for results; (2) greater flexibility for states, school districts, and schools in the use of federal funds; (3) more choices for parents of children from disadvantaged backgrounds; and (4) an emphasis on teaching methods that have been demonstrated to work (U.S.

Inclusion Versus Mainstreaming: They Are NOT the Same

Audiology students should be aware that "inclusion" and "mainstreaming" are *not* synonymous terms, although they have been used interchangeably in the past. Inclusion refers to the concept that students with disabilities deserve to have the same education as their typically developing peers, even if they are not performing anywhere near the level of their peers. These students are in a regular classroom with learning assistants.

The concept of mainstreaming, on the other hand, is based on the fact that students with disabilities may benefit from being in a general education classroom, both academically and socially, and they are usually expected to keep up with the classroom instruction, although some accommodations are allowed.

Department of Education, 2002, p. 9). It placed increased emphasis on reading at a young age, improving the quality of teachers within the United States, learning of English by all students, and providing disadvantaged students with the knowledge and skills needed to succeed. Emphasis was also placed on holding schools accountable for successes and failures of their students. A plan was outlined for testing children in grades 3 through 8 to measure outcomes of success. New vocabulary, such as "highly qualified" teachers, "scientifically based research," and "core academic subjects" were defined, and parents were given the "right to know" about the professional qualifications of their children's teachers. Early in 2010, President Barack Obama's administration put forth a "blueprint" providing incentives for states to adopt academic standards that would allow students to succeed in college and the workplace. Although it is unrealistic to think that all students will "graduate and succeed in college," it will be interesting to see how this new legislation plays out for children with disabilities.

In addition to NCLB legislation, George W. Bush signed into law another reauthorization of IDEA on December 3, 2004 (IDEA, 2004). This reauthorization is known as PL 108-446, the Individuals with Disabilities Education Improvement Act. Although the word "Improvement" is included in this version of the title of IDEA, some sources will refer to this as "IDEIA" and others (such as the U.S. Department of Education, Office of Special Education Programs) have kept the original acronym—IDEA.

Previous versions of IDEA contained language that held public agencies (such as schools) responsible for ensuring that hearing aids worn in school by children

---

The Parts of IDEA 2004

IDEA (2004) is divided into four parts:

- Part A—General Provisions
- Part B—Assistance for Education of All Children with Disabilities (3 to 21 years)
- Part C—Infants and Toddlers with Disabilities (Birth through 2 years)
- Part D—National Activities to Improve Education of Children with Disabilities

Source: http://www.nichcy.org/Laws/IDEA/Pages/Default.aspx

---

with hearing impairments were functioning properly. The 2004 reauthorization continued to contain this requirement but changed the language from "shall ensure" to "must ensure" that these devices are working. The implication here is that schools need to have a plan for checking amplification devices and documenting whether or not they are functioning properly. In addition, they should document what happens when the device/devices are not working (i.e., contact parent, contact school-based audiologist, etc.).

Changes in IDEA 2004 from the previous version (IDEA 1997) included language that set limits on related services for medical devices that are surgically implanted. This includes cochlear implants (and, by default, most likely bone-anchored implants). Schools are not responsible for cochlear implant mapping, maintaining surgically implanted devices, or replacing those devices. However, clarification is offered in the law to ensure that students with surgically implanted devices do receive related services that are deemed necessary by the IEP in order for the student to receive FAPE (e.g., speech-language therapy services, etc). Also, the law states that a public agency (such as a school) is responsible for routine checking of an external component of a surgically implanted device to make sure it is functioning properly (just as a school does for a traditional hearing aid).

To summarize, the accomplishments of IDEA and all of its reauthorizations, the following statements can be made: (1) the majority of children with disabilities are now educated in their local schools in regular classrooms among their peers without disabilities, (2) students with disabilities are graduating from high school and obtaining employment at higher rates than were seen historically, and (3) students with disabilities are enrolling in and attending colleges and universities at higher rates than were seen historically. As of the late 1990s, students with mental and physical disabilities were better off with regards to education and life-skills abilities than they ever had been in the history of the United States.

Several changes in IDEA 2004 simply aligned the special education law with NCLB (2002). The "highly qualified teacher" standards, the definition and application of core academic subjects, and the use of scientifically based research in making decisions about educational strategies were carried over from NCLB and applied in IDEA 2004.

One construct that appeared from terminology in IDEA 2004 was "Response to Intervention," or "RtI." Response to Intervention is a service delivery model that focuses on improving academic achievement with the use of scientifically-based

teaching practices. The model is said to be "designed to assure that all students have access to scientifically based instruction and a system of positive behavior supports within general education" (Johnson, 2007). One of the underlying premises of RtI is that a child may be struggling due to inadequate instruction or curriculum. The idea is that if the problem is detected early enough, and the instructional method and/or the curriculum are appropriately changed, it is possible that the child will be successful without further intervention.

Typically, RtI has three tiers of assistance that increase in intensity. According to a white paper published by the National Association of State Directors of Special Education (NASDSE) and the Council of Administrators of Special Education (CASE) in 2006, the tiered RtI model can be represented as a pyramid as follows:

- Tier I (Foundation)
  - Contains the core curriculum
  - Core curriculum should be effective for 80 to 85% of students
  - The focus of core curriculum is placed on group interventions
  - Group interventions are to be proactive and preventive
  - Core curriculum will reflect the wide variability of student performance and needs across schools.

- Tier II (Mid-Section)
  - These interventions are targeted group interventions
  - These interventions serve approximately 15% of students
  - While in Tier II, students should continue to receive Tier I instruction, as needed.

- Tier III (Tip of Pyramid)
  - These interventions are intensive, individual interventions
  - These interventions serve approximately 5% of students
  - Once students achieve targeted skill levels, the intensity and/or level of support is adjusted
  - While in Tier III, students should continue to receive Tier I and Tier II instruction, as needed.

RtI is not meant to delay the identification of a disability. At any time during the process, if the local education agency or parent thinks that the child should be evaluated for special education, appropriate steps should be taken immediately to begin the process. In the case of students with hearing loss, schools and educators will want to apply the principles of RtI to these students without precluding them from inclusion in special education, if it is appropriate.

To conclude the 2000s, the latest legislative act regarding individuals with disabilities was signed into effect on January 1, 2009 and was named the Americans with Disabilities Act Amendment of 2008, or ADAAA. This new law amended the meaning of "disability" and broadened its interpretation; however, it did not require the Department of Education to amend its Section 504 regulations.

CONCLUSIONS

Audiology students and school-based audiologists are not normally called upon to interpret the law; however, having an understanding and working knowledge of special education law will help audiologists be better informed in the practice of audiology in school settings. Furthermore, using information established in special education regulation may be helpful to audiologists who are trying to advocate for the provision of audiology services in the schools. Using the idea that audiology is a "related service" should assist advocacy initiatives.

To understand the application of the law specifically to students who are deaf/hard of hearing, the reader will need to examine case law as it has been established over the years. For a recent review of case law in the area of students who are deaf/hard of hearing, see Kreisman and John (2010) and Seaton and Johnson (2011).

REFERENCES

Americans with Disabilities Act of 1990, Public Law 101-336, 42, U.S.C. 12101 et seq.: *U.S. Statues at Large, 104,* 327–378 (1991).

Americans with Disabilities Act Amendments Act of 2008, Public Law 110-325.

Babbidge, H. (1965). *Education of the deaf: A report to the Secretary of Health, Education, and Welfare by his Advisory Committee of the Education of the Deaf.* Washington, DC: U.S. Department of Health, Education and Welfare.

Berg, F., & Fletcher, S. (1970). *The hard of hearing child.* New York, NY: Grune and Stratton.

Education for All Handicapped Children Act of 1975, Public Law 94-142, 20, U.S.C. 1401-1461: *U.S. Statutes at Large, 89,* 773–779 (1975).

Education of the Handicapped Act of 1970, Public Law 91-230.

Education of the Handicapped Amendments of 1974, Public Law 93-380.

Education of the Handicapped Act Amendments of 1986, Public Law 99-457, 20. U.S.C. 1400 et seq.: *U.S. Statutes at Large, 100,* 1145–1177 (1986).

Elementary and Secondary Education Acts of 1965, Public Law 89-10.

Elementary and Secondary Education Amendments of 1966, Public Law 89-313.

English, K. M. (1995). *Educational audiology across the lifespan: Serving all learners with hearing impairment*. Baltimore, MD: Paul H. Brookes.

Gettings, R. M. (1974). The Education Amendments of 1974: An analysis of PL 93-380. *Intelligence Report*, pp. 29–32.

Improving America's Schools Act of 1994, Public Law 103-382

Individuals with Disabilities Education Act Amendments of 1991, Public Law 102-119.

Individuals with Disabilities Education Act Amendments of 1997. Pub. L. No. 105-17, 111, Stat. 38 (1997). Codified as amended at 20 U.S.C Section 1400-1485.

Individuals with Disabilities Education Act of 1990 (IDEA), Pub. L No. 101-476, 20. U.S.C. 1400 *et seq.: U.S. Statutes at Large, 104*, 1103–1151 (1990).

Individuals with Disabilities Education Improvement Act of 2004, Pub. L. No. 108-446, 20 U.S.C. §1400 et seq. (2004).

Johnson, C. D. (2007, Spring). RtI: What it is, What it isn't. *Hands and Voices Communicator*, *X*(3), p. 1. Denver, CO: Hands & Voices.

Johnson, C. D., Benson, P. V., & Seaton, J. B. (1997). *Educational audiology handbook*. San Diego, CA: Singular Publishing Group.

Joint Committee on Audiology and Education of the Deaf. (1965). *Audiology and education of the deaf.*

Kreisman, B. M., & John, A. B. (2010). A case law review of the Individuals with Disabilities Education Act for children with hearing loss or auditory processing disorders. *Journal of the American Academy of Audiology, 21*, 426–440.

National Association of State Directors of Special Education. (2006). *Response to Intervention: NASDSE and CASE White Paper on RtI*. Available from http//:www.nasdse.org

No Child Left Behind Act of 2001, Pub. L. 107-110, 20 U.S.C. §6301 et seq. (2001).

Office for Civil Rights. (2009, March 27). Protecting student with disabilities: Frequently asked questions about Section 504 and the education of children with disabilities. Retrieved from http://www2.ed.gov/about/offices/list/ocr/504faq.html#interrelationship

Rehabilitation Act of 1973, Section 504, 29, U.S.C. 794: *U.S. Statutes at Large, 87*, 335–394 (1973).

Roeser, R. J., & Downs, M. P. (2004). *Auditory disorders in school children: The law, identification, remediation* (4th ed.). New York, NY: Thieme.

Seaton, J. B., & Johnson, C. D. (2010). Educational policy influences on educational audiology: A review of the past decade. *Journal of Educational Audiology, 16*, 20–29.

Teachers of the Deaf Act of 1961, Pub. L. No. 87-276.

U.S. Department of Education. (1994). *Goals 2000: Educate America Act*. Washington, DC: Author.

U.S. Department of Education, Office of Elementary and Secondary Education. (2002). *No Child Left Behind: A desktop reference*, Washington, DC: Author.

Educational Audiology in the Real World

Susanne Benson, M.S.
Educational Audiologist
Mat-Su Borough School District
Palmer, Alaska

I received my M.S. in Audiology from Idaho State University and began work in Alaska 3 weeks later for the Matanuska-Susitna Borough School District (locally known as Mat-Su). Prior to my arrival, the school district had contracted with a local audiologist, so I first had to take stock of what was in place, order equipment (audiometer, otoscope, etc.), and figure out where students were. I now have a small sound booth and office at one of the high schools. Our district covers about 25,000 miles, so I spend a lot of time on the road traveling between schools. It is about a 90-minute drive from my office to the rural schools at either end of the district. Most of the schools I visit monthly are in the core valley area, but it isn't uncommon for me to put 400 miles onto my mileage forms in a month.

I attend IEP meetings, check on students who have identified hearing loss to make sure their hearing aids/FM systems are working, and make sure accommodations are in place and working. I work directly with students who are new hearing aid wearers, as they adjust to wearing the aids, and I make sure they know how to use and take care of them. I also work on developing listening skills with most of our students with cochlear implants. Once a month I participate in child-find screenings, which are held for pre-schoolers, aged 3 to 5 years. I then recheck the preschoolers who don't pass in my office at a later date.

Some days I visit two to five schools, just checking equipment or doing follow-up hearing tests on students who didn't pass the nurses' screenings. Other days I have students scheduled in my office (if parents can bring them to my office), and I hope that I don't have any "no-shows," even after making reminder calls. I also try to schedule those appointments around the high school schedule, to avoid the noise of students in the halls or announcements during breaks and lunch times.

I enjoy being able to make my own schedule and driving at least once a year to the smaller outlying schools on beautiful days. I never get tired of seeing moose or eagles in the area or coming around a corner and seeing Denali (Mt. McKinley), Matanuska Glacier, or an amazing sunrise/sunset. I love being on the same schedule as my own children and having holidays, spring breaks, and summers off with them.

2

Classroom Acoustics

Donna F. Smiley and Cynthia M. Richburg

OBJECTIVES

By the end of this chapter, the reader will be able to:

1. Identify which characteristics of classroom acoustics (intensity, distance, background noise, and reverberation) affect a student's listening abilities.
2. Identify avoidable and unavoidable noise sources in a classroom.
3. Identify methods for decreasing avoidable and unavoidable noise sources in a classroom.

INTRODUCTION

Think about this. When a light bulb goes out in a classroom, no time is wasted getting that light bulb changed. It is assumed that students cannot learn if they cannot see the teacher or their materials due to poor lighting. However, little or no thought is given about the sound quality, or acoustics, in a classroom. If poor acoustics were as easy to "see" as poor lighting, would there be more diligence to improve the acoustics? The school-based audiologist is often the only professional in the school district with any information regarding classroom acoustics. This

chapter highlights the basics of classroom acoustics and provides solutions for improving the listening environment in the classroom.

IMPORTANCE OF CLASSROOM ACOUSTICS

Learning is accomplished by hearing, seeing, and experiencing. Berg (1993) estimated that students spend at least 45% of their day in activities that require listening. Therefore, students need to be able to hear what is being taught. Factors that affect a student's ability to hear the intended signal include the integrity of the listener's auditory system, the intensity of the signal, the reverberation properties of the room in which the student is listening, as well as the background noise in that room.

Children arrive in their classrooms with individual and unique auditory systems. There is evidence that the human central auditory nervous system does not reach full maturation until early adolescence (Allen & Wightman, 1994; Hartley, Wright, Hogan, & Moore, 2000; Stuart, 2005, as examples). Therefore, children in preschools and elementary schools are listening with less than perfect auditory systems because their systems are still developing. In the elementary grade levels, even children with normal peripheral hearing do not have "adult-like" auditory processing skills. In addition to immature auditory systems, the integrity of a child's auditory system can be compromised by peripheral hearing loss (either permanent or temporary) and other auditory dysfunctions, including true auditory processing disorders.

The intensity of the teacher's voice, the reverberation properties of the room in which the student is listening, and the amount of background noise in that room are all important aspects, or characteristics, of classroom acoustics. To some extent, all of these factors can be controlled or manipulated to optimize the listening experience of students in the classroom.

CHARACTERISTICS OF CLASSROOM ACOUSTICS

Intensity and Distance

The signal to which students should be listening in a classroom has two primary characteristics: intensity and distance. In most cases, this signal will be the teacher's voice; however, it could be other audio sources, such as recorded materials. First, the actual intensity, or power, of the signal may vary. Some teachers have less intense (or soft, quiet) voices; other teachers have more intense (or loud, booming) voices. Second, the distance from the signal to the student may vary. According to the *inverse square law* for sound, for every doubling of the distance from the sound source, the intensity of the sound decreases by 6 dB SPL. Therefore, the intensity of the teacher's voice rapidly decreases as the distance between the student and the teacher increases. For example, if the teacher's voice measures 65 dB SPL when she is 3 feet from the student, then at 6 feet, the intensity of her voice would be 59 dB SPL and at 9 feet, the intensity would be 53 db SPL. It would be safe to say that, when a teacher is providing whole-group teaching, she is at least 3 feet away from the closest student. Therefore, the students who are farthest away from the teacher are not hearing the same intensity of her voice as the students closest to her.

Background Noise

Children are inherently "noisy." Even teachers with excellent classroom management skills cannot eliminate all background noise in their classrooms.

In a typical classroom, there are many sources of noise (Table 2–1). Some noises are unavoidable, but others are avoidable. Aside from the noise students make themselves, noises made by the building or classroom equipment, such as the heating and cooling units (HVAC), fluorescent lighting, and computer/printer noises, are

Table 2–1. Common Sources of Noise in Classroom Settings

Sources	Examples
Students	talking, movement, coughing/sneezing
Heating, Ventilation, and Air Conditioning Systems (HVAC)	fan hum, ticking, clicking, reverberation of vents
Traffic	outdoors (cars/trucks), indoors (hallway)
Lawn maintenance equipment	lawn mowers, weed eaters, snow/leaf blowers
Playground noise	children's voices, swing sets
Computers	fan hum, keyboard noise
Janitorial equipment	floor waxers, wheels on mop bucket, vacuum cleaners
Aquarium	air compressor, bubbles
Other classes in close proximity	teachers' voices, children's voices, movement, video noise

unavoidable. In addition, noise sources from the hallway (e.g., other students, cleaning equipment) and outside of the classroom window (e.g., traffic, lawn maintenance equipment) are unavoidable. However, noises that come from classroom apparatus, such as aquariums and other classroom pets, are avoidable. That is not to say that unavoidable noises cannot be reduced, or avoidable noises cannot be altered (see discussion later in this chapter). The "take-home message" here is that none of these sources alone seems detrimental to students listening in the classroom, but the combined effects of noise sources create more difficulty listening in a classroom environment. In fact, when multiple noise sources are present at the same time, the overall loudness can be greater than that of a busy street (Jamieson, Kranjc, Yu, & Hodgett, 2004).

When audiologists use speech-in-noise testing in a clinical setting to evaluate how an individual's speech perception is affected by noise, the recorded noise source is mostly continuous (e.g., white noise or multitalker babble). However, in the classroom, noise sources are often mixed and usually are not continuous. These inconsistent noise levels lead to the false perception that background noise in a classroom is not as detrimental as it really is.

Reverberation

Reflected sound energy, known as reverberation, occurs when sound continues in a space (e.g., classroom) due to repeated reflection or scatter from the surfaces and/or objects in that space (e.g., desks, chairs; American National Standards Institute [ANSI], 2002). Reverberation time (RT) is measured by calculating the time that is required for the level of a steady sound to decay by 60 dB after the sound has been discontinued. This decay time is affected by the amount of sound absorption in a room, the room geometry, and the frequency of the sound itself (ANSI, 2002).

Research studies have shown that RTs longer than 0.5 seconds appear to degrade speech recognition for most listeners in educational environments (Crandell & Bess, 1986; Crum, 1974; Finitzo-Hieber & Tillman, 1978; Neimoeller, 1968; Olsen, 1977, 1981). RTs for unoccupied classrooms range from 0.4 to 1.2 seconds (Bradley, 1986; Crandell, 1992; Finitzo-Hieber, 1988; Knecht, Nelson, Whitelaw, & Fecht, 2002; Kodaras, 1960; McCroskey & Devens, 1975; Olsen, 1988; Ross, 1978). Therefore, because of the disparity between RTs that enhance speech recognition and those that exist in real classrooms, one can predict that the RTs in classrooms are much too long for effective speech recognition (American Speech-Language-Hearing Association [ASHA], 2005b).

It is important to note that reverberation is not always negative for speech intelligibility. The reflection of sound occurring within the appropriate time frame (not too short and not too long) assists the listener with improved sound quality, as well as speech understanding (Haas, 1972). Therefore, certain RTs are necessary in order for sounds to be perceived as normal or natural sounding.

Relationship Between the Signal, Background Noise, and Reverberation

The effects of intensity, distance, background noise, and reverberation have been discussed as separate entities. However, when combined, which is what happens in real classrooms, their effects are synergistic. That is, the combination of these properties is more problematic to listeners in a classroom than the sum of the individual effects.

The relationship between the intensity of the signal (e.g., the teacher's voice) and the intensity of the background noise, known as the signal-to-noise ratio (SNR), is an important consideration when discussing the acoustics of a classroom setting. When the SNR is decreased in the classroom, speech intelligibility decreases for the students. For instance, if the teacher's voice is measured at 65 dBA SPL and the background noise is measured at 55 dBA SPL, this would yield a SNR of +10 dB. This means the teacher's voice is 10 dB louder than the noises in the classroom. However, various studies have shown that the SNR in typical classrooms is anywhere from +5 to –7 dB (Blair, 1977; Finitzo-Hieber, 1988; Markides, 1986; Paul, 1967; Sanders, 1965) with the positive (+) number indicating a signal that is greater in intensity than the noise and a negative (–) number indicating that the signal is less intense than the noise. In a negative SNR situation, the teacher's voice could be hard for some students to hear, even if they had no hearing loss. As is evidenced by these studies, the recommended SNR is not being met in typical classrooms.

The American Speech-Language-Hearing Association's (ASHA) report, *Acoustics in Educational Settings: Technical Report* (2005b), and the American National Standards Institute (ANSI) Standard (ANSI) S12.60-2002, *Acoustical Performance Criteria, Design Requirements, and Guidelines for Schools* (2002), recommend a SNR of +15 dB to allow all individuals in a classroom to hear the spoken message well enough to receive the full meaning no matter where they are seated. No study has determined that a +15 dB SNR is absolutely necessary for students to hear well in a classroom setting; however, Nelson and Soli (2000) were able to consolidate research findings supporting the importance of this +15 dB SNR for classroom listening. Nelson and Soli (2000) pointed out that adults are able to understand familiar spoken material at SNRs of 0 dB, young children need a better SNR than adult listeners (+4 dB), students unfamiliar with the instructional language (i.e., English language learners) need an even greater SNR (+7 dB), and children with hearing loss need the greatest SNR of all (+15 dB). The deleterious and additive effect of reverberation requires an even greater SNR for all children in classroom settings, thereby supporting the recommendations of ASHA and ANSI for a +15 dB SNR in the classroom (Table 2–2).

POOR CLASSROOM ACOUSTICS

Some classroom designs inherently are poor listening environments due to their undesirable acoustic properties. For instance, open-plan (or open-concept) classrooms (i.e., classrooms that contain few interior walls) typically provide the worst acoustic environment for learning. In addition to the characteristic noise sources found in traditional classrooms, open-plan classrooms allow sound sources not typically thought of as "noise" to be part of the listening environment. For example, a teacher talking in the next classroom is a source of "noise" for a student who is not in that teacher's classroom. The noise in this situation is the other teacher's speech, and because it is speech containing a message, it may be harder for a

Table 2–2. Research Studies That Support Concepts of Signal-to-Noise Ratio (SNR) Requirements for Listening in Noise

Authors and Dates	Concepts Regarding SNR
Nilsson, Soli, & Sullivan, 1994	Adults are able to understand familiar spoken material at SNRs of 0 dB.
Elliott, 1979; Gravel, Fausel, Liskow, & Chobot, 1999; Jamieson, Kranjc, Yu, & Hodgett, 2004; Soli & Sullivan, 1997; Stelmachowicz, Hoover, Lewis, Kortekaas, & Pittman, 2000	Young children need a better signal-to-noise ratio than adult listeners (e.g., +4).
Crandell, 1996; Crandell & Smaldino, 1996b; Eriks-Brophy & Ayukawa, 2000; Hodgson & Montgomery, 1994; Mayo, Florentine, & Buus, 1997; Soli & Sullivan, 1997	Students unfamiliar with the instructional language (such as English language learners) need an even greater SNR (e.g., +7 dB).
Crandell, 1991, 1992; Crandell & Smaldino, 1992, 1995, 1996a, 1996b; Crandell, Smaldino, & Flexer, 2005; Finitzo-Hieber & Tillman, 1978; Niemoeller, 1968	Children with hearing loss who are in a classroom setting need the greatest SNR (e.g., +15 dB)

student to block out or ignore. Fewer open-plan schools are being built these days, but many existing open-plan buildings are still in use. Therefore, a school-based audiologist needs to be aware of the types of classrooms the students in his or her care go into each day.

Another poor acoustic environment for learning is a classroom that has a tall ceiling made of hard material (e.g., plaster), hard walls, and many hard surfaces. These hard surfaces tend to increase reverberation times to the point where speech intelligibility is difficult even for the best listeners.

DESIRABLE CLASSROOM ACOUSTICS

Constructing a classroom with good acoustic properties can be fairly simple. Installing sound-absorptive material on the ceiling and walls, as well as placing a rug or carpeting on the floor, can make an otherwise noisy, reverberant room suitable for learning. Constructing the midsection of the classroom's ceiling with hard surfaces to reflect sound to the back of the classroom can also improve the room's overall acoustic properties (Seep, Glosemeyer, Hulce, Linn, Aytar, & Coffeen, 2000). The ANSI (2002) standards for classroom acoustics specify the following:

1. Noise levels in unoccupied core learning spaces should not exceed 35 dBA or 40 dBA SPL, depending on the room size. (*Note:* These maximum noise levels coupled with a signal level for the teacher's voice of 50 to 65 dBA SPL should provide the appropriate SNR for students to hear the teacher, as well as their peers).

2. Reverberation time should not exceed 0.6 to 0.7 seconds, depending on room size.

SOLUTIONS FOR IMPROVING CLASSROOM ACOUSTICS

Audiologists in all practice settings should advocate for improved listening conditions. However, school-based audiologists should advocate strongly for good classroom acoustics because of the overall effects they have on the communication process. The school-based audiologist is often called on to evaluate classroom acoustics and make recommendations concerning improvements. Therefore, school-based audiologists should be familiar with standards and position statements that are relevant to classroom acoustics. Currently, the ANSI standards document (ANSI S12.60-2002) on classroom acoustics (2002), the American Academy of Audiology (AAA) position statement on classroom acoustics (2008), and three 2005 ASHA documents (i.e., a position statement [2005a], a technical report [2005b], and guidelines [2005c] for addressing acoustics in educational settings) provide excellent guidance for audiologists. Regardless of the level of involvement, from advocacy to implementation, audiologists practicing in a school setting should be knowledgeable about these documents and should be ready to provide input regarding the improvement of classroom acoustics when necessary.

In most cases, educational audiologists find themselves assisting with improving classroom acoustics in existing buildings. In some cases, they are consulted during the planning and construction phase of a new building. Regardless of the situation, the following suggestions can help to improve classroom acoustics:

1. *Reduce or eliminate unnecessary sources of background noise.* If the audiologist or the classroom teacher were to analyze the classroom environment, he or she would find unnecessary sources of noise that could be reduced or eliminated. Although it is not a popular recommendation, getting rid of classroom pets that make noise is sometimes necessary. The teacher, as an adult listener, may not realize how much noise is generated by an aquarium filter or hamster wheel. Other sources of unnecessary noise in a classroom may include fans and fan motors on older appliances (e.g., often teachers have small refrigerators in their rooms or older computers). Reducing this unnecessary noise may be as simple as adopting a classroom pet that does not require noisy equipment (e.g., Beta fish, reptiles, guinea pigs) or purchasing newer appliances.

2. *Reduce levels of background noise that cannot be eliminated.* Telling teachers to instruct students to use electric or manual pencil sharpeners at certain times of the day may reduce extraneous and unpredictable noise levels throughout the day. Providing input to administrators concerning careful selection and installation of heating and air conditioning systems can also make a tremendous difference in the noise levels in a classroom. In older buildings, a school/district might consider replacing older units when possible, or encasing them to reduce sound exposure. Desks and chairs can be noisy as they are moved across the floor. Therefore, using desk and chair feet attenuators (e.g., tennis balls, felt pads, rubber stoppers) may help to reduce the levels of extraneous and unwanted noise.

3. *Apply sound absorbing surfaces to ceilings and walls.* There needs to be a balance between sound absorption and sound reflection. If a room has materials that are either too reflective or too absorbent, the sound quality (and subsequent speech understanding) will not be optimal. In most cases, classrooms have surfaces that are too reflective. Using acoustic tiles on the ceiling and sound absorbent panels on the walls will help to absorb unwanted sound.

4. *Install carpeting on floors of classrooms.* Along with suggestion 3 above, the use of carpet in classrooms adds another absorbent material, thus reducing noise and reverberation issues. However, there are concerns about the potential for allergens and allergic reactions from some students when using carpets in high traffic areas. Maintenance and upkeep of carpet in a classroom would be critical to reduce these concerns. Ultimately, carpet in a classroom is a good way of improving the acoustics within a space.

5. *Construct classrooms with good acoustic properties.* In new school construction, classrooms should be designed with acoustics in mind. That means, architects and builders should limit the volume of the rooms, use sound absorbing materials, construct walls that limit room-to-room sound transmission, and place high noise areas (such as cafeterias and gymnasiums) away from core instructional classrooms. This concept may seem simple enough; however, many new construction classrooms still lack the

recommended acoustical properties set forth by the ANSI standard (2002).

6. *Reduce listening distance between the teacher and the students.* Teachers can be encouraged to set up their classrooms to reduce the distance between the students and themselves when they are providing whole group teaching. Changing the arrangement of classroom furniture and teaching spaces is all that may be required to reduce the distance between the teacher and the students (Siebein, Gold, Siebein, & Ermann, 2000). This suggestion is not only simple, but it requires no extra equipment or costs.

7. *Encourage the use of classroom sound-field amplification.* Soundfield amplification can improve the SNR in any classroom, no matter how large or reverberant it may be. However, addressing excessive noise and reverberation issues before using soundfield amplification is recommended. The use of soundfield amplification, as well as the use of personal FM with students who have hearing loss or other auditory disorders, is discussed further in Chapter 6.

For more detailed information on how to improve the acoustics in classrooms, see Siebein, Gold, Siebein, and Ermann's work (2000), the ASHA *Guidelines for Addressing Acoustics in Educational Settings* (2005c), and the ANSI standards (2002).

SUMMARY

The reason classrooms are not built with better acoustic properties is usually related to the expense. However, if acoustics are considered and addressed during the design phase of a building project, in the end, the cost will be lower than it would be for a classroom that has to be retrofit for acoustical modifications. Additionally, if the placement of instructional classrooms is *not* considered in relation to other areas of the building during the design phase (e.g., cafeteria, band, and gymnasium), the background noise levels for those classrooms would never be improved because moving the rooms would not be feasible. However, the good news is that there are many low-cost methods for improving the acoustics of a classroom.

Audiologists, especially those who practice in a school setting, need to be familiar with the properties of classroom acoustics, how to evaluate them, and when to make modifications and recommendations for improvements. Administrators and teachers should seek input from an audiologist when evaluating the acoustics of classrooms. Finally, instructional institutions should seek an audiologist's input when considering new construction, as well as when retrofitting existing construction.

REFERENCES

Allen, P., & Wightman, F. (1994). Psychometric functions for children's detection of tones in noise. *Journal of Speech and Hearing Research, 37,* 205–215.

American Academy of Audiology. (2008). *Position statement on classroom acoustics.* Reston, VA: Author.

American National Standards Institute. (2002). *S12.60-2002, Acoustical performance criteria, design requirements, and guidelines for schools.* Melville, NY: Author.

American Speech-Language-Hearing Association. (2005a). *Acoustics in educational settings: Position statement.* Rockville, MD: Author.

American Speech-Language-Hearing Association. (2005b). *Acoustics in educational settings: Technical report.* Rockville, MD: Author.

American Speech-Language-Hearing Association. (2005c). *Guidelines for addressing acoustics in educational settings.* Rockville, MD: Author.

Berg, F. (1993). *Acoustics and sound systems in schools.* San Diego, CA: Singular Publishing Group.

Blair, J. (1977). Effects of amplification, speechreading, and classroom environment on reception of speech. *Volta Review, 79,* 443–449.

Bradley, J. (1986). Speech intelligibility studies in classrooms. *Journal of the Acoustical Society of America, 80,* 846–854.

Crandell, C. (1991). Classroom acoustics for normal-hearing children: Implications for rehabilitation. *Educational Audiology Monograph, 2,* 18–38.

Crandell, C. (1992). Classroom acoustics for hearing-impaired children. *Journal of the Acoustical Society of America, 92,* 2470.

Crandell, C. (1996). Effects of sound field amplification on the speech perception of ESL children. *Educational Audiology Monograph, 4,* 1–5.

Crandell, C., & Bess, F. (1986, November). *Sound-field amplification in the classroom setting.* Paper presented at the American Speech-Language-Hearing Association Convention, New Orleans, LA.

Crandell, C., & Smaldino, J. (1992). Sound field amplification in the classroom. *American Journal of Audiology, 1,* 16–18.

Crandell, C., & Smaldino, J. (1995). An update of classroom acoustics for children with hearing impairment. *Volta Review, 1,* 4–12.

Crandell, C., & Smaldino, J. (1996a). Sound field amplification in the classroom: Applied and theoretical issues. In F. Bess, J. Gravel, & A. Tharpe (Eds.), *Amplification for children with auditory deficits* (pp. 229–250). Nashville, TN: Bill Wilkerson Center Press.

Crandell, C., & Smaldino, J. (1996b). Speech perception in noise by children for whom English is a second language. *American Journal of Audiology, 5,* 47–51.

Crandell, C., Smaldino, J., & Flexer, C. (2005). *Sound field amplification: Applications to speech perception and classroom acoustics* (2nd ed.). Clifton Park, NY: Thomson Delmar Learning.

Crum, D. (1974). *The effects of noise, reverberation, and speaker-to-listener distance on speech understanding.* Unpublished doctoral dissertation, Northwestern University, Evanston, IL.

Elliott, L. L. (1979). Performance of children aged 9 to 17 years on a test of speech intelligibility in noise using sentence material with controlled word predictability. *Journal of the Acoustical Society of America, 66,* 651–653.

Eriks-Brophy, A., & Ayukawa, H. (2000). The benefits of sound field amplification in classrooms of Inuit students of Nunavik: A pilot project. *Language, Speech, and Hearing Services in Schools, 31,* 324–335.

Finitzo-Hieber, T. (1988). Classroom acoustics. In R. Roeser (Ed.), *Auditory disorders in school children* (2nd ed., pp. 221–233). New York, NY: Thieme-Stratton.

Finitzo-Hieber, T., & Tillman, T. (1978). Room acoustics effects on monosyllabic word discrimination ability for normal and hearing-impaired children. *Journal of Speech and Hearing Research, 21,* 440–458.

Gravel, J.S., Fausel, N., Liskow, C., & Chobot, J. (1999). Children's speech recognition in noise using omni-directional and dual-microphone hearing aid technology. *Ear and Hearing, 20,* 1–11.

Haas, H. (1972). The influence of a single echo on the audibility of speech. *Journal of the Audio Engineering Society, 20,* 146–159.

Hartley, D. E. H, Wright, B. A., Hogan, S. C., & Moore, D. R. (2000). Age-related improvements in auditory backward and simultaneous masking in 6- to 10-year-old children. *Journal of Speech, Language and Hearing Research, 43,* 1402–1415.

Hodgson, W. R., & Montgomery, P. (1994). Hearing impairment and bilingual children: Considerations in assessment and intervention. *Seminars in Speech and Language, 15,* 174–182.

Jamieson, D. G., Kranjc, G., Yu, K., & Hodgett, W. E. (2004). Speech intelligibility of young school-aged children in the presence of real-life classroom noise. *Journal of the American Academy of Audiology, 15,* 501–517.

Knecht, H. A., Nelson, P. B., Whitelaw, G. M., & Feth, L. L. (2002). Background noise levels and reverberations times in unoccupied classrooms: Predictions and measurements. *American Journal of Audiology, 11,* 65–71.

Kodaras, M. (1960). Reverberation times of typical elementary school settings. *Noise Control, 6,* 17–19.

McCroskey, F., & Devens, J. (1975). Acoustic characteristics of public school classrooms constructed between 1890 and 1960. In *Proceedings of Noise Expo, National Noise and Vibration Control Conference* (pp. 101–103). Bay Village, OH: Acoustical Publications.

Markides, A. (1986). Speech levels and speech-to-noise ratios. *British Journal of Audiology, 20,* 115–120.

Mayo, L. H., Florentine, M., & Buus, S. (1997). Age of second-language acquisition and perception of speech in noise. *Journal of Speech, Language, and Hearing Research, 40,* 686–693.

Neimoeller, A. (1968). Acoustical design of classrooms for the deaf. *American Annals of the Deaf, 113,* 1040–1045.

Nelson, P. B., & Soli, S. (2000). Acoustical barriers to learning: Children at risk in every classroom. *Language, Speech, and Hearing Services in Schools, 31,* 356–361.

Nilsson, M., Soli, S. D., & Sullivan, J. (1994). Development of the Hearing-in-Noise Test for the measurement of speech reception thresholds in quiet and in noise. *Journal of the Acoustical Society of America, 95,* 1085–1099.

Olsen, W. (1977). Acoustics and amplification in classrooms for the hearing impaired. In F. H. Bess (Ed.), *Childhood deafness: Causation, assessment, and management* (pp. 251–266). New York, NY: Grune & Stratton.

Olsen, W. (1981). The effects of noise and reverberation on speech intelligibility. In F. H. Bess, B. A. Freeman, & J. S. Sinclair (Eds.), *Amplification in education* (pp. 151–163). Washington, DC: Alexander Graham Bell Association for the Deaf.

Olsen, W. (1988). Classroom acoustics for hearing-impaired children. In F. H. Bess (Ed.), *Hearing impairment in children.* Parkton, MD: York Press.

Paul, R. (1967). *An investigation of the effectiveness of hearing aid amplification in regular and special classrooms under instructional conditions.* Unpublished doctoral dissertation, Wayne State University, Detroit, MI.

Ross, M. (1978). Classroom acoustics and speech intelligibility. In J. Katz (Ed.), *Handbook of clinical audiology* (pp. 469–478). Baltimore, MD: Williams & Wilkins.

Sanders, D. (1965). Noise conditions in normal school classrooms. *Exceptional Child, 31,* 344–353.

Seep, B., Glosemeyer, R., Hulce, E., Linn, M., Aytar, P., & Coffeen, R. (2000). *Classroom acoustics: A resource for creating learning environments with desirable listening conditions.* Melville, NY: Acoustical Society of America.

Siebein, G. W., Gold, M. A., Siebein, G. W., & Ermann, M. G. (2000). Ten ways to provide a high-quality acoustical environment in schools. *Language, Speech, and Hearing Services in Schools, 31,* 376–384.

Soli, S. D., & Sullivan, J. A. (1997). Factors affecting children's speech communication in classrooms. *Journal of the Acoustical Society of America, 101,* S3070.

Stelmachowicz, P. G., Hoover, B. M., Lewis, D. E., Kortekaas, R., & Pittman, A. L. (2000). The relation between stimulus context, speech audibility, and perception for normal-hearing and hearing-impaired children. *Journal of Speech, Language, and Hearing Research, 43,* 902–914.

Stuart, A. (2005). Development of auditory temporal resolution in school-age children revealed by word recognition in continuous and interrupted noise. *Ear and Hearing, 26,* 78–88.

Educational Audiology in the Real World

Natalie Benafield, AuD
Educational Audiologist and Certified Teacher
Arkansas Children's Hospital (Educational Audiology/Speech
Pathology Resources for Schools Program)
Little Rock, Arkansas

The IEP conference begins with introductions. From the limited information I have been given, this meeting is expected to be contentious. The parents and the school district have been having difficulties agreeing on the amount of services the schools will provide for this student. The school speech-language pathologist introduces me as the Audiology Consultant. The parents seem relieved that I am there, but the teachers begin to look resistant. I pull out my prepared explanation, "Hello. I'm Natalie Benafield, audiologist and certified regular educator. I work for Arkansas Children's Hospital in their outreach program. I consult with the school district on matters regarding students with hearing-impairment." I can almost see the wheels turning as they process the certified teacher piece. One teacher laughs and asks how long I taught before I burned out and became an audiologist. When I tell them I worked as an audiologist for 12 years before I burned out and became a regular classroom teacher, they look at me like I'm crazy. "It's a long story," I tell them, adding, "After leaving audiology, I taught fourth grade for 5 years, worked as a school librarian for a year, and coached Junior and Senior High Quiz Bowl. I think my background helps me approach the education of children with hearing impairment from several different perspectives." What I'm thinking to myself is that my years as a teacher actually made me a better audiologist, or at least a better educational audiologist.

My current job is actually the second educational audiology position I have held. My first was before I had teaching experience. It was for the outreach program at our state's school for the deaf. It's where I fell in love with educational audiology, but also where I got burned out trying to serve too many schools with too few resources. In my particular case, two audiologists were serving 275 school districts across our state. Most educational audiologists I know are overworked. Many travel from school to school, some driving long distances. I currently work for the outreach program at a pediatric hospital, where schools contract with us to receive on-site audiology services. I have fewer schools to work with, and I'm doing a much better job for the students and teachers I serve. I still travel, sometimes long distances, but I have a much closer relationship with the schools, as I have more time to spend at each school. Some schools I visit once a month, and some once a week, depending on what we have determined is needed for the district. One day might entail attending an IEP conference, the next day I'm performing a classroom observation to make academic suggestions to a teacher; another day I'm helping the school nurse with hearing screenings, and the next I'm installing or troubleshooting soundfield systems. There are never two days that are exactly the same. I do love having summers off, but August is filled with providing professional development for teachers. Thanks to cell phones and remote computer access, I do a lot of work from my home and my car. Do

I sometimes wish I didn't have to travel and that every district had its own audiologist? Absolutely. I'm hoping that what our team is providing will help schools recognize the many services an audiologist can provide to a school district.

I realize that most audiologists don't have "regular classroom teacher" on their resume, and it's certainly not necessary to being a good educational audiologist. However, I know that I do not approach being an educational audiologist in the same way I did before I taught school. I think I'm better at it than I was before. I believe that audiologists who work in schools should have knowledge of, and respect for, the culture of schools. Schools have their own schedules, chains of command, and laws and regulations that most clinical professionals simply aren't familiar with. It's not only pediatric clinical skills and technological skills that make a good educational audiologist. Diplomatic skills and team building can be the key to success in a school setting. As a teacher, I've seen many "experts" come into schools and treat teachers as if they had nothing to contribute to the discussion on a child's education. The opportunity for collaboration was lost, which means the student was the one to lose out in the end.

I'm often asked why I became an audiologist, switched to being a teacher, and then back to an audiologist. In the clinical setting, I always felt like a piece of the puzzle was missing in serving my pediatric patients. School is such an important part of a child's life that I wanted to be involved in it. As a teacher, I missed the luxury of having time to focus on one child at a time, and I missed using my audiology training and knowledge of hearing loss. I used to feel like I was caught in the middle of two professions, but educational audiology really has given me the best of both worlds.

3

School-Age Language and Classroom Success

Dee M. Lance and Brenda L. Beverly

OBJECTIVES

By the end of this chapter, the reader will be able to:

1. Describe the foundational skills required for school success.
2. Explain the syntactic/morphologic, semantic, and pragmatic skills development in school-age children.
3. Discuss relevant issues concerning the development of narratives as they apply to school-age children.

INTRODUCTION

The first day of school is a landmark event in the lives of many children and their families. It is a day that they may both long for and dread at the same time. Children will have to navigate a complex web of mathematics and literacy skills that will allow them, one day, to acquire the ability necessary for going to college or pursuing the careers of their choice. Regardless of the chosen post-high school pathway, there are skills children must acquire to survive in a society that values literacy

and technological savvy. By the time children reach high school, they must be able to follow directions, skim reading selections, locate specific information within a text, recall information on demand, meet deadlines, take notes during presentations, plan and execute projects, participate in discussions, make logical deductions, and the list goes on (Westby, 2006). They must learn all of these abilities, with changing environments and expectations, while working through a fragmented day of stopping and starting classes.

There is no way around it—school is a language event. Language activities occur daily during *all* tasks in the classroom and school environment, not only during class periods addressing reading or language arts. School-age children use and further develop all aspects of their oral and written language abilities; listening to teacher instructions, negotiating with peers for play and work materials, articulating answers to questions, reading, and writing. School, therefore, is a particular challenge for children with language and communication impairments associated with auditory deficits. A thorough understanding of what is known about the connections between oral language skills (i.e., listening and talking) and written language skills (i.e., reading and writing) can support the effectiveness of the audiologist serving school-age children. It is critical that we view oral language skills and written language skills in an interactive framework. Children develop spoken language skills initially ahead of written language skills, starting to talk around 1 year of age, but not expected to read or write until 6 years of age. Written language skills quickly become the dominant daily modality, and the spoken language skills of older children and adults are directly shaped by their literacy development; that is, in higher education settings, many work environments, and even some social settings, one's ability to speak in a fairly formal, standardized way is expected.

Challenges of developing oral and written language can be even more difficult for children who do not exhibit typical auditory abilities. Children who are deaf or hard of hearing (d/hh) present with a variety of linguistic abilities, not unlike children with language impairment or children, in general. Students who are deaf are likely to exhibit obvious deficits and clear educational challenges that require significant accommodations from classroom teachers, such as interpreters. Students who are hard of hearing will more likely use spoken English as their primary language and spend more time in the regular classroom. As a result, their educational needs and struggles are more likely to be overlooked (Antia, Jones, Reed, & Kreimeyer, 2009). Although students who are d/hh in this century have a better chance of achieving academic success (Antia et al., 2009), this population of students is continually at risk for academic difficulties.

Preschool skills in math, reading, and attention are some of the predictors for determining how successfully children will manage school (Duncan et al., 2007). In an attempt to help audiologists better serve children who are d/hh, this chapter explains both school and language demands placed on children, regardless of hearing ability. With this information, professionals responsible for helping students who are d/hh will be prepared to support these children as they avoid pitfalls of the language-loaded curriculum.

SKILLS FOR SCHOOL SUCCESS

Before the beginning of the school year, new students will get a list of school supplies for the first day of class, supplies like markers and three-ring binders. In addition to supplies, students are expected to come to school with foundational skills in place for learning. Foundational skills are those skills that facilitate rapid gains in reading, writing, and math. Additionally, there are pragmatic or social demands placed on children that go beyond playing well with others. Children must contend with both their peer group and the academic culture. Turn-taking, functioning within small groups, and code switching between academic and peer-group interactions are just a few of the skills students are required to bring to school, or to develop quickly in school with little formal instruction. All of these demands set the background for the acquisition of literacy skills that include both mathematical and reading proficiency. The literacy demands start in preschool and advance throughout students' academic careers.

Preschoolers with typical development are increasing their ability in emergent literacy, particularly in the area of phonological awareness, or knowledge of sounds and segments in words. For example, preschoolers around the age of 3 to 4 years, begin to segment sentences into words, demonstrate an interest in sounds and rhyming games, and identify approximately ten letters of the alphabet (Shaywitz, 2003). As children get closer to school age (i.e., 4 to 5 years), about 50% of the children will be able to segment words into syllables (e.g., banana = ba-na-na), whereas 20% will be able to segment words into sounds (e.g., sat = s-a-t) and identify even more letters of the alphabet (Shaywitz, 2003). Preschoolers who exhibit strong phonological awareness skills have been found to have an easier time sounding out words (i.e., decoding) in first grade than preschoolers who have weak phonological awareness skills (Bradley & Bryant, 1983). Yet, children who are d/hh are at risk for having difficulties with decoding. In fact, Briscoe, Bishop, and Norbury (2001) found that children who are d/hh exhibit poor phonological awareness skills at ages 5 to 10 years. Clearly, preschool children (with normal hearing and hearing loss) should begin their literacy journey early

for the best possible academic outcome in reading.

One factor known to influence emergent literacy development is environment. Preschool children can be divided into two groups: children from "high print-high talk environments" and children from "low print-low talk environments" (Kuvshinoff & Creaghead, 1994). Environments that are high print-high talk include a child's home and school, where literate activities are not only valued, but are part of a family's daily activities. These activities can include, but are not limited to, joint reading time with books and magazines, paper and pencils for both joint and independent activities, using e-mail for communication, making lists, and discussing with children the things that are happening around them. In contrast, low print-low talk environments tend to have few literate activities as part of the daily routine, usually because of socioeconomic or cultural factors. As one might predict, children from high print-high talk environments have an advantage when starting kindergarten. Children from homes that are low print-low talk environments have to play catch-up when it comes to the literacy skills necessary to be successful students.

With each new teacher and/or advance in grade, classroom expectations change (Kuvshinoff & Creaghead, 1994); however, the focus of the curriculum is fairly consistent. In first through third grades, the primary focus of the classroom is developing literacy and math skills. As the children move through the upper elementary grades, they must use their literacy skills to glean information from subject texts (e.g., history and science), as well as written math problems. All of this skill development is in addition to the continued expectation that the children read fiction and nonfiction stories, write book reports, summaries, and research papers, answer questions on tests, and demonstrate accurate grammar, spelling, punctuation, and penmanship.

In middle school, all of these demands increase, and students are expected to spend about 50% of the instructional day in independent seat work that requires the ability to set priorities, organize time, and make choices about how to approach assignments (Westby, 2006). These skills call for self-regulation and self-determinism, and those with difficulty managing the linguistic demands of the classroom are at risk for deficits in both areas. Westby (2006) defines self-determinism as "having the confidence in one's abilities to achieve important goals" (p. 373) and self-regulation as "managing the internal states and external behaviors to achieve specific tasks" (p. 373). These skills are needed for the development of higher reasoning skills, which support students in setting priorities, making choices, organizing work, initiating conversations, asking for clarification, and composing comments in a timely manner.

Today's classroom is a language-loaded environment; a critical component of academic success is linguistic ability. Today's classroom is also a busy place, with increasing demands in each advancing grade. Students will have diverse backgrounds and varying abilities, all requiring the classroom teachers' time and energy to be successful. Together, students and teachers have to tackle state-mandated curricular requirements and high-stakes testing. Without the appropriate supports, students with auditory deficits are not only at risk for coming to school without the emergent literacy skills necessary to start learning

at an appropriate pace, but they are also at risk for failing to meet teacher- and state-required benchmarks.

LANGUAGE SKILLS AND DEVELOPMENT FOR SCHOOL SUCCESS

Syntax and Morphology

Typically developing children exhibit truly amazing sentence skills by the time they begin school at the age of 5 years. Their utterances will increase from simple, single words around the age of 1 year to multiple words organized in phrases to form sentences of increasing complexity. A sentence is defined as a group of related words that contains an initial noun or noun phrase, the subject, and a verb or verb phrase, the predicate. A phrase is also a group of related words, but phrases do not contain both subjects and predicates. For example, the phrase, "*my teacher*," is the subject in the sentence, "*My teacher* passed out the books on the first day of school." Likewise, "*on the first day of school*" is a prepositional phrase within the predicate of the above sentence. The structure of sentences, consisting of related words in phrases and the ordering of those words and phrases in specific languages like American English, is "syntax." "Morphology" is the language system governing small units of meaning, which include morphemes, words, and suffixes. Together, the rule-based systems of syntax and morphology comprise the grammar of a language.

Decades ago, Brown (1973) described the rapid development of syntax and morphology in children under the age of

5 years. For example, preschoolers inflect noun phrases to communicate possession (e.g., possessive pronouns such as "*your* backpack," or addition of *'s,* as in "Jen*'s* paper) and plurality (i.e., *-s* as in "pencil*s*" and "disk*s*"). They elaborate verb phrases with present progressive *-ing*, a variety of auxiliary verbs (e.g., "*is* studying," "*will* eat," and "*can't* sleep"), past tense forms (e.g., *-ed* suffix as in "color*ed*" or the irregular "*sat*"), and the third person present tense *-s* (e.g., "He write*s*," The teacher help*s*").

Children who are d/hh can exhibit delayed morphological development. Researchers have found that three early grammatical morphemes (i.e., possessive *-s*, past tense *-ed*, and the third person present verb tense *–s*) are the most vulnerable for children who are d/hh (Moeller, Tomblin, Yoshinaga-Itano, McDonald Connor, & Jerger, 2007). Acquisition of these morphemes by children who are d/hh can look inconsistent across an individual's development, and some children will achieve normal expectations for morpheme production.

Before their fifth birthdays, children begin to produce complex sentences characterized by embedded phrases and conjoined clauses (Owens, 2008). Like a simple sentence, clauses consist of a noun phrase plus a verb phrase (see example in Table 3–1). Two embedded phrases that emerge at an early age are prepositional phrases and infinitive phrases. In English, the infinitive form of the verb is the unmarked verb preceded by "*to*" as in "*to go*." Other embedded phrases are gerund and participle phrases (see examples in Table 3–1), in which words that function as verbs (i.e., playing) are used as a noun or gerund, or as a modifier or participle. Early developing conjoined sentences are created with coordinating conjunctions; that is, words such as "*and,*" "*but,*" and "*or,*" are used to connect two independent clauses to form one utterance. Initially, children use and overuse "*and,*" but increasingly they produce other conjunction words, including subordinating conjunctions (i.e., "because," "if") to conjoin clauses (Owens, 2008). Throughout the school-age years, and as students acquire written language skills, they can use elaborated and embedded phrases, and clauses to express more ideas within clauses. This acquisition of skills supports their ability to communicate more concisely detailed information. However, children who are d/hh often show comprehension and production weaknesses for complex utterances with embedded clauses, although some children who have received intense, oral language training can achieve age-level skills for complex syntactic understanding (Moeller et al., 2007).

Nippold (2007) described school-age children's increasing use of grammatical elements, which occur with less frequency in spoken utterances. One construction, known as "passive voice," is often tested as part of standardized language assessments; however, passive voice is considered to be rare in spoken language. Instead, language spoken by adults to children consists predominately of "active voice" structures, or utterances in which the subject of the sentence is also the agent of the action (e.g., "*you*" in the utterance, "*You* didn't take his boat."). In contrast, passive voice is characterized by the agent of the action in the object position of the sentence (e.g., "*you*" in "His boat was taken by *you*."), and typically developing children under the age of 9 years may interpret passive voice

Table 3–1. Sentence Complexity: Terms and Utterance Examples from Language Sample Transcripts

Terms	Example Utterance	Source (Child, Age)
Infinitive	"She wants *to pour* some milk."	TD girl, 4;3
Gerund	"I'm finished *playing* with these."	TD girl, 4;4
Participle	"I think it's called a *shooting* range or whatever."	LI boy, 11;2
	"I'm not really sure because my friend's dad found it *abandoned* on the road."	LI boy, 11;9
Complex utterance: Independent clauses *conjoined with a coordinating conjunction*	"I was riding it *and* Pawpaw ran over it at Mawmaw's."	TD girl, 4;4
	"My brother got a scooter *but* it broke."	TD girl, 4;4
	"You got to make a new one *so* the aliens don't get it."	TD boy, 4;3
Complex utterance: An independent clause and dependent clause *conjoined with a subordinating conjunction*	"I'm so funny *because* I laugh all the time."	TD boy, 3;10
	"I know, *because* they are old."	TD girl, 6;10
Complex utterance: An *embedded dependent clause that serves as the noun or object of the sentence.*	"I'll show you *what the motorcycle's trick is gonna be.*"	TD boy, 3;5
	"We can pretend *we have cups.*"	TD girl, 4;3
	"I think *we need these.*"	LI boy, 6;7
Complex utterance: An *embedded dependent clause that serves as a modifier.*	"There's so many cars *that I can't believe it.*"	TD boy, 3;5
	"You just got to do this *when you walk home.*"	TD boy 4;3

TD = typically developing; LI = language-impaired, normal hearing; Ages are years; month.

incorrectly, assuming the subject is the agent. Even with this protracted development for typically developing children, infrequent structures like passive voice are considered indicative of children's higher-level language skills, and children who are d/hh may continue to demonstrate comprehension weaknesses for passive voice well into adolescence (e.g., ages 14 to 17 years; Power & Quigley, 1973). Despite English teachers' increasing urges to avoid using passive constructions in writing, passive voice remains a preferred style in many genres. The following utterance might be associated with technical writing in our professions: "At the start of the investigation, *the story was presented* to the kindergarten children." Readers of this chapter will recognize that this sentence construction is often preferred to the active voice sentence, "At the start of the investigation, *we presented the story* to the kindergarten children."

Educators of students who are d/hh benefit from considering these rapidly expanding syntactic and morphological skills for children learning English. After all, complex and elaborated utterances emerge relatively early in the spoken and written language of children with typical language skills, and the children's competency with these forms is nothing short of remarkable. Success in school-based Language Arts curricula requires knowledge of phrase, clause, and sentence parts and their varied constructions to convey tense and agreement. Infrequent structures (e.g., passive voice constructions) are indicative of higher level language comprehension and expected of students as their writing style matures. Academic success in the upper elementary grades, and in secondary school, necessitates comprehension, production, and knowledge of these structures in spoken and written language.

Semantic Development

"Semantics," by definition, govern the meaning being conveyed in the linguistic code. Children with typical development are particularly good at learning word meanings. Around the age of 2 years, children should have a vocabulary of about 200 words. As they start first grade, typically developing children have a vocabulary of about 6,000 words, and by the time they finish high school, they are capable of exhibiting a vocabulary of 60,000 words (Pinker, 1994). Throughout our lives, our vocabulary continues to grow as we master new skills with specialized vocabulary. This mass of words

to which children have attached meaning is referred to as the "lexicon" (Pence & Justice, 2008). The receptive lexicon is the collection of words we understand, and the expressive lexicon includes the words that we can use (Pence & Justice, 2008).

How do words get stored in a child's receptive or expressive lexicon? Initially, it occurs through a process called "fast mapping." Fast mapping is the ability children possess that allows them to learn a new word with as little as one exposure to the word and its referent. We see evidence of fast mapping from the beginning of children's oral language development. For example, when the first author's daughter was a toddler, she was watching her father empty the contents of his pocket. There was some loose change, scraps of a tissue, and a pair of soft yellow ear plugs. She asked her father, "What's that?" to which he replied, "toilet paper." Little did he know that she was referring to the ear plugs and not the tissue. Until we finally corrected it, she referred to little yellow ear plugs as "toilet paper." Once a word has been fast mapped, it takes repeated exposures before the child can refine that word's meaning.

School-age children have three primary avenues for learning words. The first is vocabulary drill, or direct teaching of vocabulary words in classrooms (Nippold, 2007). Most of us have had first-hand experience with this type of lesson. Unless this type of vocabulary instruction incorporates meaningful application, other than just writing the word in a sentence, it is not very effective in changing students' lexicons (Nelson & Van Meter, 2006).

A second process for learning new words is the use of contextual cues from known words that surround unknown words (Nippold, 2007). Learning new vocabulary from the context of words is something that students with normal hearing acuity and typical language ability do readily, as it is an effective method for learning new vocabulary words. The ability to use the contextual cues of oral and written language is dependent on students' abilities to process linguistic information. Children who are d/hh can develop vocabulary skills commensurate with peers; however, auditory processing limitations associated with phonological delays may limit vocabulary development, delay strategy use for word learning, and result in below grade-level reading skills (Moeller et al., 2007). Thus, this context-based vocabulary acquisition strategy may not be available for children who are d/hh, unless they receive explicit instruction on its use.

A third mode for learning new vocabulary words is to break words down into base words, suffixes and prefixes (Nippold, 2007). To be facile readers, students must be able to break longer words down, or "chunk" them, into individual syllables or other segments, such as prefixes, suffixes, base words, and root words. The ability to break words into their root or base words and the corresponding suffixes and prefixes is a skill that is important for vocabulary devel-opment, decoding unfamiliar words, and reading comprehension, and it is known to build upon children's knowledge of English morphology.

Although word meaning is an important part of semantics, there is much more to meaning than simple or direct understandings of words. Another component of semantics is figurative language. To understand figurative language, not only do students have to comprehend the immediate context of the message being spoken, but they must move beyond the literal interpretation of the sentence to implied comparisons, as in a metaphor, or to deliberate incongruity of what is being said to what is intended, as in irony. There are four commonly used figurative language forms: similes, metaphors, idioms, and irony (Table 3–2). Not only is figurative language needed for social interactions and witty conversational exchanges, it is also central to students' academic success (Milosky, 1994). Children who are too concrete or literal in their language use and comprehension will be considered "slow on the uptake" and miss out on critical peer and academic interactions. Although preschoolers may be able to comprehend some metaphors, children's ability to comprehend and use metaphors

Table 3–2. Types of Figurative Forms Commonly Found in English

Figurative Form	Definition	Example
Simile	A comparison of dissimilar things using "like" or "as"	She was as sweet as honey.
Metaphor	An implied comparison of dissimilar things not using "like" or "as"	Love is a red, red rose.
Idioms	Sayings we use every day	A hitch in your giddy-up.
Irony	Involves the deliberate incongruity between what is stated and what is meant	You failed a test and say, "Well, that was easy."

continues to increase throughout childhood and into adolescence and adulthood (Nippold, 2007). However, children who are d/hh are at risk for having difficulty understanding and using figurative language, in part, because the development of figurative language is a skill that requires exposure and time.

Figurative language forms serve several functions. We commonly use metaphoric language to clarify unknown concepts by comparing them to known concepts or objects. Perhaps you can recall a teacher using an apple to teach the different layers of the earth. The peel is the crust of the earth, the white fruity part is the mantle, and the core of the apple is like the core of the earth. In this manner, metaphors can be used to clarify, illuminate, or explain. Successful comprehension of metaphors relies on the ability to compare dissimilar things. First, students must infer that a comparison is being made, and then students must discern the relevant similar dimensions of the two dissimilar things being compared while ignoring irrelevant similarities (Milosky, 1994). Given that successful metaphor comprehension requires this level of skill, it is no wonder that children who are d/hh are at risk for difficulty with this linguistic device.

Idioms are another figurative form that makes language interesting and rich. They are used to express an attitude, to establish group solidarity, or to be indirect. They can be as apparent as "hold on" for wait a minute or as opaque as "no quarter given" for that person who was given no mercy. The meaning of idioms can be tied to the ethnic or sociocultural group to which someone belongs, or to the dialect one speaks (Milosky, 1994). Certainly comprehension of idioms is necessary to understand informal social conversations, and much humor is conveyed through the use of idioms and metaphors.

Irony is an important linguistic tool used to shape and inform who we are as conversationalists. The only difference between irony and lying is that, for irony, the speaker says the opposite of what he wants the listener to believe. Irony extends across the whole utterance in that the intonation pattern of the statement (i.e., syllable and word stress, pauses, and fluctuation of vocal pitch), as well as the body language used, help the listener understand that the speaker's intent is actually the opposite of the words being spoken. As a student advances toward middle school, irony becomes a common vehicle for both humor and criticism from peers, as well as teachers. To comprehend and use irony, advanced conversational skills on the part of both the listener and the speaker are required. Understanding irony may be difficult for the student who is d/hh not only because of the challenge of this construct from a language standpoint, but also because acoustic cues (e.g., intonation patterns) contained within the message convey meaning that one must hear for the irony to be perceived. Students who are d/hh may not have the hearing sensitivity to perceive these acoustic cues. Semantic ability contributes to later reading comprehension and academic success in the later grades (Rand Corporation, 2002). Once children start school, semantic skill is expected to increase with exposure to classroom and written language. Children who are typically developing start school with semantic abilities that allow them to grow more words and use those words in increasingly creative and figurative ways. Children who are d/hh, however, are at risk for starting school with limited semantic ability. Specifically, these children present with receptive vocabulary skills within the "normal" range but below their hearing peers (Berent, Kelly, & Porter, 2008; Briscoe, Bishop, & Norbury, 2001).

Pragmatic Development

"Pragmatics," or the social use of language, is important to nearly every school-age child. Like many of the other linguistic skills, this skill is developed through interaction with peers. To fit in, school-age children must learn how to be competent conversationalists. As with other language skills, pragmatics develop with time and experience for children with typical language. In preschool, children's ability to maintain budding conversations often involves repetition of content and is a strategy known as "topic collaboration." During the school years, we see children becoming more advanced conversationalists because they increasingly add new information to the topic. This is a strategy known as "topic incorporation" (James, 1990). As children reach adolescence, they develop even more advanced conversational skills called "topic shading." Topic shading is the ability to move subtly from one topic to another related topic.

In theory, we expect conversations to be the meeting of two minds as they share thoughts and concepts. Yet, all of us have been in conversations where we had difficulty getting our idea across. With a few queries on the part of the listener, hopefully, we were able to repair the confusion and move on with the story. The art of conversational repair requires finesse from both the speaker and the listener to work through information that is not understood. Preschoolers can try to repair conversational breakdown, but typically they will only respond to one request for clarification (Brinton, Fujiki, Loeb, & Winkler, 1986). As children mature, their abilities to repair conversations increase (Brinton et al., 1986; James, 1990), such that, a 5-year-old child can respond to two requests for clarification. It is not until elementary school age that we expect a child to supply suitable responses to stacked sequences for a minimum of three clarification requests (James, 1990). For an example of a stacked repair sequence from a typically developing 7-year-old, see below.

Example of a stacked repair sequence from a typically developing 7-year-old.

Child's initial utterance:	"I put water in that."
Clarification request 1:	"In what, Sweety?"
Child's repair 1:	"In that thing over there."
Clarification request 2:	"I don't know what you are talking about"
Child's repair 2:	"In that thing on the counter."
Clarification request 3:	"I'm not getting it."
Child's repair 3:	"You know, the thing on the counter you scrub with."

In elementary school, children become better at responding to clarification requests and determining where the breakdown in conversation occurs. Although some children show this skill earlier, children with typical development do not consistently request clarification of a message until they are about 10 years of age (James, 1990). To request clarification, the listener must ask the speaker for additional information to reduce confusion about the message or instruction. This is of particular importance when professionals are working with children who are d/hh, as the children are often encouraged to tell or ask the teacher if they to do not understand.

Asking for help, or requesting a favor from someone, can be a tricky proposition for adults, much less children. Indirect requests, as opposed to direct requests, are a subtle, more polite way of requesting actions. If the door is open, a direct request to a family member might be, "*Shut the door.*" If the person is not as familiar, then a more polite form, an indirect request of, "*Would you shut the door for me?*" is more appropriate. Both direct and indirect requests have the same underlying intention—the door is open and the speaker wants it closed. However, the indirect request is more socially acceptable.

As many parents may attest, preschoolers tend to be direct in their requests for things, often needing prompting to use *polite forms*, like "please" and "thank you." They have a difficult time understanding indirect requests, as well. So if one said to a 4-year-old, "Isn't it a little cool in here?" He may respond by saying "yes" without understanding that you wanted him to close the door. Around the age of 6 years, children respond to many forms of direct requests, but will still not have mastered the use of indirect requests. It is not until around 8 years of age that children are able to use indirect requests because they understand the importance of being polite.

Another important aspect of pragmatic development is presupposition, or knowing what information to present so that a listener can understand a conversation. We have all been on the receiving end of a story that we could not follow. We did not know the "*she*" to whom the speaker was referring, or which "*thing*" was what. Preschool children do not have well developed presuppositional skills and will have difficulty relaying information to others if the context is not known. This difficulty is, in part, due to their lack of skill with language, but it is also based in their incorrect assumption that listeners know what they know. As children move from preschool into elementary school, their abilities with presuppositional skills advance. In general, school-age students with typical development can successfully set the context of a conversation, or explain the overall purpose of the game (Hulit, Howard, & Fahey. 2011). Additionally, they are able to organize information in a way that listeners have a good idea about the sequence of events. School-age children also pay more attention to topic relevance, providing just the right amount, and the right kind, of information needed by listeners. It is only after repeated experiences with conversations across multiple listeners and varied settings that students develop an understanding that the more pertinent, useful, or timely a topic, the more likely the topic will be readily received by listeners (Naremore, Densmore, & Harmon, 1995).

Making accurate assumptions about listeners' knowledge and establishing contexts for interactions are important skills as students advance in language arts. They will be evaluated on their ability, both written and oral, to use presuppositional skills. Conversational skills and school-age writing assignments require a complex set of language functions, and establishing a joint context for optimizing understanding between the speaker and the listener is critical for success. Additionally, presuppositional ability, in the form of accurate assumptions about teachers and curricular materials, is important for students as they demonstrate critical thinking in content courses. When answering essay questions and explaining how to solve both science and math problems, students must provide the relevant information as clearly as possible.

BEYOND THE BASICS: NARRATIVE LANGUAGE DEVELOPMENT

Expressive language in the form of narratives is a substantial accomplishment associated with school-age language ability. Narrative skills support both production and comprehension of various discourses, including conversational and written language. Narratives come in various shapes and sizes and occur in multiple contexts, including conversation, storytelling, writing fiction and nonfiction, and broadcasting ongoing events, such as a sports competition. Humans across all cultures produce narratives, although there are cross-cultural differences (McCabe & Bliss, 2003). Definitions of narratives often focus on two aspects, a unified meaning or theme and a temporal or causal sequence of ideas (Hughes, McGillivray, & Schmidek, 1997; Liles,

1993; McCabe & Bliss, 2003). When narratives consist of a unified meaning, or the key ideas cluster around a central idea, it is termed "centering." Likewise, "chaining" is the term used when the narrative has events presented in a causal or temporal order. Mature or classic narratives demonstrate both centering and chaining (Applebee, 1978). "Personal narratives" embedded in conversations are the method by which individuals tell their past experiences. Family members and friends retell shared memories through personal narratives. Personal narratives can be termed "accounts," when individuals spontaneously share their experiences (e.g., "You'll never guess what happened to me this weekend . . . "), or "recounts," when individuals are prompted to tell events or describe others' experiences (e.g., "Tell the class about your summer vacation . . . " or "You'll never guess what happened to my sister this weekend . . . "). "Stories" are fictional narratives that describe the goal-directed behaviors of characters.

Educators benefit from understanding the structure of both personal narratives and stories in order to support children's development and effective use of narratives in academic settings. The classic structure of personal narratives has been described using "high-point analysis." McCabe and Rollins (1994) indicated that a classic personal narrative includes an event that marks a high point or problem, often with several evaluative utterances, and an event that represents some resolution following the high point. Typically developing children produce classic high-point personal narratives by first grade, or the age of 6 years (see example in Table 3–3). Some personal narratives demonstrate essential elements for a chronological personal narrative, but

Table 3–3. Narrative Types: Examples Collected from Written Samples

Terms	Example	Source (Child, Age)
Personal Narratives:		
Classic High-Point	"One day I was outside rollerblading and my roller blades wouldn't stop. I was going faster and faster. My dad was standing in front of me and I hit the gravel with my knee and it dragged me along the sidewalk. I walked in the house with a straight face not crying a wink. We called my mom and told her. She was really happy that I was okay."	TD girl, age 8
Chronological	"First, I went over to my grandfather's. I rode my motorcycle."	LI boy, age 8
	"Then she talked about narratives. She had a big speech and passed out papers that they could read off of when she talked. Then she read a lot of stories to the class that she was teaching. Then she talked about how you make a story a story."	TD girl, age 8
End-at-High-Point	"My dad wouldn't let me have a friend over. I was very very sad. He just kept saying no. He was very very mad too."	TD girl, age 7
Stories:		
Complete Episode	"I see a grasshopper. He wants to skateboard. He went to the garage. He went to the place where he kept his skateboard. He looked where his skateboard*. He looked everywhere but he knows where it is in his room. He went to his room. He opened the door and surprise. It was his birthday."	TD boy, age 6;9
Pre-episodic	"I see a bee. He is making some honey. I should go inside before lots of bees come out."	TD boy, age 5;11
	"If you had no parents** I would spend my time alone trying to find new friends and a home. I would check every house in town. If I wouldn't find a friend or home I would leave the town. Go somewhere else to work."	TD girl, age 6;7
	"It was amazing. Wow. I saw a sea serpent jump out of the water. It had spikes on it. There it is! It's huge. The teeth are very sharp. There's another one! They're fighting! The other one went away. It got bigger. I can see its shadow on the water. It's jumping out of the water again and again. It jumps very high! When it got bigger, the spikes got sharper. Cool! It's getting bigger. The spikes are getting sharper."	TD boy, age 7

continues

Table 3–3. *continued*

Terms	Example	Source (Child, Age)
Multiple Episodes	"Once there was a gecko named Bobby. He got bored at standing around all day. So he decided to be a space gecko. So he went and applied for the job and then he got the job. So he went and got his suit and got food and water and then he took off into outerspace. Then he went to Pluto and his rocket ran out of fuel. So he was stuck there. Then he saw a town. He got his ray gun and started walking toward the town, and he saw a slimy green thing. It had 100 eyes, 6,000 legs, and 50 arms. 'Ahh,' Bobby yelled as the creature started walking towards him! Then the creature and Bobby started talking. They talked for at least an hour. Then they finally decided that the gecko can live with the creatures. So the creature showed Bobby around. The towns people decided to kill Bobby. So Bobby blew up the town. Boom!!! Then Bobby's creature friend gave Bobby more fuel. Bobby and the creature went back to Gecko world to prove there was life on other planets."	TD boy, age 8

TD = typically developing; LI = language impaired.

*Typically developing children may exhibit developmentally appropriate word and sentence level errors for early written narrative tasks, particularly for journal assignments that do not require proofing for a final draft. Spelling, but not grammar, has been corrected in all of the examples.

**This school journal example was prompted by the story starter, "If you had no parents . . . ," which likely led to the child's ungrammatical pronoun shift in the first sentence.

fall short of the classic high-point structure (McCabe & Rollins, 1994). That is, a chronological narrative includes a minimum of two past-tense event statements produced in a logical or causal sequence that mirrors the actual event sequence. This type of descriptive narrative is demonstrated by individuals of all ages and is often the result of the type of narrative elicitation task. McCabe and Rollins (1994) also labeled children's personal narratives as *end-at-high-point*, when children tell an event, build to the high point, but do not express a resolution or ending (see examples in Table 3–3). This narrative structure is considered typical of preschool-age children.

Similar to the elements of a personal narrative, the primary feature of a story is the "episode." Episodes consist minimally of three key components: a problem set, an attempt by the main character(s) to address the problem, and some description of the consequences or resolution of that problem (Liles, 1993; Roth & Spekman, 1986). Children's stories that do not contain these episodic elements are *pre-episodic*, similar to the chronological or end-at-high-point personal narratives. The other traditional element of a story is the setting, which precedes the episode. Settings, when explicit, tell the "who," "where," and "when" elements of the story. The episode and setting are critical components of classic story structure, or what is also termed "story grammar." Narratives, particularly fictional stories, are not as simple as what is described here. Instead, much literature, even stories written for young children, consists of multiple episodes. One episode may be embedded within another episode (e.g., Goldilocks attempts to make herself comfortable in the bears' home, while the bears take a walk to let their porridge cool.), or episodes follow one another in a series of adventures (e.g., *If You Give a Mouse a Cookie* by L. Numeroff or the *Harry Potter* series by J. K. Rowling). Children's successful reading comprehension requires tracking details (including initiating events, attempts, resolutions, and character motivations and feelings) across complex, embedded episodic structures.

Even when children produce classic narrative structures (i.e., high points with resolution or complete episodes), narratives can vary in the entertainment value, or the degree to which they evoke emotional responses. Ukrainetz (2006) described this qualitative aspect as "story art." Story art elements include introductions and explanatory elements that create increased interest, not necessarily increased factual detail. Effective stories use evaluative language, often building suspense and emotion around the problem or high point. Repetitions of key ideas or refrain-like utterances, stated moral lessons, and creative openings or endings contribute to story art. Consider any evidence of story art or "sparkle" in

the example stories in Table 3–3. Do any of the stories have creative beginnings or endings, evoke emotion, or effectively use repetition?

Development of narrative skill starts in the preschool years and increases throughout the school-age years into adulthood (Nippold, 2007). Kindergarten and early elementary-aged children tell personal narratives, produce scripts, and retell relatively simple stories. Narratives are often prompted and supported by adults who are familiar with the story content, and children may rely on pictures to create a shared context for story retelling (Ukrainetz, 2006). Around the ages of 6 to 7 years, children increasingly include all aspects of a classic story and personal narrative structure. That is, they produce complete episodes in story retelling and produce high points plus resolutions in their personal narratives (Hughes et al., 1997; Liles, 1993). By about third grade, typically developing children can generate their own stories, although picture support or shared context may be needed. Some children may not be successful at retelling stories in their entirety or generating novel stories without picture support until around the seventh grade, or ages 12 to 13 years (Nippold, 2007). From kindergarten through adolescence, children who are typically developing demonstrate narrative development through: (a) increased length and detail, (b) increased number of episodes, including multiple episodes that are linked to one another or embedded one within another, (c) more emotional detail, and (d) greater effort to entertain listeners or add story art (Nippold, 2007).

Although patterns in narrative development have been observed, differences in narrative development are also expected.

Children learn narratives in social contexts. That is, they are socialized to listen to and produce various types of narratives within their families and early preschool and school environments (Westby, 1994). Not all families and cultures create and tell stories in the same ways or for the same reasons (McCabe & Bliss, 2003; Westby, 1994). More specifically, story episode structure, as described above, is predominant in mainstream American culture, but not critical in other storytelling genres. For example, stories in many Asian cultures tend to have themes that focus on the main character's background and emphasis is placed on cultural tradition, not goal-directed behaviors of an individual (Westby, 1994).

Children who are d/hh, similar to children with language impairment, have been shown to produce fewer complete episodes at the ages of 7 to12 years than expected for non-hearing-impaired individuals (Justice, Swanson, & Buehler, 2008; Weiss & Johnson, 1993; Young et al., 1997). Ukrainetz (2006) recommended assessing four aspects of narrative production: "(1) degree of independence, (2) story grammar, (3) cohesion, and (4) story art" (p. 197). Although early elementary-age children are expected to produce narratives independently, their degree of independence is relevant because educators provide varying degrees of support for narrative success and continued development. The story grammar assessment described by Ukrainetz is dominated by evaluating the episode. Story grammar, or episodic analysis, is considered a macrostructure approach; that is, emphasis is placed on the overall text structure. Cohesion, on the other hand, is a narrative element consisting of utterance connections to create a unified text. Cohesion analysis is focused on sentence struc-

tures and word selections (particularly conjunctions and pronouns) that assist the listener or reader in creating meaning across utterances. Conjunctions used to link events in narratives include the following meanings: addition ("and," "also"); change of direction ("but," "on the other hand"); temporal ("first," "next"); causal ("because," "then"); emphasis ("most of all"); and illustration ("for example"). Maintaining cohesion through appropriate pronoun use requires that the storyteller unambiguously identify salient individuals, events, or locations prior to using a pronoun. For example, the storyteller cannot appropriately use "he" or "there" without the referents ("king" and "kingdom," for example) clearly indicated in prior utterances. Last, Ukrainetz (2006) stressed that story art factors can distinguish more sophisticated and appealing stories from those judged perfunctory.

Narrative structures, both personal narratives and stories, can be powerful teaching tools. For children who display weaknesses in narrative components, educators can target teaching those aspects of story grammar with resulting improvements in conversational skills, reading comprehension, and written expression. Additionally, narratives can be the context for targeting other skill areas, like morphology and syntax. Specifically, Swanson and colleagues have demonstrated that syntactic weaknesses (i.e., use of coordinating and subordinating conjunctions) for children with language impairment (Swanson, Fey, Mills, & Hood, 2005) and children who have cochlear implants (Justice et al., 2008) can be targeted in narrative intervention, while simultaneously addressing narrative development (e.g., explicit description of the first part of the episode, the problem set).

CONCLUSIONS

Children who talk like books and write like books have a better chance of being academically successful than children who do not. Language is everywhere at school: oral and written directions given by teachers, books on which to write reports, and science and social studies chapters with questions to answer. To successfully advance through school, students must demonstrate ever-maturing skills in oral and written language venues. To understand and express complex concepts, students need to use and understand syntactic structure that is made more complex by phrase and clause embedding. Semantics present a particular challenge for children if they have not learned the strategies for lexicon acquisition. The pragmatic use of language is needed for meaningful peer interaction. All of these components (and more) are needed for the ability to successfully produce narratives that are age-appropriate and interesting.

Students who are d/hh, and who have deficits in their oral language development, are at risk for experiencing reading disabilities and written expression weaknesses that will result in negative academic outcomes. Audiologists who are informed about the linguistic demands of the classroom are in a prime position to advocate for children who are d/hh and unable to meet those demands.

REFERENCES

Antia, S. D., Jones, P. B., Reed, S., & Kreimeyer, K. H. (2009). Academic status and progress of deaf and hard-of-hearing students in general education classrooms. *Journal of Deaf Studies and Deaf Education, 14,* 293–311.

Applebee, A. N. (1978). *The child's concept of story: Ages two to seventeen.* Chicago, IL: University of Chicago Press.

Berent, G., Kelly, R., & Porter, J. (2008). Deaf learners' knowledge of English universal quantifiers. *Language Learning, 58*(2), 401–437.

Bradley, L., & Bryant, P. E. (1983). Categorizing sounds and learning to read—a causal connection. *Nature, 301*(3), 419–420.

Brinton, B., Fujiki, M., Loeb, D. F., & Winkler, E. (1986). Development of conversational repair strategies in response to requests for clarification. *Journal of Speech and Hearing Research, 29,* 75–81.

Briscoe, J., Bishop, D. V. M., & Norbury, C. F. (2001). Phonological processing, language, and literacy: A comparison of mild-to-moderate sensorineural hearing loss and those with specific language impairment. *Journal of Child Psychology and Psychiatry, 42,* 329–340.

Brown, R. (1973). *A first language.* Cambridge, MA: Harvard University Press.

Duncan, G. J., Dowsett, C. J., Claessens, A., Magnuson, K., Huston, A. C., Klebanov, P., . . . Japel, C. (2007). School readiness and later achievement. *Developmental Psychology, 43*(6), 1428–1446.

Hughes, D., McGillivray, L., & Schmidek, M. (1997). *Guide to narrative language: Procedures for assessment.* Austin, TX: Pro-Ed.

Hulit, L. M., Howard, M. R., & Fahey, K. R. (2011). *Born to talk: An introduction to speech and language development.* Boston, MA: Pearson Education.

James, S. L. (1990). *Normal language acquisition.* Boston, MA: Allyn and Bacon.

Justice, E. C., Swanson, L. A., & Buehler, V. (2008). Use of narrative-based language intervention with children who have cochlear implants. *Topics in Language Disorders, 28,* 149–161.

Kuvshinoff, B. E., & Creaghead, N. A. (1994). Literacy in elementary school: Getting started on a lifelong journey. In D. N. Ripich & N. A. Creaghead (Eds.), *School discourse problems* (pp. 29–62). San Diego, CA: Singular.

Liles, B. (1993). Narrative discourse in children with language disorders and children with normal language: A critical review of the literature. *Journal of Speech and Hearing Research, 36,* 868–882.

McCabe, A., & Bliss, L. S. (2003). *Patterns of narrative discourse: A multicultural life span approach.* Boston, MA: Pearson Education.

McCabe, A., & Rollins, P. R. (1994). Assessment of preschool narrative skills. *American Journal of Speech-Language Pathology, 3,* 45–56.

Milosky, L. M. (1994). Nonliteral language abilities: Seeing the forest for the trees. In G. P. Wallach & K. G. Butler (Eds.), *Language, learning disabilities in school-age children and adolescents: Some principles and applications* (pp. 275–303). New York, NY: Macmillan.

Moeller, M. P., Tomblin, J. B., Yoshinaga-Itano, C., McDonald Connor, C., & Jerger, S. (2007). Current state of knowledge: Language and literacy of children with hearing impairment. *Ear and Hearing, 28,* 740–753.

Naremore, R., Densmore, A. E., & Harmon, D. R. (1995). *Language intervention with school-age children: Conversation, narrative, and text.* San Diego, CA: Singular.

Nelson, N. W., & Van Meter, A. M. (2006). Find the words: Vocabulary development for young authors. In T. A. Ukrainetz (Ed.), *Contextualized language intervention: Scaffolding preK–12 literacy achievement* (pp. 95–143). Eau Claire, WI: Thinking Publications.

Nippold, M. A. (2007). *Later language de-velopment: School-age children, adolescents, and young adults* (3rd ed.). Austin, TX: Pro-Ed.

Owens, R. E. (2008). *Language development: An introduction* (7th ed.). Boston, MA: Pearson.

Pence, K. L., & Justice, L. M. (2008). *Language development from theory to practice.* Upper Saddle River, NJ: Person Education.

Pinker, S. (1994). *The language instinct: How the mind creates language.* New York, NY: Morrow.

Power, D. J., & Quigley, S. P. (1973). Deaf children's acquisition of the passive voice. *Journal of Speech and Hearing Research, 16,* 5–11.

Rand Corporation. (2002). *Reading for understanding: Toward an R&D program in reading comprehension.* Santa Monica, CA: RAND. (ERIC Document Reproduction Service No. ED 463559)

Roth, F. P., & Spekman N. J. (1986). Narrative discourse: Spontaneously generated stories of learning-disabled and normally achieving students. *Journal of Speech and Hearing Disorders, 51,* 8–23.

Shaywitz, S. (2003). *Overcoming dyslexia.* New York, NY: Knopf.

Swanson, L. A., Fey, M. E., Mills, C. E., & Hood, L. S. (2005). Use of narrative-based language intervention with children who have specific language impairment. *American Journal of Speech-Language Pathology, 14,* 131–143.

Ukrainetz, T. A. (2006). Teaching narrative structure: Coherence, cohesion, and captivation. In T. A. Ukrainetz (Ed.), *Contextualized language intervention: Scaffolding preK–12 literacy achievement* (pp. 195–246). Eau Claire, WI: Thinking Publications.

Weiss, A. L., & Johnson, C. J. (1993). Relationships between narrative and syntactic competencies in school-aged, hearing-impaired children. *Applied Psycholinguistics, 14*(1), 35–59.

Westby, C. E. (1994). The effects of culture on genre, structure, and style of oral and written texts. In G. P. Wallach & K. G. Butler (Eds.), *Language learning disabilities in school-age children and adolescents* (pp. 180–218). New York, NY: Merrill.

Westby, C. E. (2006). There's more to passing then knowing the answers: Learning to do school. In T. A. Ukrainetz (Ed.), *Contextualized language intervention: Scaffolding preK–12 literacy achievement* (pp. 319–387). Eau Claire, WI: Thinking Publications.

Young, G. A., James, D. G. H., Brown, K., Giles, F., Hemmings, L., Hollis, J., Keagan, S., &

Newton, M. (1997). The narrative skills of primary school children with unilateral hearing impairment. *Clinical Linguistics & Phonetics, 11,* 115–138.

Educational Audiology in the Real World

Joseph A. Voglund, AuD
Audiologist working in schools
Long Beach Unified School District
Signal Hill, California

In 2000, I was working in the audiology department of a New England hospital when I read an ad in the Advance for Speech-Language Pathologists and Audiologists *for an audiologist to work in the Long Beach Unified School District in Long Beach, CA. The published salary range was quite good and the position seemed very attractive. I sent a letter of interest along with my resume, but never expected to hear from anyone. A few days later, I received a phone call from Human Resources asking me to come for an interview. I did, and I was selected as the candidate for the position. There was one condition for employment and that was that I had to earn an educational credential after hours. After some salary negotiation, I accepted the position, and my family and I moved to Long Beach. It was the best career decision I ever made.*

My beginning salary was $55,000.00 for a 10-month per year program. I was not given any funds for a moving allowance, but I felt that, over time, the benefits of the position far outweighed any moving allowance that I might have received. Family health and dental insurances were fully paid, and the District offered several plans. I was put on the same pay scale and time schedule contract as were the school psychologists and counselors (which is considered to be an administrative schedule). This contract was above the speech-language pathologists' and teachers' pay scales. I was not in the bargaining unit of the union, so I did not need to pay union dues. But I discontinued Social Security and became part of the teachers' state retirement plan.

Regarding vacation time, I had about 7 weeks off during summers. I worked only when students were in school, and if the schools were closed for vacation and holidays, I was given that time off. If I were needed during summer school, I was paid an hourly rate based on my salary.

I passed the CBEST teacher test and then worked with Dr. Carolyn Madding and Dr. O.T. Kenworthy (deceased) at California State University in Long Beach to earn my teacher credential in 2004. Doing so moved me to another pay scale in the District and offset the cost of the credential, which was about $2,500.00. Several of the audiologists in Long Beach were earning their AuD by distance education at ATSU in Mesa, AZ. I didn't want to be left out; therefore, I earned my AuD from ATSU and graduated in March, 2008. I was hooded by Dr. Tabitha Parent, who graduated a year ahead of me from Purdue University, my alma mater. And, you guessed it, I moved over another pay scale in the District. The AuD investment was about $6,000.00, but I got all of that back on income tax refunds, so the real investment was $0.00! Presently I'm earning over $92,000.00 plus $13,000.00 for health and dental through the District for a total of $105,000.00. Not bad!

So what do I do as the only educational audiologist for Long Beach Unified School District? Here's the list:

- *Perform hearing tests; some tests are done at schools when transportation is an issue, but most are done at the audiology lab where more thorough tests can be done and the family can be involved.*
- *Perform (central) auditory processing disorder evaluations.*
- *Counsel students and their families regarding hearing loss and assistive listening devices.*
- *Help with educational placement decisions. (Most of our students with hearing impairment stay in their home schools in general education with support from deaf/hard of hearing itinerant teachers, speech-language pathologists, speech specialists, SLPAs, and auditory-verbal therapists.*
- *Hold training sessions for general education teachers, support personnel, occupational therapists, physical therapists, and psychologists.*
- *Refer to California Children's Services for medical and audiological evaluations and hearing aids or implants (cochlear and BAHA).*
- *Accept referrals from school personnel, particularly the school nurses who operate the hearing screening program.*
- *Accept referrals from parents and from others outside of District personnel.*
- *Serve as a consultant.*
- *Attend individual educational plan and 504 plan meetings.*
- *Attend low incidence and related services meetings.*
- *Forge and maintain relationships with the dispensing audiologists in the area and with the implant (cochlear and BAHA) centers in the area.*
- *Work with the deaf/hard of hearing students in sign language special day classes and with general education students who use sign language.*
- *Invent and/or maintain and use electronic record keeping systems for scheduling tests, student history and census and ALD inventory.*

The District is large with over 90 schools and 88,000 students, including 300 deaf/hard of hearing students. I could never perform this job without the direct and capable assistance of two deaf/hard of hearing itinerant teachers, one early intervention deaf/hard of hearing teacher, and the technical support from a local electronics shop. I thoroughly enjoy my job. Almost everything that the staff and I do helps hard of hearing students live better lives, even with imperfect cooperation from teachers and ALD failures. My job as the audiologist for Long Beach Unified School District is the most rewarding position I have had in my life.

Some final words of wisdom: As an audiologist working in the schools, be prepared for the unexpected. For example, students implanted outside the United States may come to you without arrangements for support in the United States. In addition, I personally refrain from using the word "educational" in front of "audiologist" to describe myself. I believe I am an audiologist first and then an audiologist who works in a school system. However, I believe that associations can be described by a specialty, such as the Educational Audiology Association.

The Role of the
School-Based Audiologist

Cynthia M. Richburg and Donna F. Smiley

OBJECTIVES

By the end of this chapter, the reader will be able to:

1. Define and describe the various roles and service delivery models for school-based audiologists.
2. Discuss and describe ASHA Guidelines for service delivery in the schools and minimum competencies.
3. Describe the roles and uses of assistants.
4. Describe and discuss the equipment and facilities used in the various service delivery models.
5. Describe and discuss the roles of school-based audiologists in early intervention.
6. Describe and discuss the roles of school-based audiologists as advocates and multidisciplinary team members.

INTRODUCTION

As with any audiologist in any practice setting, school-based audiologists put on many hats and have many roles and responsibilities associated with their job descriptions. Students will get some idea of just how many different roles and responsibilities educational audiologists possess when they read the vignettes placed throughout this textbook. However, students should also be familiar with special terminology and association guidelines that will impact their future practice.

THE ROLES AND RESPONSIBILITIES OF SCHOOL-BASED AUDIOLOGISTS

Regardless of the job title, whether it is "educational audiologist," "school-based audiologist," or "audiologist employed in the schools," most school-based audiologists play several different roles. Part of their day may be spent being a diagnostic audiologist; part of their day may be spent being a technology expert. Other roles include teacher, service coordinator, instructional team member, consultant, and counselor. Still other roles include professional manager, trainer, supervisor, record keeper, collaborator, and researcher. Due to the differences among school systems and school administrations, it would be impossible to list *all* of the roles of an educational audiologist; however, all audiologists must remain cognizant of keeping their roles within the scope of practice spelled out by ASHA (2004). For a more complete description of some of the roles listed above, it is recommended that the reader access the ASHA *Guidelines for Audiology Service Provision in and for Schools* (2002) and the Educational Audiology Association's *Recommended Professional Practices for Educational Audiology* (2009).

The responsibilities of the audiologist working in a school setting will be numerous and varied between employers. Table 4–1 is a fairly comprehensive list of the responsibilities that audiologists in the schools may encounter. There are several guidelines and practice statements issued by ASHA, the American Academy of Audiology (AAA), and the Educational Audiology Association (EAA) that need to be read and reviewed regularly. These are updated with each organization's latest recommendations and protocols for providing school-based services.

LOCAL EDUCATION AGENCIES (LEA) AND COOPERATIVES

When we look at how school districts across the United States access school-based audiology services, many terms and concepts need to be described in order to make sense of it all. Each state will have its own Department of Education (DE). Under the DE within each state, there are local education agencies (LEA), which are synonymous to the term school district. An LEA, or school district, is a governmental agency that supervises the provision of instruction or educational services to the community within their local, public primary and secondary schools. Some school districts directly employ an audiologist; other school districts contract with an audiologist. Because there are many states in which school districts are small, some states have resorted to forming educational cooperative agencies, or co-ops. These co-ops employ personnel who provide specialized services (e.g., visual impairment, school psychology, behavioral intervention, etc.). In some cases, audiology services are provided to individual districts in a state under this cooperative system. Different states have their own terms for co-ops. For instance, the state of Arkansas uses the term Education Service Cooperatives (ESC), the state of New York uses the term Board of Cooperative Education Services (BOCES), the state of Pennsylvania uses the term Intermediate Unit (IU), the state of Iowa uses the term Area Education Agencies

Table 4–1. A List of the Many and Varied Responsibilities of a School-Based Audiologist

- Identifying and monitoring hearing loss
- Performing classroom observations and evaluating auditory behaviors
- Evaluating speech perception capabilities
- Selecting and fitting amplification technologies, including hearing aids, cochlear implants, frequency modulation (FM) systems
- Monitoring the use of technologies to be sure they are providing necessary benefit
- Evaluating the need for and selection of hearing assistance technologies (HAT) both personal and classroom
- Making referrals to appropriate healthcare and service providers
- Counseling parents and other team members about hearing loss and technology
- Identifying other problems, such as Auditory Processing Disorders and Auditory Neuropathy/Dys-synchrony
- Performing audiological assessments for a variety of age groups
- Performing audiological assessments for special populations (multisensory impaired, for example)
- Educating students and school personnel about the prevention of hearing loss
- Troubleshooting cochlear implants, hearing aids, and FM systems on a daily basis
- Staying abreast of current technology
- Administrating programs that serve students with hearing impairments
- Possessing some skills in American Sign Language, Signed English, or Cued Speech
- Possessing a working knowledge of the spoken language skills hierarchy
- Providing in-service trainings to staff as needed regarding hearing loss and hearing aid/cochlear implant/FM technology, etc.
- Possessing a working knowledge of special education law
- Establishing communication between the school setting and outside clinics or personal audiologists
- Calibrating equipment and analyzing classroom acoustics

Source: Excerpts from Madell and Flexer (2008). This list is not meant to be all inclusive.

(AEA), and the state of Georgia uses the term Regional Educational Service Agency (RESA). There may be other terms used; therefore, familiarizing oneself with the local terminology is recommended for anyone interested in becoming a school-based audiologist.

We would be remiss if we did not mention the fact that not all school districts are accessing school-based audiologists (Richburg & Smiley, 2009). Some districts, for one reason or another, do not believe that they need audiological services. Therefore, one should not be under the impression that every school district in every state is utilizing audiologists and audiological services. In fact, for those audiologists who practice in school settings (and those who want to), a concerted effort must be made to better educate school personnel, families of students with hearing impairments, and policy makers at federal and state levels. It is imperative to convey to these groups that school-based audiology services are *necessary* for students to benefit from the education they are receiving.

THE CONTINUUM OF SERVICE DELIVERY MODELS

Traditionally, two service delivery models are used for school-based audiology: local education agency-based services and contractual services. Determining which model to use should be based on several factors, all of which should be related to the quality and range of the services being provided. For instance, cost effectiveness is a reality of school-based services and must be taken into consideration for each model. Additionally, the number of children being served, the nature of their hearing losses, and the geographic distribution of the population being served must be taken into consideration. Finally, compliance with local, state, and federal regulations must be factored into the mix. No matter which one of these service delivery models is used, the LEA and audiologists should work to avoid duplication of services. Thereby, collaborative efforts need to take place to provide appropriate service delivery (see Chapter 10).

Local Education Agency-Based Services

These services may be more comprehensive and efficient than contractual audiol-ogy services, according to the 2002 ASHA *Guidelines for Audiology Service Provision in and for Schools.* This is because these services are provided directly by audiologists who may have more constant access to students, are more familiar with their cases, and have established a certain rapport with each child on their caseloads. Also, because the audiologists are consistently in contact with teachers, administrators, and other educational personnel, there is efficient and comprehensive daily contact and communication.

In this service delivery model, audiologists are typically employed directly by the LEA (which may be a local school district, an intermediate education agency or a cooperative program), and they are typically paid a salary and benefits. These audiologists act as the service coordinator for all students with hearing loss in the LEA, and often, become an instructional team member, working with regular and special education teachers.

Contractual Services

Although these services may not provide the same comprehensiveness and efficiency provided by local education agency-based services, there is a need for this type of service delivery in the schools. In this model, audiology services can be provided through contractual agreements that are established with a variety of agencies: audiology private practices (both for-profit and non-profit), public agencies or organizations (e.g., Optimist Club and Quota International), local speech and hearing clinics, medical facilities (such as ENT clinics or pediatric hospitals), and university training programs. Contractual services typically are provided on a fee-for-services basis, which is calculated in terms of time involved and/or number of children served.

Contracts should be written to specifically address: (1) services that are to be provided both on-site (e.g., intervention services, measurement of classroom acoustics, instruction, and teacher consultation) and off-site (e.g., reports, phone consultations, home-visit activities); (2) schedules and time lines of service delivery; (3) data that are to be collected and reported; (4) methods in which referral and follow-up are to take place, (5) guidelines for equipment, materials, and supplies usage; and (6) methods in which other appropriate personnel will receive information. The ASHA 2002 *Guidelines for Audiology Service Provision in and for Schools* state:

> Contracted audiology services have the potential to be as effective as LEA-based services, but care must be taken to ensure that the contracts are not limited in the provision of comprehensive services. Additionally, timelines, services, reports, and records must comply with federal, SEA, and LEA requirements. It is critical that contractors understand education policies and procedures, collaboration, and the multidisciplinary approach to service delivery to students with hearing loss and/or APD. (pp. 19–20)

The ASHA guidelines (ASHA, 2002) also warn of the potential for an ethical breach (i.e., conflict of interest) and disputes that may be brought about as the result of one audiologist providing services through a school contract and providing services through a private practice within the same community.

Contractual audiologists are employed by the contracting agency or agencies, and they are paid on a fee-per-service basis and typically do not receive bene-fits. These audiologists may or may not be the service coordinator for their students with hearing loss, and collaboration with regular and special education teachers may be much more difficult.

Itinerant Services

A subcategory of both school-based and contractual service delivery model would include itinerant audiological services. Itinerant audiologists are mobile audiologists who typically travel from school to school, and sometimes district to district, providing many of the services listed in Table 4–1. Like contractual services, itinerant services may be the only feasible form of service delivery that LEAs are able to offer, due to affordability or the low incidence of students who are d/hh.

RECOMMENDED WORKLOADS FOR SCHOOL-BASED AUDIOLOGISTS

When discussing the roles and responsibilities of school-based audiologists, one should be familiar with caseload and workload recommendations. It goes without saying that adequate numbers of audiologists, and ample fiscal and administrative support from the LEA, must be available to provide audiological services to children in schools. At least one full-time equivalent (FTE) audiologist for every 10,000 children (a ratio of 1:10,000) birth through 21 years of age is recommended to provide audiologic services in the schools (ASHA, 2002; Colorado Department of Education, 1998;

EAA, 2009). Note that this ratio is not based on the number of children who are deaf/hard of hearing; rather, it is based on the total number of students to be served. This is an indication of the idea that school-based audiology is really about *all* students in a school, not just the ones who are already identified as having hearing loss. Of course, there are several factors that would necessitate the lowering of those ratios due to unreasonable demands being placed on a single audiologist. For example, a large number of schools or LEAs, excessive travel times to those schools, the numbers of students with and without hearing loss or APD requiring audiological assessment and intervention services, and the quantity of devices (hearing aids, cochlear implants, FM systems) to be maintained are just some of the demands that have to be taken into account when estimating workload or caseload numbers (EAA, 2009).

USE OF AUDIOLOGY ASSISTANTS IN SCHOOL SETTINGS

Due to increases in the numbers of children diagnosed with hearing loss or auditory process disorders in U.S. schools, the expansion of audiologists' scope of practice, and changes made in state and federal health care and education initiatives, a need for support personnel, or assistants, has developed throughout the profession of audiology. Assistants are meant to help school-based audiologists provide the highest level of quality care for students while maintaining productivity and cost containment. Assistants are not recognized in all states, and some states that recognize them do not regulate their activities. Therefore, the use of and services provided by assistants are just another example of the variability of service delivery in school-based audiology.

The Educational Audiology Association (EAA, 1997) has a document, *Guidelines of the Consensus Panel on Support Personnel in Audiology*, that fully details the use of assistants in the schools. This document delineates the roles and tasks of assistants as they relate to the supervising audiologists and students. These *Guidelines* (EAA, 1997) state that licensed and certified audiologists are "the appropriate, qualified professionals to hire, supervise, and train audiology support personnel." Supervision of the assistants must be periodic and thorough. Appropriate documentation must take place to assure that students are protected and receiving the most appropriate services.

The EAA *Guidelines* (1997) list qualifications for support personnel that include the following:

1. Have a high school degree or equivalent;
2. Have communication and interpersonal skills necessary for the tasks assigned;
3. Have a basic understanding of the needs of the population being served
4. Have met training requirements and have competency-based skills necessary to the performance of specific assigned tasks; and
5. Have any additional qualifications established by the supervising audiologist to meet the specific needs of the audiology program and the population being served.

The *Guidelines* (EAA, 1997) go on to describe the type of training supervisors should provide to their assistants, and a list of activities that these support personnel are *not* to engage in is available. In general, these guidelines state that the roles and functions of assistants should be well-defined, should be influenced by the supervising audiologist's particular needs, and should remain within the skill level of the assistant. Training should be competency-based and documented fully, and supervision should be consistent with the skills and experience of the assistant. Finally, protecting the interests of students in a manner consistent with state licensure requirements and/or the Code of Ethics of the audiologist's respective professional organization(s) and employment settings remains the responsibility of the supervising audiologist.

EQUIPMENT, FACILITIES, AND MATERIALS

Any school-based audiologist's ability to carry out the roles and responsibilities of his or her job includes having access to the appropriate equipment, facilities, and materials. The equipment should be calibrated annually (or according to the manufacturer's recommendations) and maintained within the most current set of American National Standards Institute's (ANSI) standards. Equipment should be portable, and as lightweight as possible. However, it also has to be sturdy and resistant to breakage. The ASHA *Guidelines for Audiology Service Provision in and for Schools* (2002) lists much of the equipment needed to practice educational audiology. Some school-based audiologists may not have access to all of the equipment listed; however, all school-based audiologists need to have equip-

ment necessary for assessing young children and difficult-to-test children. Some of this equipment includes an otoscope, portable immittance equipment, clinical audiometer with soundfield capabilities, visual reinforcement audiometry (VRA) equipment, a CD player for use with recorded assessment materials, a portable audiometer, earmold impression materials and modification equipment, a computer for generating reports and/or tracking student data, sterilization/sanitation supplies, and a sound-level meter with calibrator. Equipment that may not be accessible to every educational audiologist (due to funding issues) includes electrophysiological equipment (e.g., otoacoustic emissions or auditory brainstem response), electroacoustic testing equipment (e.g., hearing aid analyzer or real ear system), and loaner hearing aids or hearing assistance technologies.

Facilities are harder to define as "appropriate." The term "facilities" typically refers to classrooms and offices found within schools. However, anyone who is familiar with schools knows that there is nothing "typical" or regular about the facilities found therein. Also, due to the itinerant nature of school-based audiology services, facilities for testing, assessment, and management will vary from school to school. In the practice of audiology, an acoustically appropriate test area is needed. Some school-based audiologists may have access to sound-treated test booths, but many do not. Most audiologists find a test environment in a classroom, music room, library, or other quiet area away from noise sources to perform screening or hearing assessments. Therapies are also dealt with in low-noise, if not no-noise, environments. (See Chapter 2 for more information on appropriate acoustic environments.)

Testing and screening materials should be developmentally, linguistically, and culturally appropriate for the students on the audiologist's caseload. They should also be as portable and lightweight as possible. Materials might include tests and screeners for evaluating speech, language, speechreading, functional listening, and auditory skills or supplies for providing direct and indirect intervention services (ASHA, 2002).

ADDITIONAL ROLES OF SCHOOL-BASED AUDIOLOGISTS

The Role of the Educational Audiologist in Early Intervention

In some Early Intervention (EI) and Early Hearing Detection and Intervention (EHDI) programs, school-based audiologists are part of a team of professionals whose responsibilities include hearing loss identification, intervention, prevention, and conservation in children typically younger than school age. One of the responsibilities of audiologists working with this young population includes assisting the family with decisions regarding communication options. The educational audiologist can support parents and caregivers by providing information about the features of language and communication, various communication methodologies, and the child's developmental profile. By assisting parents as they explore communication options for their child, educational audiologists can help parents chose a communication style that fits in with their family and affords the child access to the learning environment. The EAA

(2002) states that, "As educational audiologists, it is our responsibility to advocate for communication access as key to a natural environment for a child with hearing loss."

The Role of the Educational Audiologist as Advocate

English (1995) proposed that the difference between a clinical audiologist and a school-based audiologist is the school-based audiologist's role as advocate. Because children with hearing impairments are young and inexperienced, and because most of these children are not capable of advocating for themselves, the educational audiologist is one of several professionals who must step up and promote the cause and support the educational process for these children. As discussed in Chapter 10, school-based audiologists need to advocate for their students by enlightening administrators, school board members, and local and state policy makers. Ensuring that the needs of these students are not being overlooked, and ultimately helping these learners develop their own self-advocacy skills, is an important role that should not be downplayed or trivialized in the field of audiology.

The EAA published a position paper entitled *Advocacy for Audiologists Working in the Schools* in 2006. That paper describes some of the roles educational audiologists face as advocates working with students and families. It documents the roles and responsibilities that make educational audiologists uniquely qualified to ensure that all students (not just ones with hearing loss) have access to auditory information in their educational environments.

REFERENCES

American Speech-Language-Hearing Association. (2002). *Guidelines for audiology service provision in and for schools* [Guidelines]. Available from http://www.asha.org/policy .

American Speech-Language-Hearing Association. (2004). Scope of practice in audiology. *ASHA Supplement 24.*

Colorado Department of Education. (1998). *Standards of practice for educational audiology services.* Denver, CO: Author.

Educational Audiology Association. (1997). *Guidelines of the consensus panel on support personnel in audiology.* Available from: http://www.audiology.org/resources/documentlibrary/Pages/SupportPersonnelinAudiology.aspx

Educational Audiology Association. (2002). *Early detection and intervention of hearing loss: Roles and responsibilities for educational audiologists.* Available from http://www.edaud.org/associations/4846/files/Early%20Detection%20Pos09.%20stmt.pdf

Educational Audiology Association. (2006). *Advocacy for audiologists working in the schools.*

Educational Audiology Association. (2009). *Recommended professional practices for educational audiology.* Available from: http://www.edaud.org/associations/4846/files/Professional%20Practices_pos09_REVISED.pdf

English, K. M. (1995). *Educational audiology across the lifespan: Serving all learners with hearing impairment.* Baltimore, MD: Paul H. Brookes.

Madell, J. R., & Flexer, C. (2008). *Pediatric audiology: Diagnosis, technology and management.* New York, NY: Thieme Medical.

Richburg, C. M., & Smiley, D. F., (2009). The "state" of educational audiology revisited. *Journal of Educational Audiology, 15,* 63–73.

Educational Audiology in the Real World

Daniel Ostergren, AuD
Educational Audiologist
Poudre School District
Fort Collins, Colorado

I had no intention of becoming an audiologist working in an educational setting. None whatsoever. Coming out of graduate school I wanted to do research, see unusual patholo- gies—all the fun, "important" stuff. Instead, I secured a one-year position providing edu- cational audiology services to a small, northern Colorado community. It was my clinical fellowship year, and I figured I'd just move on after that. That one year has become a career spanning 25 years!

What happened? At some point, I realized that what fills my cup isn't audiology per se, it's the people. It's service. Working with children and their families is not a job or a career. It is a privilege. It gives back more than it takes, and sometimes it takes a lot (screening is tedious, but I get paid to know what to do after the screening). I have a flexible schedule, a variety of work locations, I dress casually, have time to spend with my own family, and have a great network of professional peers. Guess what? I do research, teach, serve on national/international policy committees, and consult in the private sector, as well. I guess I'm having my cake and eating it too! Shh, don't tell anyone.

SECTION II

Services in the Schools

5

Hearing Screenings in the Schools

Cynthia M. Richburg, Jackie M. Davie, and Donna F. Smiley

OBJECTIVES

By the end of this chapter, the reader will be able to:

1. Understand why screenings for hearing loss are performed in schools.
2. Identify the characteristics of an effective hearing screening protocol.
3. Recognize the resources required for implementing a screening program (equipment, staff, environment, etc.).
4. Describe follow-up procedures for children who do not pass the screening.
5. Describe effective record keeping and reporting of screening results.
6. Describe other considerations for implementing a screening program (state-directed timelines, avoidance of cold or allergy seasons, infection control, etc.).

INTRODUCTION

Screening the hearing of school-age children is just one of the many roles school-based audiologists perform. They also supervise others who perform hearing screenings. Screenings, in general, are a means of quickly and efficiently assessing a large cohort of individuals to identify those who are at a higher risk for a disorder. Screenings are typically held for individuals who are highly likely to have a disorder, or for those who can be negatively impacted if the disorder is not discovered and treated. Such is the case with children, hearing loss, and hearing screenings. If a child has an unidentified hearing loss, the loss can negatively impact his or her educational development, especially if it is not identified and treated in a timely fashion. Screening the

69

school-age population, especially in the early grades, assesses a large group of children who are in the age range likely to exhibit hearing loss caused by otitis media with effusion, as well as other acquired pathologies or congenital factors. A sound knowledge of screening protocol, follow-up procedures, record keeping, and result reporting is necessary for audiologists working in schools. This knowledge is necessary for two reasons: educational audiologists must know how to provide the services needed to identify hearing disorders in school-age children, and they must know how to abide by their state's Department of Education requirements and/or state regulations.

If audiologists are to complete hearing screenings on every child at birth, and then at regular intervals throughout their school years, the hearing screening process needs to be easy, quick, and effective at identifying children who are at risk for hearing loss. Knowing what to look for and which techniques are recommended for screening protocols should allow a school-based audiologist to implement an effective hearing screening program within his or her school district, should screenings be one of the audiologist's job responsibilities. Table 5–1 presents a list of questions that can be addressed when developing a screening protocol for a school.

THE PURPOSE OF HEARING SCREENINGS

Hearing screenings are a means of quickly identifying those who are at risk for having a hearing loss. Considering that between one and 6 out of every 1,000 children is born with a hearing loss, and nearly 10 to 15% will acquire a hearing loss during their childhood (Cunningham & Cox, 2003; Kemper & Downs, 2000; Niskar, Kieszak, Holmes, Esteban, Rubin, & Brody, 2001), the need for hearing screenings during the school-age years is well justified. The purpose of hearing screenings in the school-age population must be to identify students who have, or who are at risk for, auditory impairment that may impact communication abilities, health, education, and psychosocial function. Additionally, hearing screenings should result in recommendations for rescreening, full audiologic evaluations, or referrals for other assessment or treatment.

THE COSTS ASSOCIATED WITH OVER- AND UNDERREFERRALS

For a hearing screening protocol to be deemed acceptable, it should have good sensitivity and specificity. That is, the protocol should be able to correctly identify at least 90 to 95% of individuals with hearing loss (sensitivity) and fail no more than 5 to 10% of individuals who would be diagnosed with normal hearing (specificity; Roeser & Northern, 1981). If a protocol is not sensitive or specific enough, then there is the likelihood for too many, or not enough, referrals. Overreferring or underreferring students during the hearing screening process has "costs." These costs amount to lost time and effort on the part of staff, family, and administration. With lost time and effort comes loss of good will and willingness to continue participation in the program. Additional liabilities caused by overreferrals are associated with audiological and medical follow-up,

Table 5–1. Questions to be Addressed When Developing a Hearing Screening Protocol

- What are existing state mandates for hearing screening?
- What are the purposes of the hearing screening program?
- What resources are available to the program?
- What children will be screened and how will they be referred for screening?
- What tests will be used for screening?
- How will children who cannot respond to traditional techniques be screened?
- What personnel will be necessary for the screening program?
- What equipment will be necessary, and how will it be maintained?
- What environment will be used for the screening?
- What pass/fail criteria will be used?
- How will the screening program be organized?
- What follow-up procedure will be used for failed screenings and absentees?
- What record keeping and reporting will be used in the screening program?
- What will be done to determine the effectiveness of the screening program?

and these include: (a) the time it takes to pull a child out of a classroom for further screening, (b) the true monetary expenses associated with additional screening and/or diagnostic testing, and (c) the distress experienced by the parent or child who is left in a state of uncertainty until further testing can be completed. The cost of underreferrals can be even higher, as unidentified hearing loss has educational, social, and emotional ramifications.

HEARING DISORDERS FOUND IN THE SCHOOL-AGE POPULATION

According to the American Speech-Language-Hearing Association's *Guidelines for Audiologic Screening* (ASHA, 1997), hearing impairment for school-age children is defined as, "unilateral or bilateral sensorineural and/or conductive hearing loss greater than 20 dBHL in the frequency region most important for speech recognition (approximately 500 to 4000 Hz)" (p. 41). School-age children (ages 5 to 18 years) are at higher risk than other individuals for certain types of hearing loss. For instance, some school-age children are prone to otitis media with effusion (OME). Otitis media with effusion, commonly referred to as a "middle ear infection," has a high incidence and prevalence in the pediatric population of the United States. Otitis media with effusion is the second-most diagnosed illness in early childhood (Kaleida, 1997; Paradise, Rockette, Colborn, Bernard, Smith, Kurs-Lasky, & Janosky, 1997; Teele, Klein, Roesner, & The Greater Boston Otitis Media Study Group, 1989). Although episodes of OME usually subside in several weeks, the effusion (fluid) remains for 3 months or longer in up to 25% of the cases (Marchant, Shurin, Turczyk, Wasikowski, Tutihasu, & Kenney, 1984; Schwartz, Rodriguez, & Grundfast, 1984). Furthermore, increased episodes of OME have been associated with several risk factors, including frequent exposure to other children, lower socioeconomic status, and gender (repeated or elongated episodes being more prominent in males than females; Paradise et al., 1997). The high incidence and prevalence of OME has many health care practitioners concerned. This concern is largely due to the fact that OME has been associated with hearing loss, which for some children can cause delays in speech and language development, decreases in attention, increases in behavioral problems, and increases the risk for (central) auditory processing disorders (Fria, Cantekin, & Eichler, 1985; Gravel & Wallace, 2000; Gravel, Wallace, & Ruben, 1996; Hall & Grose, 1993; Hall, Grose, Dev, & Ghiassi, 1998; Sabo, Paradise, Kurs-Lasky, and Smith, 2003; Werner & Ward, 1997). Children with OME should be easily identified with typical screening procedures, especially if otoscopy, tympanometry, and/or otoacoustic emissions are used in conjunction with pure tones during the screening process.

Two additional hearing concerns in the school-age population include noise-induced hearing loss (NIHL) and minimal hearing impairment (MHI). These losses may be more problematic than OME because certain characteristics increase the likelihood that they will not be identified easily with typical screening procedures. That is, even with additional screening techniques (i.e., otoscopy and tympanometry), typical screening protocols do not include testing all of the frequencies affected by noise (i.e., 3000

or 6000 Hz) or all of the intensity levels included in the MHI category (i.e., 16 through 19 dBHL).

The incidence of NIHL among children and adolescents in the United States has been reported to be 12.5% (Niskar et al., 2001). However, because 6000 Hz typically is not used in screening protocols (ASHA, 1997), children with NIHL may be missed during the screening process. In fact, Meinke and Dice (2007) determined that more than half of the hearing screening protocols used in U.S. schools will identify only 22% of the students with a high-frequency noise notch, which would consequently fail to identify a potential NIHL. The authors concluded that screening protocols currently being used in schools are inadequate for the early identification of NIHL, and students are neither receiving early intervention for NIHL, nor are they receiving information on how to prevent the progression of NIHL.

Several studies have determined that young children who have hearing thresholds in the 16 to 25 dBHL range, or MHI range, can be at risk for educational, language learning, and literacy problems, as well as behavioral and socioemotional issues (Bess, Dodd-Murphy, & Parker, 1998; Stelmachowicz, Hoover, Lewis, Kortekas, & Pittman, 2000). In addition, children with MHI may be affected more adversely by poor classroom acoustics (Dodd-Murphy & Mamlin, 2002; Nelson, 2000), may end up repeating grades more often than their un-impaired peers (Bess et al., 1998; Flexer, 1994), and may experience auditory fatigue during the course of their school day. However, this minimal amount of hearing loss may not be detectable during regular hearing screenings (DeConde-Johnson, Benson, & Seaton, 1997; Northern & Downs, 2002), due to the fact that the screening level recommended for children is 20 dBHL. Therefore, screening protocols that include more measures than just pure-tone screenings prove to be more sensitive for identifying children with NIHL and MHI.

WHO SHOULD BE SCREENED?

The ASHA *Guidelines for Audiologic Screening* (1997) recommend that school-age children receive hearing screenings when they initially enroll in school, then again in kindergarten, 1st, 2nd, 3rd, 7th, and 11th grades. In addition, school-age children should be screened "as needed, requested, or mandated" (p. 42). A hearing screening should also be scheduled if a student is enrolled into a special education program, has to repeat a grade, or enters a new school system without evidence of having passed a screening. The screening guidelines (ASHA, 1997) also list several risk factors that would indicate hearing screenings should be performed in grades other than the ones listed earlier. These risk factors include a parent or guardian, health care provider, teacher, or other school professional expressing concerns about a child's hearing, speech, language, or learning abilities. In addition, risk factors include a child with:

- a family history of late or delayed onset hereditary hearing loss;
- recurrent or persistent otitis media with effusion for at least 3 months;
- craniofacial anomalies, including those with morphological abnormalities of the pinna and ear canal;
- stigmata or other findings associated with a syndrome known

to include sensorineural and/or conductive hearing loss;
- head trauma with loss of consciousness; and
- exposure to potentially damaging noise levels or ototoxic drugs (p. 42).

Children who already receive audiologic and/or otologic management on a regular basis (due to known hearing loss or disease) are not expected to participate in the school screening process. The American Academy of Audiology is in the process of developing its own guidelines for hearing screenings, and those guidelines should be another resource for school-based audiologists in the near future.

SCREENING PROTOCOLS

School-based audiologists who are responsible for, or involved with, the hearing screening program within their school districts should become familiar with the "clinical process" outlined in the ASHA screening guidelines (1997) in *Section 5. Guidelines for Screening for Hearing Impairment — School-Age Children, 5 through 18 Years.* The guidelines recommend obtaining parental or legal guardian permission prior to screening schoolchildren. In some cases, state regulations or institutional policies may take the place of the ASHA recommendations. Therefore, school-based audiologists must be aware of any local policies or regulations for appropriate screening.

Conventional or play audiometry are the screening procedures of choice; however, tympanometry and otoacoustic emission screening are options that are discussed later in this chapter. The ASHA guidelines (ASHA, 1997) recommend using supraural earphones for screening pure tones of 1000, 2000, and 4000 Hz at 20 dBHL in a quiet environment, or sound-treated booth. The quiet environment should have limited visual and auditory distractions. The ambient noise levels in that environment should abide by American National Standards Institute (ANSI; 1991) standards for pure-tone threshold testing adjusted for the 20 dBHL screening level. That is, ambient noise levels in the screening area should not exceed 49.5 dBSPL at 1000 Hz, 54.5 dBSPL at 2000 Hz, or 62 dBSPL at 4000 Hz when measured using a sound level meter with octave-band filters centered on the screening frequencies. (*Note:* Newer ANSI standards for ambient noise levels for test rooms have been established and, therefore, should be used [ANSI, 2003].) The audiometers used to screen the children should be built to meet ANSI S3.6-1996 requirements and should be calibrated annually to meet those same specifications. A daily listening check should be conducted to determine that no defects exist with the equipment, and intermittency, crosstalk, or distortion are not being produced by the earphones.

PERSONNEL

The ASHA audiologic screening guidelines (1997) limit personnel to the following practitioners when screening school-age children: (a) audiologists holding a Certificate of Clinical Competence (CCC-A) from ASHA and state licensure where applicable, (b) speech-language pathologists holding a Certificate of Clinical Competence (CCC-SLP) from ASHA and state licensure where applicable, and (c) support personnel under the supervision

of a certified audiologist. Support personnel are discussed in more detail later in this chapter.

PASS/REFER CRITERIA FOR HEARING SCREENINGS

The school-based audiologist would perform the screening protocol described above and pass a student if the responses obtained from that student (i.e., a hand raise or a play response) were judged to be reliable and consistent at the criterion intensity and frequency levels recommended. If a student did not respond in either ear to the criterion intensity level (i.e., 20 dBHL) at any one of the three frequencies screened (i.e., 1000, 2000, or 4000 Hz), the audiologist should: (1) reinstruct the student to ensure that he or she understands the screening instructions, (2) reposition the earphones over the student's ears, and (3) rescreen the student within the same screening session. If the student responds appropriately during this rescreening session, then he or she would "pass" the screening. If the student did not respond appropriately during the rescreening session, then he or she would fail the screening and be "referred" for a complete audiological evaluation. The ASHA guidelines state, "Confirm the hearing status of referred children optimally within 1 month but no later than 3 months after initial screening."

RECORDING KEEPING AND REPORTING

It is important to document the results of hearing screenings with a written form to indicate the child's name, screening results, and any recommendations being made for rescreening, full assessment, and/or referral. It is important to also indicate who will be performing the follow-up procedures. Parents and guardians should be given a copy of the child's hearing screening results and the appropriate actions required, if necessary.

It is the responsibility of the screening personnel to place all screening information into students' files; this includes original copies of letters of referral and screening results. The school nurse is typically the professional responsible for the maintenance of student health records; therefore, the nurse should maintain a log of student referrals and actions being requested of parents and guardians. The school-based audiologist or the school nurse (depending on the protocol used in the school) should follow up on student progress 2 weeks after referrals have been made. The audiologist or nurse should also notify the teachers of any referred student. Teachers then have an obligation to be aware of the possibility of hearing problems impacting student performance. Likewise, teachers should document and report relevant information back to the school audiologist or nurse, when necessary.

ADDITIONAL SCREENING PROTOCOL OPTIONS

As mentioned earlier, pure tones are not the only measure or technique that a school-based audiologist can use during hearing screenings. Depending on state or school district regulations (as well as availability of equipment), otoscopy, tympanometry, and/or otoacoustic emissions

may be used in conjunction with pure tones during the screening process. The reader must realize that adding some of these measures may result in confounding results or overreferrals. Determining which screening measures to incorporate requires knowledge about their usefulness with screenings.

Inappropriate Screening Options

Before we describe the additional screening protocol options, something should be said about what the 1997 ASHA screening guidelines deem as "inappropriate" measures. Inappropriate screening measures would include screening with speech stimuli instead of frequency-specific stimuli. Also, nonconventional instrumentations (such as handheld screeners), noncalibrated signals (such as noisemakers or whisper tests), and group screening procedures have been listed as unsuitable options for screening hearing. Finally, the 1997 Guidelines list transient evoked otoacoustic emissions (TEOAE) and distortion product otoacoustic emissions (DPOAE) as inappropriate screening measures. However, the reader should be advised that the American Academy of Audiology Childhood Hearing Screening Guidelines plan to include TEOAE and DPOAE options for screening in the near future. It is assumed that updated ASHA screening guidelines will follow suit.

Otoscopy

Although it is beyond the scope of this chapter to describe otoscopy and otoscopic inspections in detail, we note that a visual inspection of the outer ear, ear canal, and tympanic membrane of both ears using an otoscope should be completed if screeners plan to perform tympanometry prior to pure tone screening. Due to the possibility of spreading infection, infection control strategies (including purchasing disposable specula) should be implemented. A more detailed discussion on infection control is provided later in this chapter.

Tympanometry Screening

Again, it is beyond the scope of this chapter to describe tympanometry measures in detail; however, the use of tympanometry as a screening measure must be discussed. Because support personnel may be providing school screenings, the professional in charge of setting up the screenings should provide tympanometers that can quickly and easily provide the measurements (i.e., ear canal volume, peak admittance/compliance, and possibly gradient) looked at during screenings. The tympanometers must meet the ANSI S3.39 (1987) standards for instruments to measure acoustic immittance. A 226 Hz probe tone is appropriate for screening school-age children, and multifrequency tympanometry is not recommended. As with portable audiometers, a screening tympanometer should be lightweight and durable enough to withstand the rough treatment associated with school screenings.

The screening guidelines (ASHA, 1997) provide pass/fail criteria for determining if middle ear pathologies exist, and screeners are expected to refer a student for a medical examination of the ears if:

- Drainage is observed;
- Visual identification of previously undetected structural defects of the ear are noted;
- Ear canal abnormalities are apparent (e.g., obstructions, impacted cerumen, foreign objects, blood or other secretions, stenosis, atresia, otitis externa, perforations, or other abnormalities of the tympanic membrane); and
- A tympanic membrane perforation is suspected because of the tympanometric equivalent ear canal volume (Vec) being greater than 1.0 cm^3 and accompanied by a flat tympanogram.

School-age children, under the ASHA (1997) screening guidelines, should exhibit tympanometry screening results falling within these ranges: Peak Admittance (Ytm) >0.3 mmho and Tympanic Width (TW) <200 daPa.

The reader should be advised that the screening guidelines (ASHA, 1997) briefly describe the long-running debate that exists over whether or not mass school screenings should even include screening for middle ear status. The guidelines do not support or condemn the use of tympanometry and state that the screening program's administrator must determine whether or not to screen for middle ear status, "based on circumstances specific to the goals of a given screening program" (p. 11).

Otoacoustic Emissions

The mechanisms and measurement techniques of otoacoustic emissions are also outside the scope of this chapter. However, readers who are familiar with OAE testing can appreciate the idea that students with middle ear disorders and/or cochlear hearing loss greater than 30 dBHL will not produce these emissions (Probst, Lonsbury-Martin, Martin, & Coats, 1987). Therefore, OAEs may be useful as a screening measure.

Otoacoustic emission (OAE) screeners are automated, lightweight, and fairly portable. Most devices come with the ability to present different types of stimuli for either TEOAE or DPOAE screenings. They also come with an assortment of disposable (or reusable) probe tips. The handheld devices present pass/refer test results that require no interpretation from the person completing the screening. The devices come from the manufacturer with a default pass/refer criteria (e.g., 4 out of 4 frequencies or 3 out of 4 frequencies). Most of the devices also give error messages to inform the screener of a poor seal, blockage, or high background noise levels. OAE screeners, like tympanometry screeners, require calibration and general maintenance. Some screeners have portable printers that allow the test results to be printed at the test site, and some screeners have the ability to store multiple runs for transferring results back to an office.

Limitations to using OAEs as a screening for hearing impairment do exist. OAEs are not a true test of hearing and only assess function up to the cochlear outer hair cell. The function of the cochlear inner hair cells and auditory nerve is therefore left unknown. If an OAE screening were the only assessment tool implemented, a child having normal outer hair cell function and abnormal function further up the auditory pathway, as seen in cases of auditory neuropathy (Rapin & Gravel, 2003; Starr, Picton, Sininger, Hood, & Berlin, 1996), may be missed (i.e., incorrectly identified as not having a hearing loss). In addition, because the current ASHA guidelines do not recommend OAE screenings, there are no set guidelines to offer assistance at this time. The AAA guidelines to be released soon, however, are expected to contain some recommendations.

IMPLEMENTING SCREENING PROTOCOLS

Once a school-based audiologist has determined which criteria and measures will be used for his or her school system, other technicalities must be in place to implement an effective screening program. The actual screenings are fairly simple; however, the procedures that are completed before and after the screenings are just as important as the screenings themselves.

Scheduling of Screenings

Well in advance of the actual screenings, the school-based audiologist (or person in charge of school screenings) should consult with the school's principal and nurse to determine which grades will be screened (if state or Department of Education mandates exist), which dates and times will be used, what (if any) support staff will be trained, and how the parent notification process will proceed. The principal and nurse will assist the audiologist in determining how the screenings fit into the daily and monthly schedule that already exists for the school.

Paperwork Necessary for Screenings

Several forms are necessary to correctly document hearing screenings. Figure 5–1 is an example of the letter that would be written to parents and guardians to obtain permission to screen their child. This letter should clearly explain the purpose of hearing screenings, why identifying hearing loss in children is important, and the dates on which students will be screened. Lines should be supplied for the child's full name and birthdate. In addition, a line should be provided for the

Birdsdale Elementary School
445 North Valley Road
Pottsville, PA 15757
884-663-8376

Dear Parent/ Guardian,

    With your child entering or currently enrolled in school, it is crucial that he or she hears properly and is able to perceive the information that is being provided in school. It is also important that if any hearing loss is present, it is identified and dealt with quickly.

    This letter is to request permission to screen your child's hearing. On the day of the screenings, your child will wear headphones and be asked to indicate that a tone was heard by raising his or her hand. He or she may also have the middle ears checked for any medical conditions.

Hearing screenings will take place between September 20, 2011 and October 4, 2011.

Parent/Guardian Name_____ Child Name_____

(Check One)

    _____**I give consent for my child to have his/her hearing screened.**
    _____**I do not give consent for my child to have his/her hearing screened.**

Childs Birth Date (MM/DD/YYYY): _____

If you **DO** give consent, please provide the information requested below. Circle response:

1. Does your child have any known hearing loss? Yes   No   Which ear(s)? _____
2. Does your family have any known history of hearing loss since birth? Yes   No
   If yes, please describe below:

3. Does your child have a history of ear infections, tubes, other ear surgeries, etc.? Yes   No
   If yes, please describe below:

4. Has your child had a recent cold or suffer from allergies? Yes   No

_____   _____
Parent's Signature   Date

Figure 5–1. Example of permission letter to be sent to parents and guardians prior to hearing screenings.

parent or guardian to write in their name(s) and another line should be provided for the actual signature(s). The letter should clearly state that the parent or guardian does or does not give permission for their child to be screened. The letter should contain easily understood terms, using words that a person with a 7th- or 8th-grade reading level could understand (Kutner, Greenburg, Jin, & Paulsen, 2006). This letter can also be an excellent source to gain more information about the child's hearing history. That is, some short questions can be written for parents or guardians to provide information about the child's family history of hearing loss, history of ear infections, current status of colds or upper respiratory infections, and any concerns the parents/guardians themselves may have about the child's hearing. Office staff should help to make copies of screening forms and permission slips for parents and guardians to sign prior to the screenings.

Another form that is needed and can be written prior to initiating screenings is the form that will be stored in the students' records. Figure 5–2 is an example of this type of form. This form should contain information concerning the frequencies screened and the intensity level used as the criterion. Notes can be made concerning passing and failing results, such as which ear at which frequencies failed to elicit a response from the student. This form can also have information concerning both the initial screening results, as well as the rescreening results. Recommendations for follow-up can be typed in and checked off accordingly. Again, the form should have a line for the student's complete name and birthdate.

A third form should be used to report the screening results to the students' parents. This form can be in a template format, whereby appropriate items are checked off for each student's independent screening results. Figure 5–3 is an example of this form, and the reader can see that a summary of the child's screening results and the recommendations for follow up are written in clear, easy-to-read terminology with some specific directions for parents to follow.

Educating Teachers and Administrators

Prior to starting the screenings, the school-based audiologist (or person in charge of the screening process) should take some time to educate teachers and administrators about what to expect and how they can help make the process run smoothly. By requesting some specific rooms that are known to be quiet and suitable for screenings, an audiologist can help educate administrators about appropriate screening environments. Also, by providing advance notification to classroom teachers, and by developing a plan for volunteers and teachers to adhere to on the days of screenings, the screening process can be less confusing and take less time. Simply providing basic directions for how teachers and/or administrators can get entire classes to the screening location will keep the stream of children coming and make the process faster.

Training Volunteers and Support Staff

The school-based audiologist may be the professional responsible for training the volunteers and support staff who will ultimately be performing the screenings. Therefore, depending on how many vol-

Gatorville Elementary School
Hearing Screening Documentation

Child's Name: _____

Child's Date of Birth _____

Screening Date _____

Place a √ in the box if the child responds at an intensity of 20 dBHL. Place an X in the box if the child does not respond. Write CNT if child could not be screened. Write DNT if frequency was not screened.

	500 Hz	1000 Hz	2000 Hz	4000 Hz
Right Ear:				
Left Ear:				

Pass Criteria: Child passes if he/she responds to all frequencies at an intensity of 20dBHL.
Refer Criteria: Child will be referred for further screening or testing if he/she does not respond at any one of the frequencies presented at 20dBHL.

Place a checkmark in the appropriate box:

PASS:	FAIL:

Referral made to:_____

Additional Comments:

Figure 5–2. Recording form to be kept in child's school records.

Gatorville Elementary

222 Longview Pike
Anytown, USA 12345
722-566-4477
Principal: Daniella Long
dlong@gatorville.us.k12.edu

Dear _____,

Your child, _____, did not hear all of the sounds presented to him/her at the appropriate loudness during the hearing screenings that were performed on September 21, 2011 and October 1, 2011 at Gatorville Elementary School. Because of this, he/she did not pass the hearing screening. Results obtained today are from a screening only and indicate that your child should have a more complete audiological evaluation to determine if a hearing loss is present.

I would like to stress the importance of ensuring that your child is hearing all of the information being presented to him/her in the classroom. Hearing is one of the main methods for learning. I strongly urge you to have your child's hearing evaluated more fully. If a hearing loss is found, measures can be taken to remedy the problem. I thank you in advance for your cooperation.

Please sign below if you give permission for your child to have a complete hearing evaluation here at school, or take the information below to an audiologist of your choice. Please have the results of that evaluation sent directly to my office to be maintained in your child's records.

Signed,

Suzie P. Smith

Educational Audiologist
722-566-4747

I, _____, give my permission for my child,_____, to have a complete hearing evaluation at Gatorville Elementary School. I understand that I will be notified of the results of that evaluation. _____   _____
                                                    Parent/Guardian Signature   Date

Hearing screening results obtained on_____

A "√" in the box indicates that the child responded at an intensity of 20 dBHL: An "X" indicates the child did not respond at 20 dBHL: CNT=could not test   DNT=did not test

	500 Hz	1000 Hz	2000 Hz	4000 Hz
Right Ear:				
Left Ear:				

Figure 5–3. Example letter to be sent to parent or guardian.

unteers or staff are being trained, the appropriate time should be scheduled to ensure that these screeners know why hearing screenings are important, what is to be accomplished with the hearing-screening process, what equipment is going to be used, how to operate the equipment, what paperwork is involved, and what they as screening personnel are and are not able to say to children (and even parents/guardians). Allowing the volunteers to obtain hands-on practice while the audiologist is around to answer questions and demonstrate the equipment is crucial for training volunteers and staff. Also, allowing these screeners to obtain some real-life practice with school-age children while the audiologist supervises is important for an efficient and successful screening program. This is especially the case if otoscopy, tympanometry, OAEs, and/or play audiometry techniques are to be used during the screenings.

If the school speech-language pathologists are involved with the screenings, they may already be knowledgeable about screening procedures and not require a lot of training. However, if tympanometry or OAE screenings are performed, they must be supervised by the audiologist.

Whether or not the school-based audiologist is responsible for the entire screening process, he or she will be responsible for performing the follow-up services, including diagnostic evaluations, referrals to other agencies, and educational management processes.

EVALUATING PROGRAM EFFECTIVENESS

The positive predictive value (PPV) of the hearing screening program can be examined to evaluate the effectiveness of the program. That is, the proportion of patients who are referred on for follow-up and who have been *correctly* identified as needing that follow-up can provide the director of a screening program with much-needed information regarding the effectiveness of that program. To obtain the PPV, the program director would need to obtain feedback from the audiologists and physicians who conducted further testing on any students referred to them. Learning the results of those evaluations and whether or not a student was truly (true positive) or falsely (false-positive) identified as having a middle ear (ME) disorder and/or hearing loss will allow the program's director to calculate the program's PPV. This value would be calculated by dividing the number of students who truly have a ME disorder and/or hearing loss by the sum of the number of true positives and false-positives and then multiplying by 100. The higher the PPV value, the more likely the program is correctly identifying students who truly have ME disorders and/or hearing loss. The school-based audiologist would be interested in knowing this information even if he or she was not the director of the screening program because the audiologist needs to know if the screenings yielded any newly identified children for his or her caseload.

SCREENING ISSUES TO KEEP IN MIND

The reader needs to be aware that there are inconsistencies and differences in the screening programs across school districts. Also, some topics concerning screening do not fit into the categories already addressed; therefore, this section discusses some of those topics.

Inconsistencies in Screening Protocol

The ASHA guidelines (1997) contain criterion intensities and frequencies that are just guidelines. In fact, Meinke and Dice (2007) surveyed states within the United States regarding their hearing screening protocols and reported that the intensity criterion used ranged from 15 to 30 dBHL and the frequency criterion ranged from three to six tones. There were multiple combinations of testing protocol (e.g., 20 dB at 1000, 2000, and 4000 Hz; 25 dB at 500 Hz then 20 dB at 1000, 2000, and 4000 Hz; and 20 dB at 250, 500, 1000, 2000, 4000, and 8000 Hz), and many states used protocols that were not consistent with ASHA guidelines.

Inconsistencies in Personnel Responsible for Screening

In addition to the protocol inconsistencies, not every school system employs an audiologist to provide hearing screenings. Some school systems direct the school speech-language pathologists to complete the screenings on their students. These speech-language pathologists should be performing the screenings according to ASHA guidelines, but the state regulations and local school district mandates will ultimately dictate what protocols are used. In some states (e.g., Pennsylvania and Arkansas), the school nurses are responsible for conducting the hearing screenings as mandated by state regulations or departments of education. This group of professionals, therefore, has its own set of screening requirements and protocols.

Use of Volunteers as Support Personnel

Trained volunteers can be used (usually under the supervision of an audiologist,

speech-language pathologist, or nurse) to carry out hearing screenings within a school district. The levels of training and experience among these individuals varies, but training for these volunteers should include information on: (a) the purpose or rationale behind hearing screenings; (b) screening equipment setup, checks, and basic troubleshooting procedures; (c) typical behaviors of children during screenings and ways to handle these behaviors; (d) how the screening program will operate; and (e) how the results of the program will be reported to parents and teachers. These volunteers should also be informed that their role does not include diagnosing hearing loss or directly reporting screening results to parents or teachers. Finally, all volunteers should obtain supervised practice under the direction of an audiologist, including hands-on practice using the equipment and school-age subjects.

Access to an Appropriate Screening Environment

Few school administrators truly have the ability to provide an acoustically appropriate screening environment. As a school-based audiologist, you may be offered rooms within the building that do not meet ANSI S3.1 (1991) standards for ambient noise levels, yet you will be expected to pursue the screening process regardless of this fact. It will be up to the school-based audiologist in charge of screenings to determine if the screening environment is "appropriate enough" to conduct screenings. Asking school staff to remove offending noise sources, or alter typical noisy routines, during the time screenings are taking place is not too much to request. Mentioning that, "we want to make sure we are getting accurate results for the children" may be enough to get staff cooperation.

Times to Avoid Scheduling Screenings

As alluded to earlier, state agencies and departments of education will mandate when screenings have to occur in many states. However, the school calendar also has to be taken into account when trying to schedule screenings. For instance, the school nurse has to complete vision and scoliosis screenings around the same time hearing screenings need to take place (usually in the fall, shortly after school starts). Some teachers may have field trips scheduled on specific days, and many schools have professional development days for teachers each year. Therefore, all of those examples include dates in which screenings would need to be avoided.

Other dates to avoid include the time of year when cold and flu season would create a number of absences in students. In addition, if possible, the times of the year when seasonal allergies could affect tympanometric screenings should be avoided. Finally, months in which snow and ice may increase the likelihood for school closings should be avoided.

Infection Control

Incorporating "universal precautions" and infection control procedures are very important during screenings of children, due to the possibility of passing an infection from one child to another. Risk from exposure to microorganisms varies depending on the screening tests used. Microorganisms can pass from student to student directly or indirectly. Any time a probe tip is used, the opportunity for contact with cerumen becomes an infection control issue. Cerumen is not considered to be an infectious material; however, because cerumen has the potential of containing blood or other infectious substances, it should be treated as if it contains infectious materials at all times (Kemp, Roeser, Pearson, & Ballachanda, 1995).

The screener should wash his or her hands as often as possible with disinfecting soap or disinfecting lotion when soap is not practical. Additionally, decontaminating, cleaning, disinfecting, and/or sterilizing multiple-use equipment before reuse should be carried out according to facility-specific infection control policies and procedures and according to manufacturer's instructions. Cleaning and disinfecting the equipment (i.e., earphones, probe tips, etc.) will eliminate the possibility of passing around infection and head lice. These procedures also ensure the safety of the patient and clinician and adhere to standard health precautions (e.g., prevention of bodily injury and transmission of infectious disease).

REFERENCES

American National Standards Institute. (1987). *Specifications for instruments to measure aural acoustic impedance and admittance (aural acoustic immittance)* (ANSI S3.39-1987). New York, NY: Author.

American National Standards Institute. (1991). *Maximum permissible ambient noise levels for audiometric test rooms* (ANSI S3.1-1991). New York: Author.

American National Standards Institute. (1996). *Specifications for audiometers* (ANSI S3.6-1996). New York: Author.

American National Standards Institute. (2003). *Maximum permissible ambient noise levels for audiometric test rooms* (ANSI S3.1-R2003). New York, NY: Author.

American Speech-Language-Hearing Association. (1997). *Guidelines for audiologic screening* [Guidelines]. Retrieved from ASHA Web site: http://www.asha.org/policy.

Bess, F. H., Dodd-Murphy, J., & Parker, R. A. (1998). Children with minimal sensorineural hearing loss: Prevalence, educational performance, and functional status. *Ear and Hearing, 19*(5), 339–354.

Cunningham, M., & Cox, E.O. (2003). Hearing assessment in infants and children: Recommendations beyond neonatal screening. *Pediatrics, 111*(2), 436–440.

DeConde-Johnson, C., Benson, P., & Seaton, J. (1997). *Educational audiology handbook.* San Diego, CA: Singular.

Dodd-Murphy, J., & Mamlin, N. (2002). Minimizing minimal hearing loss in the schools: What every classroom teacher should know. *Preventing School Failure, 46*(2), 86–92.

Flexer, C. (1994). *Facilitating hearing and listening in young children.* San Diego, CA: Singular.

Fria, T. J., Cantekin, E. I., & Eichler, J. A. (1985). Hearing acuity of children with otitis media with effusion. *Archives of Otolaryngology, 111*, 10–16.

Gravel, J. S., & Wallace, I. F. (2000). Effects of otitis media with effusion on hearing in the first 3 years of life. *Journal of Speech, Language, and Hearing Research, 43*(3), 631–644.

Gravel, J. S., Wallace, I. F., & Ruben, R. J. (1996). Auditory consequences of early mild hearing loss associated with otitis media. *Acta Oto-Laryngologica, 116*(2), 219–221.

Hall, J. W., III, & Grose, J. H. (1993). Short-term and long-term effects on the masking level difference following middle ear surgery. *Journal of the American Academy of Audiology, 4*(5), 307–312.

Hall, J. W., III, Grose, J. H., Dev, M. B., & Ghiassi, S. (1998). The effect of masker interaural time delay on the masking level difference in children with history of normal hearing or history of otitis media with effusion. *Ear and Hearing, 19*(6), 429–433.

Kaleida, P. H. (1997). The COMPLETES exam for otitis. *Contemporary Pediatrics, 14*, 93–101.

Kemp, R. J., Roeser, R. J., Pearson, D. W., & Ballachanda, B. B. (1995). *Infection control for the professions of audiology and speech-language pathology.* Chesterfield, MO: Oaktree Products, Inc.

Kemper, A. R., & Downs, S. M. (2000). A cost-effective analysis of newborn hearing screening strategies. *Archives of Pediatric and Adolescent Medicine, 154*(5), 484–488.

Kutner, M., Greenburg, E., Jin, Y., & Paulsen, C. (2006). *The Health Literacy of America's Adults: Results from the 2003 National Assessment of Adult Literacy (NCES 2006-483).* U.S. Department of Education, Washington, DC: National Center for Education Statistics.

Marchant, C., Shurin, P., Turczyk, V., Wasikowski, D., Tutihasu, M., & Kinney, S. (1984). Course and outcome of otitis media in early infancy: A prospective study. *Journal of Pediatrics, 104*(6), 826–831

Meinke, D. K., & Dice, N. (2007). Comparison of audiometric screening criteria for the identification of noise-induced hearing loss in adolescents. *American Journal of Audiology, 16*, S190–S202.

Nelson, P. B. (2000). Improving acoustics in American schools. *Language, Speech, and Hearing Services in Schools, 31*, 354–355.

Niskar, A., Kieszak, S., Holmes, A., Esteban, E., Rubin, C., & Brody, D. (2001). Estimated prevalence of noise-induced hearing threshold shifts among children 6 to 19 years of age: The Third National Health and Nutrition Survey, 1988–1994, United States. *Pediatrics, 108*(1), 40–43.

Northern, J. L., & Downs, M. P. (2002). *Hearing in children* (5th ed.). Baltimore, MD: Lippincott Williams & Wilkins.

Paradise, J. L., Rockette, H. E., Colborn, D. K., Bernard, B. S., Smith, C. G., Kurs-Lasky, M., & Janosky, J. E. (1997). Otitis media in 2253 Pittsburgh-area infants: prevalence and risk factors during the first two years of life. *Pediatrics, 99*, 318–333.

Probst, R., Lonsbury-Martin, B., Martin, G., & Coats, A. (1987). Otoacoustic emissions in ears with hearing loss. *American Journal of Otolaryngology, 8*(2), 73–81.

Rapin, I., & Gravel, J. (2003). Auditory neuropathy: physiologic and pathologic evidence calls for more diagnostic specificity. *International Journal of Pediatric Otorhinolaryngology, 67*(7), 707–728.

Roeser, R. R., & Northern, J. L. (1981). Screening for hearing loss and middle ear disorders. In R. R. Roeser & M. P. Downs (Eds.), *Auditory disorders in school children* (pp. 120–150). New York, NY: Thieme-Stratton.

Sabo, D., Paradise, J., Kurs-Lasky, M., & Smith, C. (2003). Hearing levels in infants and young children in relation to testing technique, age group, and the presence or absence of middle-ear effusion. *Ear and Hearing, 24*(1), 38–47.

Schwartz, R. H., Rodriguez, W. J., & Grundfast, K. M. (1984). Duration of middle ear effusion after acute otitis media. *Pediatric Infectious Disease Journal, 3*, 204–207.

Starr, A., Picton, T. W., Sininger, Y., Hood, L. J., & Berlin, C. I. (1996). Auditory neuropathy. *Brain, 119*(3), 741–753.

Stelmachowicz, P. G., Hoover, B. M., Lewis, D. E., Kortekas, R. W. L., & Pittman, A. L. (2000). The relationship between stimulus context, speech audibility, and perception for normal hearing and hearing-impaired children. *Journal of Speech and Hearing Research, 43*, 902–914.

Teele, D. W., Klein, J. O., Chase, C., Menyuk, P., Rosner, B. A. & the Boston Otitis Media Study Group. (1990). Otitis media in infancy and intellectual ability, school achievement, speech and language at 7 years. *Journal of Infectious Diseases, 162*, 685–694.

Werner, L., & Ward, J. (1997). The effect of otitis media with effusion on infants' detection of sound. *Infant Behavior and Development, 20*(2), 275–279.

Educational Audiology in the Real World

Krista Yuskow, AuD, and Sarah Burns, MS
Educational Audiologists
Edmonton Regional Educational Consulting Services
Edmonton Public Schools
Edmonton, Alberta, Canada

Welcome to Edmonton, Alberta where two educational audiologists don touques,[1] mittens, and snow boots before trekking out across the cold, Canadian tundra; audiometers and tympanometers in hand.

Within the Edmonton Public School Board is Edmonton Regional Educational Consulting Services (ERECS), a team of multidisciplinary professionals who provide assessment, consultation, and in-services to schools whose students fit "the mandate" and for whom service is requested within northern Alberta. Within ERECS are two educational audiologists, Sarah Burns and Krista Yuskow. We make up a 1.4 full-time employee position, and like all audiologists in Alberta (and as required by the Health Professions Act) are registered with the Alberta College of Speech Language Pathologists and Audiologists. We are only two of a multidisciplinary team of 40 consultants in the areas of adapted physical education, educational audiology, education behavior programming, education of the deaf and hard of hearing, education of the visually impaired, occupational therapy, physical therapy, psychology, and speech-language pathology. All ERECS consultants provide service to severely sensory-impaired multihandicapped students, 2½ to 20 years of age throughout northern Alberta. These students have been previously identified with a provincial code indicating a severe disability, inclusive of cognitive, physical, multiple, medical (including autism), deafness, blindness, hearing, vision, communication, as well as students for whom there is a suspicion of hearing loss, vision loss, or pervasive developmental disorder.

The degree of hearing loss for which "severe" funding is allocated is a pure-tone average, or high frequency pure-tone average, of 71 dB HL in the better ear. The dollars from this funding are allocated to the schools for the purposes of programming, accommodations/ modifications, assistive technology, and classroom supports. Students with PTAs or HF PTAs of 41 dB HL in the better ear are identified as "moderate," and as a result, schools receive less than 1% of the severe funding allocation. Students with mild hearing loss, unilateral hearing loss, or auditory processing disorders are not allocated any funding, nor are they identified by a code that would distinguish them as requiring additional educational supports.

Not being familiar with the geography of Alberta, you may be wondering just how far "throughout northern Alberta" encompasses. Alberta's land mass totals 661,190 km² (260, 000 mi²), which means that Sarah and Krista together cover approximately 130,000 square miles of land mass.

---

[1]Touque: a woolen cap: a cylindrical stocking cap of double-thickness wool or synthetic yarn, worn in winter. [Late 19th century. Via Canadian French from French *toque*.]

The farthest point of travel is a First Nations community, Fort Chipewyan. In the summer and autumn months, Fort Chipewyan is accessible by plane only, as there are no access roads. However, during the winter months Fort Chipewyan is auto-accessible via frozen rivers, which are otherwise known as "ice roads." First Nations reservations, Hudderite or Mennonite colonies, and White Russian communities are all fair game for us. In the average school year, we serve approximately 200 students in 32 different school jurisdictions at an average of 15 hours per contract. The demographic that we serve include both sensory multihandicapped and single-sensory hearing impaired students.

Due to the structure of the Canadian socialized medical system, students in Alberta are typically diagnosed and fit with hearing aids and personal FM (which are paid for by the province) before educational audiology services are provided. Educational audiologists work with dispensing audiologists, implant teams, schools, and families to check personal FM systems and/or soundfield systems. They also verify fittings and provide in-services to school personnel on the topics of amplification technology and the access to auditory information. Because a majority of classrooms in northern Alberta (kindergarten through 6th grade) are fit with soundfield amplification systems, the management of multiple amplification systems (personal and soundfield) is a primary responsibility for us. For students suspected of having a hearing loss, ERECS audiologists provide audiologic assessments with portable diagnostic equipment, referring to a diagnostic center if indicated. Commensurate with the responsibilities of many educational audiologists, we also provide consultation and assessment in the areas of auditory processing, room acoustics, and vocal fatigue.

We were involved in a project with Alberta Infrastructure, which resulted in Alberta being the first state or province with minimal standards for classroom acoustics. Then, in response to the vast number of audio-visual companies inappropriately supplying classrooms with soundfield amplification, and again in consort with Alberta Infrastructure, we helped to develop minimal standards for classroom amplification systems. The result was the Soundfield Systems Guide for Schools *accessible at http://www.infras.gov.ab.ca/home/index.asp. Although sections on the research and support for soundfield amplification were removed by editors, the document remains a useful support and guide for school administrators who find themselves making decisions regarding the purchase of classroom amplification systems.*

Although we recognize the organizational and financial restrictions that seem to be the reality of many school jurisdictions today, we both remain enthusiastic and passionate about our work. We feel deeply for the students we serve, sometimes shedding a tear or two for students who meet administrative limitations or resistance. We also laugh, mostly at ourselves and the peculiar situations we find ourselves in. Being an educational audiologist is full of challenges and surprises that provide an ongoing learning curve, opportunities for authentic and true-to-life professional development, as well as a heartfelt appreciation for all the incredible students who continue to do incredible things. Thank you to all of our incredible students who demonstrate persistence, evoke hope, inspire greatness, and who truly are our teachers.

6

Amplification for the Classroom

Donna F. Smiley and Cynthia M. Richburg

OBJECTIVES

By the end of this chapter, the reader will be able to:

1. Identify the controversies surrounding the responsibility of school districts for providing students with hearing aids.
2. List the functions school-based audiologists and other school personnel are responsible for completing when assisting students with their amplification devices (i.e., listening checks, functional listening checks, documentation, and follow-up plans).
3. Determine which personal FM system or classroom soundfield amplification system is most appropriate for use with a student who is deaf/hard-of-hearing.
4. Identify verification and validation procedures for personal FM systems.
5. List the rationale and options for classroom soundfield amplification systems.

INTRODUCTION

If you ask a school-based audiologist to list the tasks that he or she spends the most time focusing on during the workday, hearing technology in the classroom would be close to the top of that list. With that in mind, the focus of this chapter is to familiarize the reader with amplification and hearing assistance technology (HAT) that will be encountered in a preschool or school setting. Personal FM systems and classroom soundfield amplification will receive the most attention. The selection, fitting, and programming of hearing aids will not be covered in this text; however, some of the responsibilities that school-based audiologists have with personal hearing aids, as well as bone anchored implants (BAI), will be discussed. Similarly, cochlear implants (CI) are covered in a separate chapter; therefore, the reader is referred to Chapter 12 for information and questions regarding CI in the school setting.

HEARING ASSISTANCE TECHNOLOGY: THE RESPONSIBILITIES OF THE LOCAL EDUCATION AGENCY

There are a variety of answers to the question, "What is the responsibility of a school district to provide either personal amplification devices or hearing assistance technology for a student?" Some of those answers may be dependent on whether or not the student has an IEP (discussed in Chapter 1). Unfortunately, sometimes the answer to this question is based on an administrator's personal opinion and not necessarily grounded in law or regulation. The best way for a school-based audiologist to approach this topic is to be armed with information about what is written in regulations and standards (and in some cases, what is *not* written in these regulations or standards). After all, misinformation can be harmful to the overall success of a student, as well as to the credibility of the audiologist.

IDEIA and Hearing Assistance Technology

The field of audiology uses the term "hearing assistance technology," or HAT, to refer to the various amplification devices used by students within the classroom setting. However, special education regulation uses the term "assistive technology" because these laws are not always referring to hearing or amplification while dictating what public agencies (schools) must provide to students with disabilities. Therefore, the reader will see both terms used in this chapter.

IDEIA: *Personal Hearing Aids*

Historically, public agencies have not been held responsible for providing personal devices (i.e., eyeglasses or hearing aids) to a child with a disability, regardless of whether or not the child is attending school. However, if the personal device is not a surgically implanted device and a child's IEP team determines that the child requires the device to receive a free, appropriate public education (FAPE), the public agency must ensure that the device is provided to the student at no cost to the student's parents. This precedent was set by a letter to Dr. Peter Seiler (who at the time was Superintendent of the Illinois School for the Deaf) in 1993 from Thomas Hehir (who was the Director of the Office of Special Education Programs [OSEP]). Dr. Seiler had asked the OSEP office to respond to his inquiry about whether or not a school district was responsible for purchasing hearing aids (assistive technology) under IDEA if the device was listed on the student's IEP. A copy of this letter may be found on the Listen Up Web site (http://www.listen-up.org/rights2/osep1.htm).

The debate over whether or not school districts should be responsible for personal hearing aids for a student is multifaceted. On one side of the argument, schools do not have endless resources (as some may think). However, on another side of the argument, schools do not want to spend hours every day providing instruction to students who cannot hear what is being taught simply because the students do not have amplification devices. The reality is that many IEP teams will shy away from listing personal amplification in the assistive technology portion of the IEP because: (1) they either do not want to have the district held responsible for those personal devices or (2) they may have been instructed not to list the personal devices at all. However, the interpretation from the OSEP still exists; if the student needs the personal device(s) to receive a free, appropriate public education, then the school district is responsible for providing the device.

Regardless of whether or not the personal hearing aids are provided by the school, the family, or some other agency, IDEIA (2004) provides clear direction for the routine checking of hearing aids worn in school by children with hearing impairments. The regulation instructs the public agency to ensure that hearing aids, as well as the external components of surgically implanted devices, are functioning properly (§300.113). The specifics of how the school-based audiologist may be involved with this task are discussed later in this chapter.

IDEIA: Assistive Technology Devices and Services

The requirement that every child who has an IEP be considered for assistive technology has existed through several revisions of IDEA (Mittler, 2007). In §300.105, IDEIA (2004) charges public agencies with ensuring that that assistive technology devices and/or assistive technology

services (see the box that follows for definitions) are made available to a child with a disability if required as a part of the child's special education (§300.36), related services (§300.34), or supplementary aids and services [§§300.38 and 300.114(a)(2) (ii)]. In addition, under §300.324 (a)(2)(v) —a section referred to as "special considerations"—the IEP team must consider whether the child needs assistive technology devices and services.

For students who are deaf/hard of hearing (d/hh) or who have other auditory dysfunctions, assistive technology certainly includes such devices as personal FM systems and/or classroom soundfield amplification systems. IDEIA (2004) defines not only the assistive device (§300.5), but it also defines the services that assist the child in the selection, acquisition, and use of the device. For the school-based audiologist, these services should include the functional assessment of the device in the student's routine environment, the selection of the appropriate device for the student, and the training and technical assistance on how to use the device appropriately (which should be provided to the student, school staff, and family).

There is one final issue regarding IDEIA's (2004) directives as they pertain to assistive technology. Section 300.105(b) states that on a case-by-case basis, a child may use his or her school purchased assistive devices at home or in other settings *if* the child's IEP Team determines that the child needs access to those devices in order to receive FAPE. Obviously, this leaves some room for interpretation by IEP Teams; however, many school-based audiologists have made the case that a child needs their assistive technology at home if they are to benefit (i.e., receive FAPE) from their education.

**Assistive Technology Device and
Service as Defined by IDEA 2004**

§300.5 Assistive technology device

Assistive technology device means any item, piece of equipment, or product system, whether acquired commercially off the shelf, modified, or customized, that is used to increase, maintain, or improve the functional capabilities of a child with a disability. The term does not include a medical device that is surgically implanted, or the replacement of such device.

§300.6 Assistive technology service

Assistive technology service means any service that directly assists a child with a disability in the selection, acquisition, or use of an assistive technology device. The terms include:

(a) The evaluation of the needs of a child with a disability, including a functional evaluation of the child in the child's customary environment;

(b) Purchasing, leasing, or otherwise providing for the acquisition of assistive technology devices by children with disabilities;

(c) Selecting, designing, fitting, customizing, adapting, applying maintaining, repairing, or replacing assistive technology devices;

(d) Coordinating and using other therapies, interventions, or services with assistive technology devices, such as those associated with existing education and rehabilitation plans and programs;

(e) Training or technical assistance for a child with a disability or, if appropriate, that child's family; and

(f) Training and technical assistance for professionals (including individuals providing education or rehabilitation services), employers, or other individuals who provide services to, employ, or are otherwise substantially involved in the major life functions of that child.

Section 504 and Hearing Assistance Technology

The specifics of Section 504 of the Rehabilitation Act of 1973 were discussed in Chapter 1. Much inconsistency exists in terms of whether or not students with 504 plans are provided with access to assistive technology. The Office for Civil Rights (OCR) in the U.S. Department of Education states that "an appropriate education for a student with a disability under Section 504 regulations could consist of education in regular classrooms, education in regular classes with supplementary services, and/or special education and related services" (http://www2.ed.gov/about/offices/list/ocr/504faq.html). This wording would lead the school-based audiologist to believe that students with 504 plans *would* be eligible for assistive devices; however, we continue to hear from school-based audiologists who report that their school districts do not provide personal FM for students who have 504 plans.

One approach for making the argument that a student should have a personal FM system under Section 504 is to use the terminology of the act itself. Section 504 is a law designed to prevent discrimination based on having a disability. It prohibits the exclusion from participation in activities *and* prohibits the denial of benefits of a program. In addition, Section 504 requires public schools to provide students with disabilities appropriate educational services designed to meet their individual needs to the same extent that the needs of students without disabilities are met. As an example, the school-based audiologist could argue that a student who is d/hh does not have the same access to auditory information students with normal hearing have without

the use of a personal FM system. Therefore, denying the student access to that auditory information constitutes discrimination, excludes him from an activity, and denies him the benefits of the educational program.

PERSONAL AMPLIFICATION DEVICES

It is not within the scope of this text to cover the selection and fitting of personal hearing aids or BAIs. Anecdotal data would suggest that most school-based audiologists are not dispensing hearing aids. However, information relevant to the role of the school-based audiologist in managing these personal amplification devices will be covered.

Routine Checking of Personal Amplification Devices

As mentioned earlier in this chapter, for students who have an IEP, the law clearly states that public agencies are responsible for ensuring that hearing aids worn by students in schools are functioning properly. For students who have 504 plans, it is possible to include a provision that the student's personal amplification also be checked by school personnel on a routine basis.

Because school-based audiologists often provide services to many students, in different buildings and maybe even in different school districts, it is necessary to train other personnel who are building-based to perform these checks on personal amplification. In addition, it is assumed that the school-based audiologist will have provided instruction to school personnel on how these devices work and how to take care of them. Therefore, the focus in this chapter is on the ways to ensure that personal amplification devices are working.

Listening Checks

The most common way to ensure that personal amplification devices are working is via a listening check. This is typically performed with a hearing aid stethoscope, or stethoset, by a person who is considered to have normal hearing. Although this procedure may be familiar to audiologists, it most likely will not be to other school personnel. The two boxes that follow provide examples of handouts that may be used by the school-based audiologist to give to school personnel who will be doing the listening check. The first box explains a listening check for a hearing aid, and the second explains how to perform a listening check for a BAI.

How to Check a Hearing Aid

Supplies needed: Hearing aid stethoscope or stethoset, extra hearing aid batteries, hearing aid battery tester, earmold blower (optional), ear wax removal tool (optional), hearing aid cleaning brush (for in-the-ear models)

Steps for checking a hearing aid:

1. Check hearing aid parts to make sure that there is no damage or obstruction
   a. Case of hearing aid—Is it cracked or broken?
   b. Earmold—Is the tubing coming out? Is it plugged with wax?
   c. If the earmold has excessive wax or moisture in the tubing, remove the earmold from the hearing aid and, using the earmold blower, clean the earmold out.
   d. If there is a problem that cannot be fixed quickly, notify the appropriate individual (i.e., school-based audiologist and/or parent)

2. Check the battery
   a. Batteries should be tested to make sure that they are functioning. Hearing aid battery testers are available for purchase online, as well as from some audiologists. Battery testers usually indicate whether the battery is "good" or "needs replacing."
   b. Replace the battery when needed. If you are concerned that batteries are being replaced too often, notify the appropriate individual. This could be the sign of a problem.

3. Listen to the hearing aid
   a. This requires the use of a special hearing aid stethoset or stethoscope. Place the hearing aid on the stethoset/stethoscope and engage the battery (this is typically the way that hearing aids are turned off and on). Listen to the sound quality of the hearing aid when speech is being introduced. Use the Ling 6-sounds (oo, ah, ee, sh, s, m) to listen for sounds of different

frequencies. Listen for differences or problems that may not have been there the last time you listened to the hearing aid.

If there are any problems with the hearing aid, document the issue and notify the appropriate person about the problem.

How to Check a Bone-Anchored Implant (BAI)

Supplies Needed: BAI test rod, extra batteries, battery tester

Steps for checking a BAI:

1. Check the BAI processor to make sure there is no damage
   a. Case of processor—Is it cracked or broken?
   b. If there is a problem that cannot be fixed quickly, notify the appropriate individual (i.e., school-based audiologist and/or parent)

2. Check the battery
   a. Batteries should be tested to make sure that they are functioning. Battery testers are available for purchase online, as well as from some audiologists. Battery testers usually indicate whether the battery is "good" or "needs replacing."
   b. Replace the battery when needed. If you are concerned that batteries are being replaced too often, notify the appropriate individual. This could be the sign of a problem.

3. Listen to the bone-anchored device
   a. This requires the use of a special test rod (typically obtained from the manufacturer of the BAI device). Snap the BAI processor on the test rod. Hold the test rod against the skull bone behind the ear (of the person performing the listening check). The listener should then plug both ears and introduce sound to see if he or she can hear via the BAI device. This will obviously take two people—one person to hold the BAI in place and the listener can then plug his or her own ears. The Ling 6-sounds (oo, ah, ee, sh, s, m) may be used to listen for sounds of different frequencies. Listen for differences or problems that may not have been there the last time you listened to the BAI device. (NOTE: If you are working with a student who is wearing a BAI device on a soft headband, you can place the sound processor directly on your skull bone behind the ear without the use of the test rod—all other directions apply).

If there are any problems with the BAI device, document the issue and notify the appropriate person about the problem.

Functional Listening Checks

Another way to check the function of amplification devices would be to ask the student to either detect or identify speech sounds. The most common tool used for this type of functional listening check is the Ling 6-sounds. The Ling 6-sounds represent speech sounds from low to high frequency (See the following box for more in-depth information regarding the Ling 6-sounds). Detecting the Ling sounds is appropriate for children with lower auditory skills. Ultimately, the best use of the Ling sounds for a functional listening check would be to have the student repeat the sound that he or she hears while wearing the amplification device. If the audiologist or teacher produces the /s/, then the student would repeat that sound. The goal would be for the student to be able to identify the sound without visual cues (i.e., auditory input only).

Using a functional listening check instead of a hearing aid stethoscope could be useful with older students who may be embarrassed if the audiologist or teacher asks them to remove their hearing aids

---

Ling Six-Sounds

The Ling Six-Sounds (Ling 1976, 1989, and 2002) were developed by Dr. Daniel Ling. The six sounds were selected to represent familiar speech sounds from the speech spectrum (250–8000 Hz). Ling proposed the use of isolated phonemes to correspond to low, middle, and high frequency sounds.

Ling Six-Sounds and Example Words

m	mug
ah	bat
ee	he
oo	do
sh	dish
s	sit

Cochlear Americas has a downloadable document that contains illustrations of and activities to use with the Ling Six-Sounds (http://www.cochlear.com/files/assets/Ling%20cards.pdf).

References
Ling, D. (1976). *Speech and the hearing-impaired child: Theory and practice.* Washington, DC: Alexander Graham Bell Association for the Deaf.
Ling, D. (1989). *Foundations of spoken language for the hearing-impaired child.* Washington, DC: Alexander Graham Bell Association for the Deaf.
Ling, D. (2002). *Speech and the hearing impaired child* (2nd ed.). Washington, DC: Alexander Graham Bell Association for the Deaf and Head of Hearing.

every day. It is also useful with students who utilize CIs, as there is not a way to "listen" to the implant in the same way that the student listens with the implant. It is important to note that using a functional listening check may not be as effective with students who utilize amplification in cases of single-sided hearing loss. The normal hearing ear may interfere with ensuring that the amplification device is working. For a more in-depth explanation of the use of the Ling 6-sounds, refer to Smiley, Martin, and Lance (2004).

Documentation

Although IDEIA (2004) does not provide specifics for how schools should document the proper function of hearing aids worn by students, it stands to reason that there must be some record to prove that a school is upholding this regulation. Therefore, best practice would suggest that some type of form be used to document amplification checks. Figure 6–1 is an example of a form developed by Dr. Joanna Wakefield (The EARS Program at Arkansas Children's Hospital) for use in school settings. The school-based audiologist should develop a documentation form, train school personnel to use the form, and then ensure that documentation is kept in the appropriate place.

Follow-Up Plans

A plan should be implemented to specify what should happen if the amplification is not working. Some of the issues to be addressed in the follow-up plan should include:

- Who will be contacted when the amplification is not working? (i.e., parent, school-based audiologist, etc.)

- At the building level, who is responsible for making contact with the person above?
- Is there any provision for backup amplification while the primary amplification is out of commission?

Notations should be made on the documentation forms of the steps that are to be taken when the amplification is not functioning properly.

PERSONAL FM SYSTEMS

A student's ability to listen in an academic setting is impacted by many factors. As discussed previously in Chapter 2, the effects of distance, noise, and reverberation can be detrimental to any listener, especially listeners whose auditory systems are compromised. Additional factors affecting a student's ability to access auditory information in the classroom include qualities related to the speaker, as well as qualities related to the listener.

- **Qualities of the Speaker**—intent of message, language and speech patterns, accent, and vocal quality
- **Qualities of the Listener**— developmental age, language and vocabulary skills, knowledge base, attention, and listening skills

All of these factors have an impact on the child's ability to access and ultimately use the auditory information in the classroom.

The school-based audiologist is the professional particularly interested in overcoming the acoustical factors that are often present in the classroom. For many children with hearing loss and other auditory dysfunctions, personal FM systems (sometimes referred to as personal HAT)

Daily Hearing Aid/FM Check Chart

STUDENT NAME (L, F, M)		DOB		GRADE	SEX
SCHOOL		STUDENT #		DATE OF LAST AUDIO	
STAFF RESPONSIBLE/TITLE				CURRENT DATE	
RIGHT HEARING AID MAKE	MODEL			SERIAL #	
LEFT HEARING AID MAKE	MODEL			SERIAL #	
TRANSMITTER MAKE	MODEL			SERIAL #	
RECEIVER(S) MAKE	MODEL			SERIAL #	

WEEK OF:_____	M	TU	W	TH	F	NOTES
WEARS AID(S)						_____
BATTERY OK						_____
HA LISTENING CHECK (LING SOUNDS) ☐ Student wearing device ☐ Stethoscope	AH / E SH / U S / M	AH / E SH / U S / M	AH / E SH / U S / M	AH / E SH / U S / M	AH / E SH / U S / M	_____
FM LISTENING CHECK						_____
ACTION (Call parent, call Audiology, etc.)						_____
OTHER						_____
WEEK OF:_____	M	TU	W	TH	F	_____
WEARS AID(S)						_____
BATTERY OK						_____
HA LISTENING CHECK (LING SOUNDS) ☐ Student wearing device ☐ Stethoscope	AH / E SH / U S / M	AH / E SH / U S / M	AH / E SH / U S / M	AH / E SH / U S / M	AH / E SH / U S / M	_____
FM LISTENING CHECK						_____
ACTION (Call parent, call Audiology, etc.)						_____
OTHER						_____
WEEK OF:_____	M	TU	W	TH	F	_____
WEARS AID(S)						_____
BATTERY OK						_____
HA LISTENING CHECK (LING SOUNDS) ☐ Student wearing device ☐ Stethoscope	AH / E SH / U S / M	AH / E SH / U S / M	AH / E SH / U S / M	AH / E SH / U S / M	AH / E SH / U S / M	_____
FM LISTENING CHECK						_____
ACTION (Call parent, call Audiology, etc.)						_____
OTHER						_____
WEEK OF:_____	M	TU	W	TH	F	_____
WEARS AID(S)						_____
BATTERY OK						_____
HA LISTENING CHECK (LING SOUNDS) ☐ Student wearing device ☐ Stethoscope	AH / E SH / U S / M	AH / E SH / U S / M	AH / E SH / U S / M	AH / E SH / U S / M	AH / E SH / U S / M	_____
FM LISTENING CHECK						_____
ACTION (Call parent, call Audiology, etc.)						_____
OTHER						_____

REV 5/1/10 (Used with permission of Dr. Joanna Wakefield, EARS Program @ Arkansas Children's Hospital)

Figure 6–1. Daily hearing aid and FM check chart.

provide a solution for some of the listening difficulties encountered in the classroom. Therefore, the general principles of determining candidacy for personal FM, as well as selecting and fitting personal FM devices, are discussed. For a more in-depth and comprehensive review of these procedures, the reader is referred to the *Clinical Practice Guidelines: Remote Microphone Hearing Assistance Technologies for Children and Youth Birth–21 Years* published by the American Academy of Audiology (2008; http://www.aud iology.org/ resources /document /library/ Documents/HATGuideline.pdf).

The Basics of Personal FM

Personal FM systems use a frequency modulated (FM) signal to wirelessly transmit the speaker's voice to the student. The speaker (e.g., the teacher) wears a transmitter that serves as the wireless microphone, while the listener (i.e., the student) wears a receiver (or receivers) that receives the FM signal. The concepts behind providing personal FM in a classroom setting center on providing the student with the best possible signal. The teacher's voice becomes the best possible signal because it is wirelessly transmitted directly to the student's ear, thereby, overcoming the issue of distance (as discussed in Chapter 2). In addition, because the teacher typically wears the remote microphone (wireless transmitter) within 6 inches of her mouth, her speech is the auditory signal closest to the microphone. This close proximity helps cut down on reverberation issues and improves the signal-to-noise ratio (teacher's voice is the signal; everything else is noise). Current research behind best practice suggests that a personal FM

system should increase the level of perceived speech in the listener's ear by at least 10 dB relative to speech reception via the hearing aid only (AAA, 2008; ASHA, 2002).

Transmitter Options

Personal FM systems are available from several manufacturers. Transmitter options will vary from company to company; however, there are some standard features available in the current market. For instance, personal FM system transmitters are typically made to be worn by the speaker. However, some transmitters can also be passed around from speaker to speaker or placed in the middle of a group (e.g., on a conference table). The microphone options should be taken into consideration when advising the user of the system on placement options. If the microphone has a directional (versus omnidirectional) option, the user would need to point the microphone toward the source of choice (e.g., toward the speaker and not the audience). Personal FM transmitters come with several different microphone styles (Figures 6–2 and 6–3). Some have a built-in microphone (e.g., Phonak's EasyLink+), whereas other transmitters use an external microphone that is lapel or boom style (e.g., Oticon's Amigo T30 or Phonak's Inspiro).

Receiver Options

Some FM receivers are designed to work with hearing aids, BAIs, or CIs, whereas other receivers are designed to be worn without hearing aids. Ear-level FM receivers that can be used in conjunction with other personal amplification devices can be categorized as either *universal receivers*

Figure 6–2. Phonak EasyLink+ transmitter, a personal FM transmitter with built-in microphone option. (Photo courtesy of Phonak LLC.)

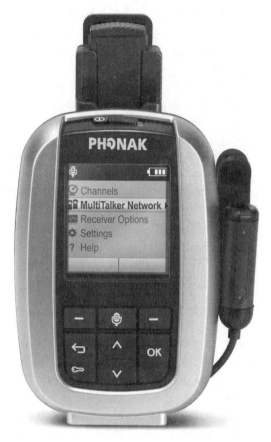

Figure 6–3. Phonak Inspiro transmitter, a personal FM transmitter with lapel style microphone option. (Photo courtesy of Phonak LLC.)

(Figure 6–4) or *integrated receivers* (Figure 6–5). Universal receivers are typically compatible with all behind-the-ear hearing instruments that are direct audio input (DAI) compatible. In order to couple a universal receiver with a hearing aid, there has to be either a special battery door that allows the receiver to be plugged in, or an audio shoe that couples the universal FM receiver to the hearing aid. Special universal FM receivers that are made to be coupled with BAIs and CIs also exist.

Integrated FM receivers are designed to take the place of a behind-the-ear hearing aid battery door. These receivers are usually made specifically for a certain brand, model, or line of hearing aid or cochlear implant. For ear-level receivers, the gain and frequency output characteristics of the personal FM system are determined from the hearing instrument settings and programming (AAA, 2008).

For students who wear hearing aids that are not DAI capable (e.g., in-the-ear styles or behind-the-ear aids with no DAI), an induction loop style of receiver can be used (Figure 6–6). This type of receiver, however, requires that the hearing instrument have a functioning and active t-coil.

Personal FM receivers that are used independently of a hearing aid or other amplification device do exist. These stand-alone receivers are available in ear-level styles (e.g., Phonak's iSense) or body worn styles that are coupled with earphones or headsets (e.g., Oticon's R5). These types of devices may be useful for students with normal peripheral hearing sensitivity in one or both ears who benefit from improvements in signal-to-noise ratios in the classroom environment (e.g., unilateral hearing loss, attention issues, processing issues, etc.).

Candidacy for Personal FM

School-based audiologists are essential in the process of determining who is an appropriate candidate for the use of a personal FM system. According to AAA (2008), children and youth who have any of the following concerns *may* be candidates

Figure 6–4. Phonak MLxi universal receiver. (Photo courtesy of Phonak LLC.)

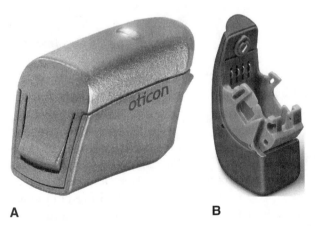

A

B

Figure 6–5. Integrated FM receivers. **A**. Oticon Amigo R12 dedicated receiver. (Photo courtesy of Oticon.) **B**. Phonak ML12i integrated receiver. (Photo courtesy of Phonak LLC.)

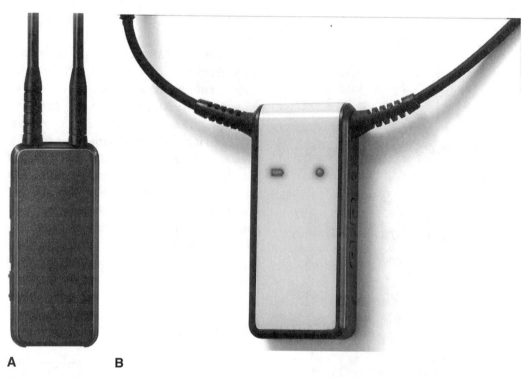

A   B

Figure 6–6. Neckloop style FM receivers. **A.** Phonak MyLink+ neckloop FM receiver (Photo courtesy of Phonak LLC.) **B.** Oticon Amigo arc FM neckloop receiver (Photo courtesy of Oticon.)

for remote microphone HAT (which in the AAA document includes classroom soundfield amplification, discussed later in this chapter):

■ Hearing loss
■ Auditory processing disorders
■ Learning disabilities
■ Auditory neuropathy/ dys-synchrony
■ Language delay/disorder
■ Attention deficits
■ English as a second language

Once there is documented evidence for any one of the above concerns, the next step for deciding whether or not to implement the use of a personal FM system with a particular student is to consider the acoustical environment, the social and emotional factors, the functional issues, and the support system of the individual (AAA, 2008). This candidacy process is more complex than simply answering the question, "Does the individual have an audiometric hearing loss?"

Personal FM System Selection

Deciding on the specifics of a personal FM system for any given student involves consideration being given to the student's audiological and developmental history and status. Additionally, the school-based audiologist must consider the listening environment in which the student functions in order to make an appropriate device selection. Aside from the size of the room, the location of the teacher in the room, and the additional sources of noise within and around the room, other technological considerations need to be taken into account. For instance, the audiologist must determine what other personal FM systems are being used in the same building. Will the FM signals be compatible, or will students be picking up the signals from other students' systems? The school-based audiologist must consider the "wearability" of the device for each individual student. Will the student be self conscious wearing the device, or will she only wear the device in certain settings due to social or peer influences? Last, the school-based audiologist must consider funding issues (AAA, 2008). If the school system is not responsible for providing the personal FM system, will the student's family be able to pick up the additional costs? All of these issues become crucial to the process of determining who can and will benefit from personal FM.

Implementation of the Personal FM System

Once a personal FM system has been selected, the performance of the device needs to be verified and validated. The reader is referred to the 2008 AAA Guidelines for comprehensive instructions on how to accomplish these analyses and procedures in a manner that is specific to best practice.

The Verification Process

Verification procedures are used to determine whether or not the personal FM device is functioning according to pre-determined targets (AAA, 2008). Verifica-

tion may be accomplished with electro-acoustical analysis, real ear measurements, as well as behavioral verification procedures. Verification procedures may differ depending on whether or not the FM system is being utilized in conjunction with hearing aid(s), cochlear implant(s), or by itself (i.e., ear level FM only).

Electroacoustical analysis with personal FM systems measures the performance of the device in terms of sound amplitude and signal-to-noise ratio (AAA, 2008). One of the primary goals of electroacoustical analysis when personal FM systems are being utilized with other hearing devices (i.e., personal hearing aids) is to verify transparency. Transparency is obtained when equal inputs to the wireless (FM system) and local (hearing aid) microphones generate equal outputs from the hearing device (AAA, 2008).

Real ear verification procedures are useful when an ear-level FM only is used. The priority in this case is to measure input levels in the ear canal of the user, especially the maximum output levels.

Behavioral verification procedures typically include formal and informal evaluation of speech recognition in noise, with and without the personal FM system. These types of procedures can be utilized in all conditions of FM use (i.e., in conjunction with hearing aids, cochlear implants, or ear-level FM only). Behavioral verification procedures are extremely important with students who use personal FM in conjunction with cochlear implants because electroacoustical analysis and real-ear measurements cannot be utilized with cochlear implants for verification.

The Validation Process

Validation procedures are used to ensure that the student is receiving optimal speech input via the personal FM system, and they should be ongoing. Additionally, the validation process should include both objective and subjective measures and may include self-assessments, observation questionnaires (completed by teachers and parents), and functional evaluations completed in the student's learning environment (AAA, 2008).

In the validation process, the audiologist determines if the personal FM system provides the student with full audibility and intelligibility of speech to the same extent that the student is able to recognize speech in an ideal listening condition. In addition, the validation process helps to establish whether or not the device provides full audibility of self and others, as well as whether or not the device reduces the deleterious effects of distance, noise, and reverberation (AAA, 2008).

Training and Technical Assistance to School Staff, Students, and Families

The school-based audiologist should be aware that the users of personal FM systems, their teachers, and family members will need training in order for the device to be used effectively. If the teacher never wears the transmitter correctly, then the student cannot get the intended benefit from the device. Topics that should be covered with students, teachers, parents, and other school personnel should include (AAA, 2008):

- Basic function of the device (e.g., how to turn off/on)
- Appropriate use of the device (e.g., when should the device be used)
- Care and maintenance of the device
- Basic troubleshooting of the device

Although initial training of the users of these systems is important, ongoing technical assistance is also crucial for students to receive maximum benefit. School-based audiologists should frequently check on teachers, students, and other personnel to make sure that they are using the device correctly and consistently.

Using FM for Sound Transmission

A specific band of radio frequencies have been set aside for use of personal FM systems in the United States. Older FM systems utilized the 72 to 76-mHz frequency range; however, newer systems use the 216 to 217-mHz frequency range. A receiver on one frequency range is not compatible with a transmitter on the other frequency range. This is unfortunate because it reduces a school's ability to use older equipment that is still functional with newer equipment.

Using FM for sound transmission in schools requires the school-based audiologist to be conscious of, and keep a record for, which FM channels are being used at any given time. For example, if Student A is using channel N01, Student B cannot use that channel at the same time because the systems will interfere with one another. Student B may hear Student A's teacher or vice versa. Each manufacturer of personal FM systems has its own coding strategy for assigning a frequency to a "channel." The school-based audiologist needs to be familiar with each manufacturer's coding scheme and be aware of how it interacts or overlaps with other manufacturers' schemes. There are cases in which a single channel for one manufacturer actually overlaps two channels for another manufacturer. School-based audiologists should contact specific manufacturers to inquire how their coding scheme may overlap with other manufacturers' coding schemes.

If two or more students in the same classroom wear personal FM systems, in most cases it would be possible to use one transmitter for all of the students. This would be accomplished by "syncing" all of the students' receivers to one common channel. Then, if these students separate into different classrooms for the next class period, each student can take his or her own transmitter and resync the receiver to the assigned FM channel. This task becomes somewhat complicated when equipment comes from different manufacturers. Also, the students involved with this process have to be at an appropriate age- and independence-level to complete this task successfully. There is no "magic" age level; however, the school-based audiologist will need to work closely with the student and teachers to determine at what level of independence a given student will be able to function.

Growing Applications for the Use of Personal FM Systems

The application of personal FM systems has grown from simply allowing a student to hear a teacher lecture in the classroom to allowing that student to interface (via their personal FM system) with multimedia devices. In the classroom, the school-based audiologist should assess the listening needs of the student and determine how to interface the personal FM system with all audio sources. For example, when students use personal computers for classroom activities, the student with a personal FM system should use the FM device instead of the computer's headphones. Interfacing can be accomplished with an auxiliary cord that patches the personal FM transmitter into the computer headphone jack.

CLASSROOM SOUNDFIELD AMPLIFICATION

The basic premise of the classroom soundfield amplification system is much like that of the personal FM system. The teacher wears a wireless microphone and his or her voice is transmitted to a receiver. However, in the classroom soundfield amplification system, the output is via a speaker or speakers (the receiver). This setup allows all students in the classroom to hear the teacher's voice and, therefore, access the increased signal-to-noise ratio being provided by the system.

Rationale for the Use of Classroom Soundfield Amplification

Classroom soundfield amplification systems have been used in classrooms for more than three decades. In 1978, the Mainstream Amplification Resource Room Study (MARRS) began and lasted for 13 years. The MARRS project used a wireless FM microphone system to amplify the teacher's voice above background noise with the purpose of allowing all students, no matter where they were seated in the classroom, to hear with equal clarity (Ray, 1988). The end results of this study indicated that, with the use of the system, the teacher's oral instructions were enhanced (improved signal-to-noise ratio), teacher vocal fatigue was lessened, and students' academic achievements were improved (Ray, 1988). Since that time, many studies have documented the value of the use of classroom soundfield amplification systems (see the suggested reading list at the end of this chapter for some of those studies).

Sound Transmission for Classroom Soundfield Amplification Systems

Classroom soundfield amplification systems have used FM sound transmission in the past and continue to do so in the pres-

ent. However, infrared sound transmission has also become popular for classroom soundfield systems. Infrared systems use a light wave to transmit sound. There are advantages and challenges to both FM and infrared sound transmission (refer to Table 6–1 for a complete list). Ultimately, the decision to use FM or infrared sound transmission will need to be based on the characteristics and needs of the classroom and building.

Options for Classroom Soundfield Amplification Systems

As with personal FM systems, classroom soundfield amplification systems come

Table 6–1. Advantages and Challenges of Infrared and FM Sound Transmission

Sound Transmission	Advantages	Challenges
Infrared	• Uses "line of sight" transmission; cannot spill over into another classroom • Transmission stops at the classroom door; teacher does not have to remember to turn off when she leaves to go down the hall	• Does not work well in large spaces because infrared transmission does not have the range that FM transmission does • Because of the need for "line of sight," infrared transmission does not work well in oddly shaped rooms (e.g., L-shaped)
FM	• Works well in large classrooms or spaces; FM transmission has a greater range than infrared transmission • Works well in oddly shaped rooms (e.g., L-shaped; odd corners); radio waves can bend and go through walls	• There exists the chance for interference from other FM signals • Sometimes FM signals are sensitive to large amounts of metal, wiring, or electricity in the environment • May pick up some interference from computers • FM signals have enough range that a teacher must remember to turn off her transmitter when leaving the room; otherwise, the students may overhear conversations outside of the classroom

in many shapes and sizes. Several of the options provided by manufacturers are described below.

Transmitter Options for Classroom Systems

Some transmitters have a built-in microphone; others have an external microphone that is either a lapel-style or boom-style microphone (Figure 6–7).

Many classroom soundfield amplification systems come with a pass-around microphone that can be used by team teachers or guests in the classroom. In addition, teachers have reported that they allow students to use the pass-around microphone when asking questions or making presentations to the class. This feature has been very popular with classroom teachers because students are excited to present information or ask questions when they are allowed to use the microphone. In addition, students with softer voices are more likely to be heard when using the microphone.

Speaker Configuration Options for Classroom Amplification Systems

Classroom soundfield amplification systems come with a variety of speaker configurations. Some example configurations are single, stand-alone speakers, ceiling

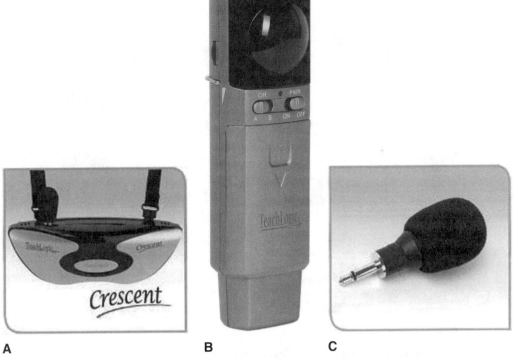

A **B** **C**

Figure 6–7. Transmitter examples for soundfield and microphone styles. **A.** Crescent transmitter from Teachlogic. **B.** Pendant transmitter from Teachlogoic. **C.** Plug-in mic from Teachlogic. *continues*

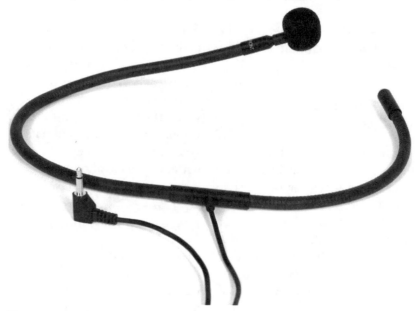

D

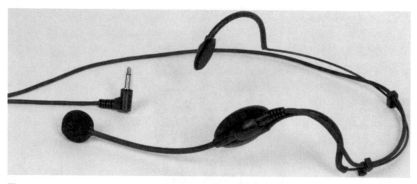

E

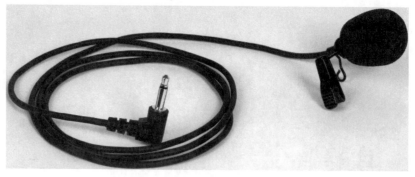

F

Figure 6–7. *continued* **D.** Collar mic from Teachlogic). **E.** Headset mic from Teachlogic. **F.** Lapel mic from Teachlogic. (Photos Courtesy of Teachlogic.)

mounted speakers (one to six in a classroom), and side wall mounted speakers (one to four in a classroom). Decisions regarding the most appropriate speaker configuration for a given classroom should be made based on individual classroom characteristics and available funding.

INTERFACING PERSONAL FM SYSTEMS WITH CLASSROOM SOUNDFIELD AMPLIFICATION

More and more classrooms are using soundfield systems. Therefore, there is a very good chance that a child with a personal FM system will be assigned to a classroom already containing soundfield amplification. Fortunately, there are several methods for interfacing personal FM systems with classroom soundfield amplification systems; however, the most common method is to directly patch the personal FM system transmitter into the soundfield receiver. Regardless of the method, however, the school-based audiologist should be the professional who determines how to go about patching the personal FM system of each child to the classroom's soundfield system. Also, the audiologist must patch the two systems without expecting the classroom teacher to wear two microphones (i.e., one for FM system and one for the soundfield system). If two or more students are wearing personal FM in the same classroom, the method described earlier in this chapter should be applied to the personal FM system transmitter and receivers first, then the personal FM transmitter can be patched into the soundfield system receiver.

There is an added benefit to using soundfield systems in classrooms where there are students who also utilize personal FM systems. This benefit arises when the soundfield system has both a teacher transmitter and a pass-around transmitter. In this scenario, the teacher can establish a "class rule" making it a requirement that all students speak into the pass-around transmitter (i.e., microphone) when asking or answering questions. This method of classroom management ensures that the student wearing the personal FM system hears the comments, questions, and presentations of his or her peers, which is beneficial to the child's learning and social development.

CONCLUSIONS

The school-based audiologist will spend an enormous amount of the workday focused on the amplification needs of students in the academic setting. Local education agencies have a responsibility to provide students with disabilities (and, in some cases, all students) access to the auditory information being presented in the academic setting. School-based audiologists are the appropriate professionals to manage these devices in the classroom setting.

It is the responsibility of the school-based audiologist to stay current on the topic of amplification for the classroom. Advances in technology will continue to improve and change the landscape in the field of classroom amplification. Manufacturers of amplification devices tend to keep their Web sites updated with information about their products and features; therefore, these Web sites have the ability to provide current and accurate information about technology and any advances. Continuing education sessions can also provide practitioners with updated information regarding this topic. The reader is advised that the individual devices (pieces of technology) change in this area very rapidly. However, the basic concepts for improving speech understanding in classrooms remain steady.

SUGGESTED READINGS

Although this list is not inclusive, the following items may provide the reader with a deeper understanding of research evidence that exists in the area of hearing assistance technology.

Cornwell, S., & Evans, C. (2001). The effects of sound field amplification on attending behaviors. *Journal of Speech-Language Pathology and Audiology, 25*(3), 135–144.

Crandell, C. (1996). Effects of sound field FM amplification on the speech perception of ESL children. *Educational Audiology Monograph, 4,* 1–5.

Crandell, C., Flexer, C., & Smaldino, J. (2005). *Sound field amplification: Applications to speech perception and classroom acoustics* (2nd ed.). Clifton Park, NY: Thomson Delmar Learning.

Edwards, D., & Feun, L. (2005). A formative evaluation of sound-field amplification systems across several grade levels in four schools. *Journal of Educational Audiology, 12,* 59–66.

Flexer, C. (2002). Rationale and use of sound field systems: An update. *Hearing Journal, 55*(8), 10–18.

Lewis, M. S., Crandell, C. C., Valente, M., & Horn, J. E. (2004). Speech perception in noise: Directional microphones versus fre-

quency modulation (FM) systems. *Journal of the American Academy of Audiology, 15,* 426–439.

Schafer, E., & Thibodeau, L. (2003). Speech recognition performance of children using cochlear implants and FM systems. *Journal of Educational Audiology, 11,* 15–26.

Thibodeau, L. (2010). Benefits of adaptive FM systems on speech recognition in noise for listeners who use hearing aids. *American Journal of Audiology, 19,* 36–45.

REFERENCES

American Academy of Audiology. (2008). *AAA clinical practice guidelines: Remote microphone hearing assistance technologies for children and youth birth–21 years.* Reston, VA: Author.

American Speech-Language-Hearing Association. (2002). *Guidelines for fitting and evaluation of FM systems.* Rockville, MD: Author.

Individuals with Disabilities Education Improvement Act of 2004. 20 U.S.C. §1400 et seq. (2004).

Ling, D. (2002). *Speech and the hearing impaired child* (2nd ed.). Washington, DC: Alexander Graham Bell Association for the Deaf and Head of Hearing.

Mittler, J. (2007). Assistive technology and IDEA. In C. Warger (Ed.), *Technology integration: Providing access to the curriculum for students with disabilities.* Arlington, VA: Technology and Media Division (TAM).

Smiley, D. F., Martin, P. F., & Lance, D. M. (2004, May 3). Using the Ling 6-Sound Test everyday. *AudiologyOnline.* Retrieved June 24, 2011 from http://www.audiologyonline.com/articles/arc_disp.asp?id=728

Ray, H. (1988). *Mainstream amplification resource room study (MARRS): A national diffusion network project.* Norris City, IL: Wabash & Ohio Valley Special Education District.

Educational Audiology in the Real World

Laurie Allen, AuD
Educational Audiologist
Keystone Area Education Agency
Dubuque, Iowa

When I was in graduate school, I did not plan to work in the schools. But I ended up doing my school practicum right before graduating with my master's degree from the University of Iowa in 1978. I traveled rural roads seeing kids in small schools. I did a lot of testing and hearing aid checks in school libraries, nurses' offices, and sometimes even locker rooms. All along the way, the students, school staff, and parents were happy to see me and grateful for my services. I was hooked.

I am one of four educational audiologists working for a state area education agency (AEA), which provides support services to schools in an eight county area. I have approximately 13,000 students on my caseload, birth to 21 years. My main duties include hearing evaluations, troubleshooting hearing instruments and classroom amplification equipment, ordering FM devices, verifying instrument fittings, in-servicing school staff, students, and parents, advocating for children with hearing loss, data collection, and documentation. I serve one large public school district and a small parochial district.

I am fortunate to have a wonderful audiometrist who screens students (Head Start and grades K, 1st, 2nd, and 7th) and then assists me with the more challenging children. She can hold a child on her lap, steady a probe tip in an ear, and comfort an anxious child while I am turning the dials and recording the test results. We make a good team. Testing is done both in the schools and at our office diagnostic center.

Lessons I have learned:

1. *The educational audiologist is the watchdog when it comes to verifying children's hearing instrument fittings. Unfortunately, there are many dispensers who still do not incorporate real ear verification as part of their fitting protocol. This results in having children sitting in school wearing hearing aids which were "first fit" by their dispensers. The children are underamplified, which reduces their access to normal conversational speech. This is a barrier to learning and is addressed in IDEA. Unfortunately, adding an FM system coupled to the child's hearing instruments will not help if these instruments are not set to provide an appropriate amount of gain. I would suggest that you ask your local dispensers about their fitting protocols. Ask parents to sign an exchange of information form so that you can obtain test results from their child's dispenser. Work hard to build rapport with your local dispensers.*

2. *Classroom amplification equipment is not appropriate for all children with hearing loss. In most cases, children with more than mild degrees of hearing loss need an FM device that couples directly to their hearing instruments. I will never forget the time when I was persuaded into using a classroom amplification system for an aided first*

grade student. The teacher consistently wore the classroom FM transmitter and also prided herself in having a "loud" voice. Later in the year, I ordered a personal FM system on a trial basis for this student. The expression on his face still haunts me after all these years. The joy and wonderment of being able to really hear showed clearly in his eyes. I knew, at that moment, that this child needed this type of FM system, and the minimal amplification provided by the classroom system was not enough. Fortunately, it is now possible to connect a student's personal FM device with a classroom amplification system so that every child is able to hear their teacher clearly without the teacher having to wear multiple microphones. This arrangement makes for a win-win situation for everyone.

3. *Simulated hearing loss software is a valuable tool for the educational audiologist. It is a tremendous tool that can be used to:*

   - *help convince parents that their child's hearing loss needs to be addressed.*
   - *reinforce teachers' use of FM equipment and the need for other accommodations*
   - *educate school staff and administrators for whom hearing loss can be an invisible barrier to learning. Student performance and academic success are directly related to the student's ability to access information in school. It is advantageous for your school principal and/or special education director to understand the impact that hearing loss has on a student's academic performance.*

   Being an educational audiologist offers a fulfilling and challenging career helping children and their families. It enables you to provide a large variety of services. One day you may be taking sound pressure readings in the high school band room, meeting with a student and their vocational rehabilitation counselor, or rescreening newborn babies. Every day is different and gives you the opportunity to positively impact the life of a child. What could be more rewarding?

7

The School-Based Audiologist and Hearing Loss Prevention/ Hearing Conservation Programs

Cynthia M. Richburg and Donna F. Smiley

OBJECTIVES

By the end of this chapter, the reader will be able to:

1. Describe why hearing loss prevention/hearing conservation programs in schools are so important.
2. Describe who should be responsible for providing hearing loss prevention/ hearing conservation programs to students.
3. Describe why current school curricula do not typically include instruction on hearing loss prevention/hearing conservation.
4. Describe the hearing loss prevention/hearing conservation programs that are currently available.

INTRODUCTION

Because the prevalence of noise-induced hearing loss (NIHL) is increasing among school-age children (Cooley Hidecker, 2008; DeConde Johnson & Meinke 2008; Folmer, 2006; Niskar, Kieszak, Holmes, Esteban, Rubin, & Brody, 1998; Shargorodsky, Curhan, Curhan, & Eavey, 2010), all school-based audiologists should possess a thorough understanding of the consequences of this type of loss and the impact it can have on the educational and socio-emotional characteristics of students. Identification of students with NIHL is only a small part of any educational audiologist's responsibilities concerning hearing conservation. In fact, in many schools, it is the audiologist's responsibility to develop an active hearing loss prevention, or an active hearing conservation, program that is age-appropriate for the students. If the school-based audiologist is not the main provider of this service, then the audiologist should collaborate with other educators (e.g., science and health teachers) to disseminate the information contained in a hearing loss prevention/hearing conservation program. Whether the school system refers to the services as a hearing loss prevention program, or as a hearing conservation program, the goals for educating students, school employees, and parents should remain the same for personnel involved in this educational mission: raise public awareness about NIHL in school-age children, inform educators about existing programs and curricula on hearing conservation, and propose state and federal legislation for implementing and maintaining hearing conservation instruction at multiple grade levels throughout a student's educational training.

NOISE-INDUCED HEARING LOSS AND ITS CAUSES

When the human ear is exposed to loud noise (whether constant or impulse) without being adequately protected, the resulting consequence can be NIHL. It is beyond the scope of this chapter to fully discuss the pathological changes in cochlear structures caused by noise. However, audiology students should be familiar with the three types of hearing loss caused by exposure to noise: noise-induced temporary threshold shift (NITTS

or TTS), noise-induced permanent threshold shift (NIPTS or PTS), and acoustic trauma.

A NITTS is the temporary reduction in hearing sensitivity following exposure to loud sound. This temporary reduction in hearing can last from less than one hour to as much as a few days (Feuerstein, 2002). A person with a NITTS may experience a reduction in hearing sensitivity, tinnitus, and/or aural fullness, but all of these conditions dissipate as hearing recovers. An NIPTS is a permanent reduction in hearing sensitivity, which arises when full recovery from a NITTS does not occur. An NIPTS also may result in tinnitus and/or aural fullness. NIPTS is typically slow and progressive, and therefore, a person is often unaware of any hearing difficulty until it is too late. Acoustic trauma results from exposure to a single, impulsive, and intense stimulus, such as an explosion, gunshot, or firework. The resultant hearing loss may also be accompanied by tinnitus and/or aural fullness, but the loss is permanent and does not recover fully.

Both NITTS and NIPTS result from swelling of the cochlear hair cells. With NITTS, the swelling resolves and the cochlear structures return to their normal orientation and placement. However, with NIPTS and acoustic trauma, the swelling of the hair cells results in some of the cells rupturing. The hair cells may also become distorted and the stereocilia may fuse, which would keep them from transmitting energy effectively to the hair cells (NIH, 1990). In addition to these cellular changes, with acoustic trauma, the tympanic membrane (TM) may be ruptured, which in turn may disarticulate the ossicular chain. Therefore, an NIPTS will result in a sensory, or cochlear, loss, whereas acoustic trauma may result in either a sensory loss or a mixed loss, due to the conductive nature of the loss caused by a perforated TM and/or ossicular discontinuity.

Because of the increased use of personal listening devices (e.g., MP3 players, iPods, CD players), and because of direct and incidental exposure to noisy machinery (e.g., farm equipment, snowmobiles, all-terrain vehicles, motorcycles), technology (e.g., video games, movie theatres, concert sound systems), and environmental noise pollution (e.g., traffic noise, gunfire, fireworks), more and more school-age children are acquiring NIHL (Cooley Hidecker, 2008; DeConde Johnson & Meinke, 2008; Folmer, 2006; Niskar, Kieszak, Holmes, Esteban, Rubin, & Brody, 1998). Therefore, it is essential for today's schoolchildren to learn about NIHL and develop healthy hearing habits to prevent the consequences associated with NIHL.

THE IMPORTANCE OF HEARING LOSS PREVENTION/HEARING CONSERVATION

Even though the high-frequency hearing loss detected in the studies on NIHL in school-age children would often be classified as minimal or mild, there are many reasons why NIHL should be identified and prevention of further loss should be addressed in schools. First of all, NIHL may not be easily detected during regular hearing screenings that use 20 dB HL across the frequencies recommended by the American Speech-Language-Hearing Association (ASHA, 1997; Meinke & Dice, 2007). Noise-induced hearing loss *may* be identified at 4000 Hz; however, Meinke and Dice (2007) discovered that over half

of the school-based hearing screening protocols used throughout the United States would identify only 22% of students who have a high-frequency noise notch. Therefore, many students with NIHL would not fail their hearing screenings at school. Screening hearing at 6000 Hz would give an educational audiologist a clearer picture of a student's past exposure to noise, as well as a better idea of the degree of high-frequency loss.

Although debate continues over the importance of identifying minimal hearing impairment (MHI) in school-age children, there is increasing evidence that MHI has significant consequences for education, language learning and literacy, and for behavior and socioemotional development (Bess, Dodd-Murphy, & Parker, 1998; Gillon, 2000, 2002; Jarvelin, Maki-Torkko, Sorri, & Rantakallio, 1997; Johnson, Stein, Broadway, & Markwalter, 1997; Pakulski & Kaderavek, 2002; Rvachew, Ohberg, Grawburg, & Heyding, 2003). Additional research has documented that children with MHI repeat classes more often than students with normal hearing, and the economic and psychological costs of grade repetition are substantial (Bess et al., 1998; English & Church, 1999; Flexer, 1994). Blair, EuDaly, and Benson (1999) estimated that there are as few as one child, and as many as seven children, in *every* elementary school classroom who has some degree of auditory-based learning problem. Of great concern is the fact that many students with mild or unilateral hearing losses are not considered eligible for services from special education personnel, including educational audiologists. Therefore, it is vital that professionals working with school-age children have an accurate understanding of NIHL and its possible ramifications.

Can A Love of Music Cause Hearing Loss?

Many studies have documented the fact that musicians, including school-age students in band and choir classes, are at risk for developing noise-induced hearing loss (NIHL; Jerger & Jerger, 1970; Jurman, Karmody, & Simeon, 2004; Royster, Royster, & Killion 1991; Westmore & Eversden, 1981). In addition to these students, the band and choir instructors are at risk for NIHL (Cutietta, Klich, Royse, & Rainbolt, 1991). In fact, Cutietta and colleagues (1991) found high-frequency hearing loss present in 45% of elementary and high school music teachers under the age of 40.

It is difficult to predict the risk for NIHL based on the number of practice sessions to which a musician is exposed (Early & Horstman, 1996; Jerger & Jerger, 1970). Also, the characteristics of practice sessions (e.g., length of time, room size, construction materials used in the rooms, numbers of instruments played in each session, etc.), in conjunction with the sound pressure levels generated by various instruments, make it difficult to predict the degree and permanence of a high frequency hearing loss (Jerger & Jerger, 1970). However, Early and Horstman (1996) found that many high school marching band and concert band members exceed the OSHA allowable limits for noise levels even though these musicians may only practice 1 to 3 hours at a time.

Chasin (2006) presented a table listing various musical instruments and the average output of those instruments (in dB[A]). According to Chasin (2006), a violin ranges from 85 to 105 dB(A), a saxophone from 75 to 110 dB(A), a flute from 92 to 105 dB(A), a French horn from 92 to 104 dB(A), a trombone from 90 to 106 dB(A), and a trumpet ranges from 88 to 108 dB(A). All of these instruments, if played loud enough and long enough, have the potential to create NIHL for students who play them.

Even more alarming, findings by Early and Horstman (1996) indicated that the students in two separate high school marching bands and one high school concert band were exposed to noise dose ratings exceeding the 50% noise dose criteria in which an individual should be included in a hearing conservation program, according to OSHA guidelines. With each group, five dosimeters were used and noise doses of as much as 71.8% were measured.

One should be aware that the OSHA standard protects against hearing loss in the speech frequencies, but it does not protect against hearing loss in the higher frequencies, frequencies important for musicians. Also, tinnitus and pitch perception problems are even more troubling to musicians than actual hearing loss. Therefore, providing hearing conservation information and solutions to students in school bands and choirs should be included in an educational audiologist's armada of responsibilities and roles.

References

Chasin, M., (2006). Hearing aids for musicians, *Hearing Review, 13*(3), 24–31.

Cutietta, R. A., Klich, R. J., Royse, D., & Rainbolt, H. (1994). The incidence of noise-induced hearing loss among music teachers. *Journal of Research in Music Education, 42*(4), 318–330.

Early, K. L., & Horstman, S. W. (1996). Noise exposure to musicians during practice. *Applied Occupational and Environmental Hygiene, 11*(9), 1149–1153.

Jerger, J., & Jerger, S. (1970). Temporary threshold shift in rock and roll musicians. *Journal of Speech and Hearing Research, 13*, 218–224.

Jurman, S., Karmody, C., & Simeon, D. (2004). Hearing loss in steel band musicians. *Otolaryngology-Head and Neck Surgery, 131*(4), 461–465.

Royster, J. D., Royster, L. H., & Killion, M. C. (1991). Sound exposures and hearing thresholds of symphony orchestra musicians. *Journal of the Acoustical Society of America, 89*(6), 2793–2803.

Westmore, G. A., & Eversden, I. D. (1981). Noise-induced hearing loss and orchestral musicians. *Archives of Otolaryngology, 107*(12), 761–764.

THE LACK OF HEARING LOSS PREVENTION/HEARING CONSERVATION PROGRAMS IN SCHOOLS

In response to the increasing numbers of school students being identified with NIHL, for years many experts have recommended implementing hearing loss prevention/hearing conservation programs in primary and secondary educational settings (Chermak & Peters-McCarthy, 1991; Folmer, 2008; Meinke & Dice, 2007; Montgomery & Fujikawa, 1992; Roeser, 1980). Yet, despite the availability of hearing loss prevention/hearing conservation programs, basic instruction on hearing preservation and the subsequent materials associated with instruction remain absent in schools (Ahlstrand, 2009; Folmer, 2002; Folmer, Griest, & Martin, 2002).

More than 20 years ago, Lass, Woodford, Lundeen, Lundeen, and Everly-Myers (1986) asserted that hearing conservation education should receive the same attention as antismoking, antidrug, and teen pregnancy campaigns receive, especially as NIHL is totally preventable if proper precautions are taken. Yet, even with experts in the field stressing the need for hearing loss prevention/hearing conservation in the schools, Chung, Des Roches, Meunier, and Eavey (2005) still reported that most teenagers consider NIHL a much smaller risk than the other health concerns they are frequently warned about in school courses (i.e., alcohol and substance abuse, sexually transmitted diseases, depression, weight problems, smoking, and acne).

If the programs and materials are available, you may be asking yourself why then are hearing conservation practices not being taught in most schools? The main reason lies in the fact that there are no educational agencies, policies, or mandates requiring hearing conservation be taught in schools within the United States. The Occupational Safety and Health Administration (OSHA), the National Institute for Occupational Safety and Health (NIOSH), and the Centers for Disease Control and Prevention (CDC) are agencies that focus on assuring safety and healthful working conditions for men and women in the workplace; however, there is no such organization (not even the U.S. Department of Education) that regulates noise exposure for children in schools or mandates that hearing protection education be taught in school curricula. For more information about OSHA and NIOSH, see the box that follows.

There are additional reasons why hearing loss prevention practices remain absent from most schools' curricula. For example, there is a general lack of public awareness regarding NIHL, and lack of public awareness regarding NIHL in school-age children is no different. The average person on the street is not aware of the risks associated with excessive noise exposure. Likewise, most students, teachers, school administrators, and parents are not aware of the problems associated with NIHL in school students (EAA, 2009; Folmer, 2002).

Another reason hearing loss prevention or hearing conservation is not typically seen in school curricula is due to the lack of effective dissemination of programs that currently exist (e.g., Crank it Down!, Dangerous Decibels™, and Know Noise). There are many hearing loss prevention/hearing conservation programs available to schools and teachers these days, many of which use games, simulations of hearing loss, instruction on anatomy and physiology of the ear, and hands-on experience with hearing protectors incorporated into their lesson plans. (These programs will be discussed more thoroughly later in this chapter). Yet, even with the abundance of information about hearing loss prevention, and the available materials needed to make the topic palatable and understandable to young children, getting teachers and administrators to assist educational audiologists in distributing the information has been a major obstacle.

Finally, according to Folmer (2002), there is a problem with maintaining the continuity of hearing conservation instruction among the relatively small numbers of audiologists, school nurses, health teachers, coaches, and volunteers who might have presented hearing conservation curricula in the past. That is, even if a conservation program is initiated within a school, often the professional offering the curricula retires, leaves for a different position, or has to stop presenting the information for other reasons. Therefore, the perpetuation of the instruction is missing because another professional will fail to pick up where the first professional left off. All of these reasons for the lack of hearing conservation curricula in the schools must be addressed and overcome if NIHL is ever going to be fully understood and appreciated by students, parents, and school personnel.

OSHA and NIOSH

The Occupational Safety and Health Act of 1970 created the Occupational Safety and Health Administration (OSHA) and the National Institute for Occupational Safety and Health (NIOSH). Both of these agencies are crucial to the prevention of hearing loss and dissemination of information concerning the effects of noise on hearing. Yet, neither organization sets standards for schools. The OSHA standards do not cover school, farming, and recreational settings common to adolescents. NIOSH recommendations are not binding unless they are adopted by a regulatory agency. Therefore, a regulatory agency is needed to address noise-induced hearing loss (NIHL) in school-age children and hearing loss prevention education in schools throughout the United States.

The Occupational Safety and Health Administration (OSHA)

OSHA, a division of the U.S. Department of Labor, developed noise level standards in 1983 for industry. The concept of noise level exposure, which is the amount of allowable time an individual may be exposed to a certain level of noise, was established to protect industry workers' hearing. Hearing conservation programs were mandated for noise levels exceeding 85 dBA for an exposure period greater than eight hours. OSHA determined the amount of allowable time an employee may be exposed to a noise level, even with hearing protection. The time limit was meant to preserve hearing and reduce the amount of NIHL seen in workers. Standards exist for industry, mining, and the military. However, as mentioned in this chapter, people are exposed to excessive noise levels in many settings for which no standards or regulations exist.

The National Institute for Occupational Safety and Health (NIOSH)

NIOSH is a division of the Centers for Disease Control and Prevention, which is part of the Department of Health and Humans Services. NIOSH, like OSHA, seeks to protect workers, assist employers with safety issues, and continues to research improvements in the workplace environment. NIOSH develops and establishes occupational safety and health standards. The standard set by NIOSH differs from OSHA's standard, however. The noise exposure level set forth by OSHA allows for a larger increase in environmental noise before a reduction in exposure time. The NIOSH standard does not allow for as large an increase in environmental noise before a change in exposure time takes place.

ADDRESSING THE LACK OF HEARING PROGRAMS IN SCHOOLS

In 1988, Frager and Kahn found that one half of health teachers using health textbooks lacked sufficient information for teaching hearing conservation. They concluded that health textbooks should, "discuss and illustrate what can be done to minimize hearing health risks related to prolonged exposure to loud sounds and help children develop better judgment regarding the use of hearing protection" (Frager & Kahn, 1988, p. 179).

Since that time, many studies have shown that people who are educated about NIHL and hearing loss prevention techniques are more likely to use hearing protection at a future date, both in recreational situations and in occupational situations (Chermak, Curtis, & Seikel, 1996; Chermak & Peters-McCarthy, 1991; Florentine, 1990; Kanekama & Downs, 2008; Knobloch & Broste, 1998). Therefore, research findings support the argument for educating students and school personnel about the causes and effects of noise on hearing.

COLLABORATING WITH EDUCATORS FOR DISSEMINATING HEARING CONSERVATION MATERIALS

To many, hearing loss is a low priority. A person's loss often has to become severe enough to interfere with the ability to communicate before it is recognized and addressed. However, for those of us in the profession of Audiology, hearing loss and hearing loss prevention are a high priority and something we think about routinely. It is because we are in the field of Communication Sciences and Disorders that we are so aware of the consequences and causes of hearing loss, and it is up to us to work with school personnel, parents, and students to get our message across. There is an entire chapter on the topic of collaboration in this book (Chapter 10), and some of the ideas for working with other school personnel listed in that chapter could be used for the purposes of establishing and maintaining an active hearing conservation program in your school district. However, not all professionals or school personnel listed in Chapter 10 are essential to the establishment of hearing conservation programs and hearing loss prevention education. In general, it is very likely that the only professionals who will have any type of responsibilities associated with hearing conservation education will be the educational audiologist, the school nurse, the speech-language pathologist, the science or health teachers, and the school principal. In fact, audiologists have the primary responsibility of providing hearing loss prevention education, according to the scope of practice established by the American Academy of Audiology (2004) and the American Speech-Language-Hearing Association (2004). In addition, the Individuals with Disabilities Education Act (IDEA; 2004) specifically defines audiology services to include "the creation and administration of programs for prevention of hearing loss" (see Chapter 1 for complete definition of audiology in IDEA, 2004). Audiologists are charged with determining the content of the hearing conservation instruction provided in their schools, as well as making the curricula relevant to the various age groups.

DEVELOPING AND IMPLEMENTING PROGRAMS FOR SCHOOL-AGE CHILDREN

Over the last 30 or more years, many articles have been written addressing the development and implementation of hearing loss prevention/hearing conservation programs (Anderson, 1991; EAA, 2009; Lass, Woodford, Lundeen, Lundeen, Everly-Myers, McGuire, et al., 1987). Most experts recommend several topics for inclusion in hearing preservation/conservation instruction: instruction on normal and disordered auditory structures, types and causes of hearing loss, the effects of noise on hearing, tinnitus, aural fullness, and other warning signs of NIHL, and recommendations for the prevention of NIHL. The Educational Audiology Association's document entitled *Recommended Professional Practices for Educational Audiology* (EAA, 2009) describes the process of delivering these services as:

- Provision of a comprehensive hearing conservation curriculum that focuses on the process of hearing and hearing loss prevention;
- Collaboration with other school professionals (e.g., nursing staff, classroom teachers, administrators) to develop materials and design activities to disseminate information through coursework (e.g., science, health), as part of a school-wide health fair, or through formal presentations in schools and community events;
- Provision of current resources and materials for school staff, administrators, parents, and students regarding state and federal standards (OSHA, 1993); and
- Provision of information about and access to hearing protection devices and equipment. (EAA, 2009, p. 2)

As mentioned earlier, the information provided to school-age children should correspond with their grade and understanding levels. According to Folmer (2002), audiologists should encourage teachers to include hearing loss prevention messages into lesson plans in several different classes (e.g., music, science, health, physics/math) in several different grades (e.g., 1st, 4th, 7th, and 10th). Likewise, school-based audiologists should encourage their speech-language pathology colleagues to incorporate hearing loss prevention messages into their lesson plans.

EXAMPLES OF CONSERVATION PROGRAMS AVAILABLE TO SCHOOL-BASED AUDIOLOGISTS

Folmer, Griest, and Martin (2002) identified 29 organizations that produced or disseminated hearing conservation curricula and materials that were meant to be presented to school-age children. The list is not all inclusive, but it is an excellent example of the plethora of hearing conservation materials that are available to teachers, administrators, and educational audiologists. We have included a short list (Table 7–1) of some of the more comprehensive hearing conservation programs aimed at school-age students.

Table 7–1. Comprehensive Hearing Prevention/Conservation Programs

Program	Web Site	Description
Dangerous Decibels®	http://www.dangerousdecibels.org	A public health campaign designed to reduce the incidence and prevalence of NIHL and tinnitus; Has three components: education, exhibitry, and research
Listen Smart: Safely Handling the Power of Sound	Produced by Dan Beck; available via EAA (http://www.edaud.org) and H.E.A.R. (http://www.hearnet.com)	A video that features interviews with popular musicians talking about NIHL; offers useful tips on hearing protection
It's a Noisy Planet	http://www.noisyplanet.nidcd.nih.gov	A campaign of NIDCD aimed at 8- to 12-year-olds to teach them to avoid hearing loss from overexposure to loud noise
Listen to Your Buds	http://www.listentoyourbuds.org	A public education campaign sponsored by ASHA aimed at preventing NIHL by helping parents teach their children how to use personal audio technology safely
Turn It to the Left®	http://www.turnittotheleft.com	A public education campaign sponsored by AAA with the goal of raising public awareness about the risks of NIHL and how to prevent it
It's How You Listen That Counts®	http://www.earbud.org	A campaign targeted at 7th to 12th graders produced by the House Research Institute

CONCLUSION

Although hearing loss prevention or hearing conservation programs are less commonly provided by school-based audiologists than would be hoped, these programs are nonetheless important to the service delivery of school-age children. School-based audiologists should be leading the efforts to promote these programs and the outcomes they can provide for all school-age students. In light of the fact that so many programs already exist and are readily available to the consumer, schools should be at the forefront for teaching children how to preserve their hearing.

REFERENCES

Ahlstrand, V. (2009). *Perceptions of sound exposure and hearing preservation by high school juniors in north central Pennsylvania.* Unpublished doctoral research project, Bloomsburg University of Pennsylvania, Bloomsburg, PA.

American Academy of Audiology. (2004). *Scope of practice.* Retrieved from: http://www.audiology.org/resources/documentlibrary/Pages/ScopeofPractice.aspx

American Speech-Language-Hearing Association. (1997). *Guidelines for audiologic screening* [Guidelines]. Available from: http://www.asha.org/policy

American Speech-Language-Hearing Association. (2004). Scope of practice in audiology. *ASHA Supplement 24.*

Anderson, K. L. (1991). Hearing conservation in the public schools revisited. *Seminars in Hearing, 12,* 340–364.

Bess. F. H., Dodd-Murphy, J. & Parker, R. A. (1998). Children with minimal sensorineural hearing loss: Prevalence, educational performance, and functional status. *Ear and Hearing, 19*(5), 339–354.

Blair, J., EuDaly, M., & Benson, P. (1999). The effectiveness of audiologists' information sources for classroom teachers. *Language, Speech, and Hearing Services in Schools, 30,* 173–182.

Chermak, G., Curtis, L., & Seikel, J. (1996). The effectiveness of an interactive hearing conservation program for elementary school children. *Language Speech and Hearing Services in Schools, 27,* 29–39.

Chermak, G., & Peters-McCarthy, E. (1991). The effectiveness of an educational hearing conservation program for elementary school children. *Language Speech and Hearing Services in Schools, 22,* 308–312.

Chung, J., Des Roches, C., Meunier, J., & Eavey, R. (2005). Evaluation of noise-induced hearing loss in young people using a Web-based survey technique. *Pediatrics, 115,* 861–867.

Cooley Hidecker, M.J. (2008). Noise-induced hearing loss in school-age children: What do we know? *Seminars in Hearing, 29,* 12–28.

DeConde Johnson, C., & Meinke, D. (2008). Noise-induced hearing loss: Implications for schools. *Seminars in Hearing, 29,* 59–66.

Educational Audiology Association. (2009). *School-based audiology advocacy series: Noise and hearing loss prevention education.* Retrieved from http://www.edaud.org

English, K., & Church, G. (1999). Unilateral hearing loss in children: An update for the 1990s. *Language Speech and Hearing Services in Schools, 30,* 26–31.

Feuerstein, J.F. (2002). Occupational hearing conservation. In J. Katz (Ed.), *Handbook of clinical audiology* (pp. 567–583). Baltimore, MD: Lippincott Williams & Wilkins.

Flexer, C. (1994). *Facilitating hearing and listening in young children.* San Diego, CA: Singular.

Florentine, M. (1990). Education as a tool to prevent noise-induced hearing loss. *Hearing instruments, 41*(10), 33–34.

Folmer, R. L. (2002). *Why aren't hearing conservation practices taught in schools?* Retrieved from: http://www.audiologyonline.com/articles/article_detail.asp?article_id=354

Folmer, R. L. (2006). Noise-induced hearing loss in young people. *Pediatrics, 117,* 248–249.

Folmer, R. L. (2008). Hearing loss prevention practices should be taught in schools. *Seminars in Hearing, 29,* 67–80.

Folmer, R. L., Griest, S. E., & Martin, W. H. (2002). Hearing conservation education programs for children: A review. *Journal of School Health, 72*(2), 51–57.

Frager, A. M., & Kahn, A. (1988). How useful are elementary school health textbooks for teaching about hearing health and protection? *Language, Speech and Hearing Services in Schools, 19,* 175–181.

Gillon, G. T. (2000). The efficacy of phonological awareness intervention for children with spoken language impairment. *Language, Speech, and Hearing Services in Schools, 31,* 126–141.

Gillon, G. T. (2002). Follow-up study investigating benefits of phonological awareness intervention for children with spoken language impairment. *International Journal of Language and Communication Disorders, 37,* 381–400.

Individuals with Disabilities Education Improvement Act of 2004. 20 U.S.C. §1400 et seq. (2004).

Jarvelin, M., Maki-Torkko, E., Sorri, M. J., & Rantakallio, P. T. (1997). Effect of hearing impairment on educational outcomes and employment up to the age of 25 years in northern Finland. *British Journal of Audiology, 31*(3), 165–175.

Johnson, C. E., Stein, R. L., Broadway, A., & Markwalter, T. S. (1997). "Minimal" high-frequency hearing loss and school-age children: Speech recognition in a classroom. *Language, Speech, and Hearing Services in Schools, 28*, 77–85.

Kanekama, Y., & Downs, D. (2008). A university-based hearing conservation program for high school students. *Proceedings of the 9th International Congress on Noise as a Public Health Problem*, pp. 152–158.

Knobloch, M. J., & Broste, S. K. (1998). A hearing conservation program for youth working in agriculture. *Journal of School Health, 68*(8), 313–318.

Lass, N., Woodford, C., Lundeen, C., Lundeen, D., & Everly-Myers, S. (1986). The prevention of noise-induced hearing loss in the school-aged population: A school educational hearing conservation program. *Journal of Auditory Research, 26*, 247–254.

Lass, N., Woodford, C., Lundeen, C., Lundeen, D., & Everly-Myers, S., McGuire, K., . . . Phillips, R. (1987). A hearing conservation program for a junior high school. *Hearing Journal, 40*, 32–40.

Meinke, D., & Dice, N. (2007). Comparison of audiometric screening criteria for the identification of noise-induced hearing loss in adolescents. *American Journal of Audiology, 16*, S190–S202.

Montgomery, J., & Fujikawa, S. (1992). Hearing thresholds of students in the second, eighth, and twelfth grades. *Language, Speech, and Hearing Services in Schools, 23*, 61–63.

NIH Consensus Statement. (1990). Noise induced hearing loss. *NIH Consensus Statement, 8*(1), 1–24.

Niskar, A., Kieszak, S., Holmes, A., Esteban, E., Rubin, C., & Brody, D. (1998). Prevalence of hearing loss among children 6 to 19 years of age: The third national health and nutrition examination survey. *Journal of the American Medical Association, 279*, 1071–1075.

Pakulski, L. A., & Kaderavek, J. N. (2002). Children with minimal hearing loss: Interventions in the classroom. *Intervention in School and Clinic, 38*(2), 96–104.

Roeser, R. J. (1980). Industrial hearing conservation programs in the high schools (protect the ear before the 12th year). *Ear and Hearing, 1*(3), 119–120.

Rvachew, S., Ohberg, A., Grawberg, M., & Heyding, J. (2003). Phonological awareness and phonemic perception in 4-year-old children with delayed expressive phonology skills. *American Journal of Speech-Language Pathology, 12*, 463–471.

Shargorodsky, J., Curhan, S.G., Curhan, G. C., & Eavey, R. (2010). Change in prevalence of hearing loss in U.S. adolescents. *Journal of the American Medical Association, 304*(7), 772–778.

Educational Audiology in the Real World

Kym Meyer, MS
Educational Audiologist and Certified Teacher
Director, The Outreach Partnership Program (TOPP)
The Learning Center for the Deaf
Framingham, Massachusetts

Educational audiology was unheard of in the majority of Massachusetts' public schools until the late 1990s. The schools for the deaf in our state have always had audiologists, and that is how I started my educational audiology career 3 years after finishing my audiology degree. For several years, I worked as the educational audiologist at The Learning Center for the Deaf (TLC) in Framingham and Randolph, MA. The job was wonderful, and it encompassed everything I loved about audiology: language and education. As a former deaf educator, having a high degree of sign language fluency, I could converse with all Deaf students and staff. I enjoyed sitting down and explaining, in American Sign Language, hearing technology to Deaf people who wanted to understand more. I tested hearing of all the students, did middle ear screenings, fit hearing aids, attended IEP meetings, and got to know the children and their families. I really loved my work.

A few years later, we received telephone calls from public schools who were struggling with the technology that their hard of hearing students were using. The schools were desperate to contract with TLC to have someone come out and "fix" these problems (the schools did not yet know they were requesting educational audiology services). In addition to my "day job," I would go to the public schools to troubleshoot FM equipment and train teachers on what hearing loss really meant (and that hearing aids did not make their student's hearing "normal"). I would also educate these districts about educational audiology as a related service under IDEA. The number of requests from public schools grew and, after discussion with my administration, we knew that these services could no longer be delivered in a piecemeal way. I gave up my position as TLC's educational audiologist and began concentrating on providing contract educational audiology services to public schools through a newly developed department at TLC, called The Outreach Partnership Program (TOPP).

For many years, I was TOPP's only employee, and my job was to drive thousands of miles each year to provide educational audiology services around the state. Through networking, word got out among special education directors that educational audiology services were important in order to provide access to children with hearing loss. Now our program contracts with four educational audiology consultants and four teachers of the deaf consultants, who provide services in their "catchment" area (the section of the state that they travel in), and I am the TOPP Director. In many cases, the educational audiologists and teachers of the deaf work together to provide services. TOPP educational audiologists provide a variety of services: functioning as the school liaison to the child's clinical audiologist (who does the testing and hearing aid fittings), fitting FM equipment, training classroom teachers, attending IEP meetings, and providing the expertise in hearing loss and CAPD to the school district. This expertise is even more important when a child with hearing loss is being evaluated for a learning disability or an autism spectrum disorder. It is important to identify all the needs that may affect the child's ability to access the curriculum and not to assume that the issues the child has are a result of the hearing loss. Working within a team approach (with the classroom teacher, special educator, behavior consultant, speech-language pathologist, school psychologist, etc.) is critical to the academic success of these children.

Educational audiology services are still not delivered consistently in our state. Providing contract services can mean different things to different school districts. One district may contract with TOPP to provide educational audiology services for one specific student (although we may be aware that there are other students with hearing loss in the district). Another district may request that educational audiology services be provided to all hard of hearing students. And most districts still do not have an educational audiologist.

In addition, audiologists around Massachusetts have worked together to form the Massachusetts Educational Audiology (MEA) Task Force. MEA's goal is to network with special education directors and other educators about educational audiology services. Other schools for the deaf and clinical audiology settings have developed their own contract educational audiology services to public schools. Hopefully, through education, we can continue to inform special education directors and the MA Department of Elementary and Secondary Education of the need to provide educational audiology as a related service to their students to fulfill MEA's mission—consistent educational audiology services for all children with hearing loss in Massachusetts' public schools.

I still love being an educational audiologist and participating in the successes of my public school students.

SECTION III

Management

Classroom Management

Natalie J. Benafield and Donna F. Smiley

OBJECTIVES

By the end of this chapter, the reader will be able to:

1. Identify the effects of hearing loss on a student and how they might be manifested in the classroom.
2. List some common characteristics of students who are deaf/hard of hearing.
3. Discuss some accommodations and modifications for the classroom that are appropriate to consider for students who are deaf/hard of hearing.
4. Identify academic issues for students who are deaf/hard of hearing.

"Full inclusion occurs when the child 'fits in' within the typical social and academic life; the child feels engaged and has peers with whom he or she appropriately interacts; and the child functions well within the social context of learning." (Rhoades, 2006)

INTRODUCTION

Providing technical assistance to school personnel during the day-to-day classroom management of students who are deaf/hard of hearing (d/hh) is one of the most vital roles the school-based audiologist plays. However, it is probably the area in which these audiologists are least prepared. But, the school-based audiologist is *more* than just the person who provides technical support for equipment issues. He or she is an educator and an advocate, as well. The audiologist needs to be able to educate teachers and other school personnel about hearing loss because these professionals are often unaware of the impact hearing loss has on early learning experiences and school readiness. Likewise, school administrators may need assistance with interpreting and applying laws or regulations for dealing with students who are d/hh. Thus, the school-based audiologist is the ideal person to educate, advocate, *and* provide the technical support needed in school settings for children who are d/hh.

In general, the expertise that a school-based audiologist can bring to the school environment should make administrators' and classroom teachers' jobs easier. Often, school personnel may see audiologists as outsiders—audiologists are not teachers, after all. Consequently, school-based audiologists (whether contracted or district-employed) should work to develop relationships with school personnel so that they are considered a member of the student's team, not just an outsider who provides expert input. The audiologist's actions should promote cooperation and not evoke territorialism or hostility from other school team members. For example, a school-based audiologist could volunteer to help the science teacher with a science unit on the topic of noise and its effects on hearing. A discussion about the sense of hearing and how audiologists test hearing might be of interest to students at all grade levels. These gestures should help teachers see school-based audiologists as a part of the collaborative school team, not merely as outsiders.

The educational and advocacy tasks discussed previously require knowledge that is not necessarily needed in a clinical setting. Therefore, school-based audiologists must be informed about the skills needed to become educators *and* advocates within the school environment. This chapter provides practical information about the classroom management of students who are d/hh, and how the school-based audiologist can be involved with that aspect of the educational system.

EFFECTS OF HEARING LOSS AND ITS MANIFESTATION IN THE CLASSROOM

As you probably know, the effects of hearing loss cannot be described or categorized by audiometric thresholds alone. Each person with hearing loss is unique, and how hearing loss affects each person is also unique. For children who are d/hh, many issues contribute to how their hearing loss manifests itself in the classroom. Factors that impact and influence successful outcomes for a child with hearing loss are discussed below.

Child's Age at Onset and Identification

Two important factors for obtaining successful outcomes for a child with hearing loss include: (1) the child's age at the onset of hearing loss and (2) the age at which the child is identified with the loss. In many cases, more deleterious effects are seen when hearing loss occurs before the development of language (i.e., prelingually) than when the hearing loss occurs after the development of language (i.e., postlingually). In addition, the closer the identification of hearing loss occurs to the time of the onset, the better the outcome is expected to be for the child. Therefore, the goal for any child born with hearing loss is to identify that hearing loss as soon after birth as possible.

Degree, Type, and Configuration of Hearing Loss

The degree, type, and configuration of hearing loss also contribute to the overall outcomes for a child with hearing loss. However, due to early identification processes and amplification options, these factors may not have as much effect as they once did. For example, in the past, a child with a profound hearing loss was much more at risk for developing atypical speech and language patterns than a child with a mild hearing loss. However, in recent years, the development and use of cochlear implants has changed the "access" that children with profound hearing loss have to speech and language information. This access has allowed these children to have more typical speech and language patterns. Children with lesser degrees of hearing loss may actually have a harder time academically because their hearing loss is less evident than the hearing loss in children with more severe losses. Therefore, children with lesser degrees of hearing loss, or fluctuating conductive hearing loss, may be overlooked (or even assumed to have other issues), when in fact their hearing loss is the cause of their academic struggles.

Use of Amplification

Depending on the communication option chosen by a family (see the box that follows for a full explanation of communication options), appropriate amplification is critical for school success with children who want to use spoken communication as their primary mode of communication. Chapter 6 provides a deeper discussion on the use of amplification. However, it is important to note here that the school-based audi-

ologist plays a vital role in ensuring that amplification worn by children in school settings is being used properly and is in good working order on a day-to-day basis.

Appropriate Intervention

Appropriate intervention is another factor that will influence the academic success of the student who has hearing loss. There are many opinions, or "schools of thought," on exactly what *appropriate intervention* is for children who are d/hh. However, no one intervention strategy works for every child. It is not the purpose of this text to provide an exhaustive review of available early intervention strategies for children who are d/hh (for more information on this topic, see Cole & Flexer [2010] or Nittrouer [2009]). It is sufficient to say that intervention needs to be provided early and by professionals who have experience and knowledge about hearing impairment.

Family Support

Family support is also important in the overall outcome for the child who is d/hh. Parents and guardians are important components in the learning of all children, and this is especially true for the child with hearing loss. A parent or guardian will spend much more time with their child who is hearing impaired than will professionals who are involved with the intervention process. Therefore, regardless of the communication modality that a family chooses for their child, it is critical for the family to be involved in helping the child learn in that modality. If a family chooses for their child to be a manual communicator (i.e., to use sign language),

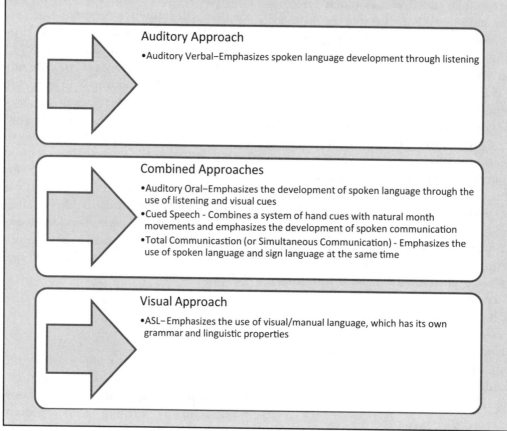

Communication Options

In many cases, by the time a child reaches school age, the family will have made decisions about the child's communication modality. However, it is important for the school-based audiologist to be aware of the communication options available to a child and his or her family. Also, in some cases, children may need to change an approach to their communication modalities, even after starting school.

Auditory Approach
- Auditory Verbal–Emphasizes spoken language development through listening

Combined Approaches
- Auditory Oral–Emphasizes the development of spoken language through the use of listening and visual cues
- Cued Speech - Combines a system of hand cues with natural month movements and emphasizes the development of spoken communication
- Total Communicastion (or Simultaneous Communication) - Emphasizes the use of spoken language and sign language at the same time

Visual Approach
- ASL–Emphasizes the use of visual/manual language, which has its own grammar and linguistic properties

then the family members also need to learn sign language in order to provide a communication-rich environment for the child. If a family chooses for their child to use spoken communication, then it is important for the family to be diligent in ensuring that the child has appropriate and functional amplification *and* that the child uses it during all waking hours.

Additional Influential Factors

As with all children, the personality, the natural talents and abilities, and the strengths and weaknesses of each child who is d/hh will contribute to his or her overall success in school. Communication differences in a child with hearing loss may be magnified when that child is quiet and shy, whereas a child who is more naturally outgoing may be unfazed by his or her communication differences. Parents often wonder if their children would have been more talkative, or friendlier, if they had had normal (typical) hearing. Educational audiologists can help those parents remember that all children have different personalities, and those different personalities contribute to who the children are, and who they will become, as a person.

Among children who are d/hh, it is estimated that nearly 25% have one or more disabilities in addition to hearing loss (Bhasin, Brocksent, Avchen, & Braun, 2006). Some of the disabilities that commonly co-occur with hearing loss are intellectual disabilities, learning disabilities, emotional or behavioral disabilities, and cerebral palsy. The presence of disabilities in addition to hearing loss increases the complexity of educating these students.

Every child who is d/hh will have a different story when he or she shows up in the school setting. Some children will have been identified early, but not amplified appropriately. Other children will have late-onset hearing loss, and all children will come with different levels of family support. Read the cases included in this chapter to see how the factors described in this section interact and affect each other in children who are d/hh.

Case 1: Katie

Katie is a 5th grade student in the Excelsior School District. She is 11 years of age and has profound sensorineural hearing loss, bilaterally. Katie's hearing impairment was not identified until she was 4 years old. At that time, her hearing impairment was in the severe range and, therefore, she was fit with traditional hearing aids. Katie's family was committed to full-time hearing aid use and ensured that she received appropriate services for her hearing impairment.

When Katie entered school for kindergarten, she did not have age-appropriate language skills, and therefore, she repeated Kindergarten. By the time she was in 3rd grade, her hearing loss had progressed to the profound range in both ears, which then made her a candidate for a cochlear implant. Her family chose the option of a cochlear implant, and Katie received her first implant during the middle of her 3rd grade school year. Her other ear received a cochlear implant during the summer between the 3rd and 4th grades.

Today, Katie is working at grade level in all subject areas in school. She receives speech and language services at school to address some of her syntactical and semantic language issues, as well as monitor her speech production. She uses a personal FM system and has the support of a school-based audiologist. Katie is an example of how a child who receives appropriate intervention and has strong family support can overcome being identified with hearing loss late.

Case 2: Charles

Charles is a 1st grade student at Wicket Elementary School. Psycho-educational evaluations indicate that Charles has a normal, nonverbal IQ. He is in the regular classroom and receives pull-out, specialized instruction for reading and math. In addition, he receives speech-language therapy every school day for 30 minutes. However, in spite of these specialized services, Charles is falling farther and farther behind his classmates. There are concerns that he may need to receive more of his academic instruction in a special education classroom.

Charles has a family history of hearing loss and, therefore, he was identified not too long after birth with moderate to moderately severe sensorineural hearing loss, bilaterally. Hearing aids were fit by 3 months of age. However, Charles' mother was not able to care for him and he was sent to live with his grandmother. He did not wear his hearing aids consistently until he entered kindergarten. When he entered kindergarten, his language skills were at the 2-year-old level. Charles is an example of how, even when identification is made early and appropriate amplification is fit, inconsistent use of that amplification, weak intervention, and limited family support impact the language and academic progress of a child.

Case 3: Paige

Paige is a 5-year-old kindergarten student in the Spring School District. She did not pass her newborn hearing screening 24 hours after birth. She was rescreened a week after birth and still did not pass the screening. She was immediately scheduled for a follow-up hearing assessment with a local pediatric audiology clinic. At 3 weeks of age, she was diagnosed with severe sensorineural hearing loss bilaterally and fit with hearing aids by 2 months of age. The family immediately began receiving intervention from a speech-language pathologist who had expertise in spoken communication. When Paige entered kindergarten, she had language and speech skills that were commensurate with her hearing peers. She is receiving all of her academic instruction in the regular classroom and uses a personal FM system at school and home. She is an example of how early identification, early amplification, appropriate intervention, and strong family support can result in school readiness. We hope that with universal newborn hearing screenings (i.e., early identification) and continued advances in hearing technology, kids like Paige will become the norm.

CHARACTERISTICS OF CHILDREN WHO ARE D/HH IN THE CLASSROOM

Children who are d/hh will come in all shapes and sizes. No two students will have the same combination of characteristics; however, there are some common characteristics that are seen across groups of children who are d/hh. In addition to some of the characteristics already discussed in this book (i.e., speech and language issues presented in Chapter 3), another characteristic seen in children who are d/hh is the appearance of being immature, or having social skills that are not grade appropriate. These children may also seek reassurance more often than their same-grade peers. They may be more distracted by visual and auditory stimuli. Also, children with hearing impairments may be more tired, or "fatigued," at the end of the day, due to the effort and energy they give to listening.

Finally, there is the potential for the appearance of behavior problems in children who are d/hh, but this potential is actually less about behavior and more about frustration or misunderstanding. Frustration caused by not being accepted may look like anger toward peers. Frustrations about academic success may look like anger toward teachers. Misunderstanding of instructions may look like defiance in a class. A student's desire to fit in, especially in the middle school, junior high, and high school grades, may lead to behaviors such as apathy, disrespect, refusal to wear amplification, or refusal to attend therapy.

School-based audiologists can play an important role in helping teachers understand these behaviors and their possible solutions. However, audiologists must not enable students to blame inappropriate behaviors solely on their hearing loss. Therefore, helping teachers and students set appropriate expectations for behavior is an important responsibility for school-based audiologists.

APPLICATION OF LEGISLATION/ REGULATION FOR SCHOOL-AGE STUDENTS WHO ARE D/HH

In Chapter 1, the legislative mandates that affect the education of all children with disabilities were presented and described. In this section, we look at the application of these legislative mandates and federal regulations to school-age children who are d/hh. We apply the most current reauthorizations or updates of these laws and regulations. (*Note:* The 2004 reauthorization is referred to here as IDEIA because that is the formal term used for this most recent update of IDEA.)

IDEIA (2004)

When considering whether or not a student qualifies for special education under IDEIA (2004), the student needs to have a documented disability. In an audiological case, a student may have a documented hearing impairment. However, in addition to being diagnosed, the hearing impairment must adversely affect educational performance before a student receives services under IDEIA (2004). There is no exact formula for determining "adverse effect." However, the educational team (which includes the parent) must look at all available data (e.g., testing, class work, etc.) to determine if the disability is having an adverse effect on the child's educational performance. If it is determined that the disability is having an adverse effect, then the team can design a plan for special education services as needed.[1]

This special plan is called an Individualized Education Program (IEP; see the box that follows for a detailed description of the general content requirements of an IEP). In the IEP, specifications about a student's placement (which must occur in the least restrictive environment), needed modifications, and accommodations are listed. (These last two issues are discussed in more detail in the next section of this chapter.)

The concept of least restrictive environment (LRE) has been a basic tenet of IDEIA since the early days of the law. There is a strong preference in IDEIA (2004) for educating children with disabilities in the regular educational environment. However, it is important to note that the LRE provisions in the IDEIA (2004) make it clear that supplementary aids and services are critical to support the education of children with disabilities in regular classes. In addition, there must be a continuum of alternative placement options for children with disabilities (Rebhom & Kupper, 2007). This requirement for a continuum of alternative placements substantiates the idea that the determination of LRE must be done on an individualized basis. Figure 8–1 illustrates placement options. Note that the left end of the continuum is the placement that would be less restrictive, whereas the right end of the continuum is the placement that would be more restrictive (Rebhorn & Smith, 2008).

Continuum of alternative placements includes:

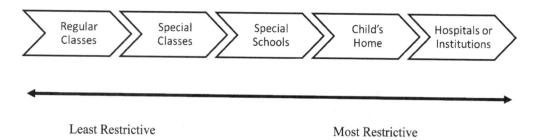

Figure 8–1. Continuum of alternative placements.

---

[1]Although the federal regulation gives some information about qualification for special services, there are states that are more descriptive with how students will be qualified for services in their individual state regulations. However, state regulations do have to line up with federal regulations. Be sure to familiarize yourself with the specific state's regulations in which you are practicing.

General Content Requirements of an Individualized Education Program

As used in Section 300, the term individualized education program, or IEP, means a written statement for each child with a disability that is developed, reviewed, and revised in a meeting in accordance with 34 CFR 300.320 through 300.324. An IEP must include:

- A statement of the child's present levels of academic achievement and functional performance.
- A statement of measurable annual goals, including academic and functional goals designed to:
  - Meet the child's needs that result from the child's disability to enable the child to be involved in and make progress in the general education curriculum; and
  - Meet each of the child's other educational needs that result from the child's disability.
- A description of benchmarks or short-term objectives for children with disabilities who take alternative assessments aligned to alternative achievement standards.
- A description of:
  - How the child's progress toward meeting the annual goals described in 34 CFR 300.320(a)(2) will be measured; and
  - When periodic reports on the progress the child is making toward meeting the annual goals (such as through the use of quarterly or other periodic reports, concurrent with the issuance of report cards) will be provided.
- A statement of the special education and related services and supplementary aids and services, based on peer-reviewed research to the extent practicable, to be provided to the child, or on behalf of the child.
- A statement of any individual appropriate accommodations that are necessary to measure the academic achievement and functional performance of the child on State and district-wide assessments consistent with section 612(a)(16) of the Act; and if the IEP Team determines that the child must take an alternate assessment instead of a particular regular State or district-wide assessment of student achievement, a statement of why the child cannot participate in the regular assessment and why the particular alternate assessment selected is appropriate for the child. [34 CFR 300.320(a)] [20 U.S.C. 1414(d)(1)(A)(i)]

Reference

Rebhorn and Küpper (2007).

It is beyond the scope of this text to fully cover all of the aspects of IDEIA (2004) and its application to students who are deaf or hard of hearing. For more information on this topic, we would recommend that the reader access the training curriculum produced by the National Dissemination Center for Children with Disabilities (NICHCY), *Building the Legacy/Construyendo el Legado: A Training Curriculum on IDEA 2004* (http://www .nichcy.org/Laws/IDEA/Pages/Building TheLegacy.aspx).

504 Plans

If an educational team decides that a child is not eligible for special education services, or if a child is never referred for consideration of special education services (because it is not deemed necessary) even though the child has a hearing impairment, he or she may be in need of a 504 Plan, which is a written plan of accommodations (Refer to Chapter 1 for an overview of Section 504 of the Rehabilitation Act of 1973 and eligibility criteria). Section 504 provides reasonable accommodations to students with disabilities so that they will be able to benefit from and access their education in the same way as their peers who do not have disabilities do. It is the experience of these authors that the use of 504 plans for children who are d/hh (and who do not need

special education services) varies widely depending on the school district. For instance, some school districts formulate 504 plans for every student who is d/hh. Other school districts insist that a student needs to be "struggling" in order to have a 504 plan. In our opinion, ensuring that a student has consistent access to his or her amplification may provide the justification needed to have a 504 plan for most students who are d/hh. An extensive list of possible accommodations for students who are deaf or hard of hearing is provided in the box that follows.

ACCOMMODATIONS AND MODIFICATIONS IN THE CLASSROOM

Educational modifications and educational accommodations are two different constructs. Sometimes, even school personnel will use them interchangeably when, in fact, they mean two very different things in the educational setting.

Modifications involve changing the content and performance expectations for what a student should learn. Examples of modifications that might be made for a student who is d/hh are:

■ using a different curriculum that is written at a lower level of understanding

Accommodations for Students Who Are Deaf or Hard of Hearing

This list is a comprehensive list of possible accommodations for students who are deaf/hard of hearing. The best way to use this list is to consider the needs of the student and then pick accommodations that address those needs. The educational audiologist may find that giving a "laundry list" to a teacher is overwhelming and often meaningless. However, if the audiologist picks five or six of these accommodations to address a student's specific needs, this action will be more meaningful to the teacher and will make it easier for the teacher to incorporate a few accommodations at a time. Later, once the initial accommodations have become second nature, other accommodations can be used to address the student's continuing needs.

Teaching Strategies and Tools

- Use visual aids:
  - Charts
  - Maps
  - Graphs
  - Photos
  - Captioned films and videos
  - Overhead projector
  - PowerPoint slides
  - Written outlines or summary of materials
- Avoid talking to the class while facing the board
- Use speaker cues:
  - Cuing is when the teacher or interpreter indicates who is speaking in a given moment
  - Students who are d/hh may not be able to find (or localize) sounds with their hearing aid or cochlear implant
  - Cuing helps the student to follow conversations, discussions, or lectures
- Repeat other students' comments and questions:
  - The student who is d/hh may miss the presentation content while trying to identify the speaker
  - The student may not see the speaker well, and therefore, may miss out on speechreading cues
- Use teacher cues:
  - Cuing the context or topic helps the student who is d/hh make predictions about transitions, presentations, lectures, or conversations
  - Sometimes students miss the first part of a lecture or discussion because they are still trying to figure out the topic. Cuing will help to facilitate the student's attention to the topic.

- Use vocabulary and concepts:
  - Remember that many students who are d/hh have missed some vocabulary and concept development because of their hearing loss
  - Some students get stuck on a certain word or concept and miss everything thereafter
  - Preteaching vocabulary and concepts can be helpful. This can occur either in the regular classroom, resource room, speech-language therapy session, or at home with the parents

Communication Strategies

- Remember the student's visual communication needs:
  - Make sure that the student who is d/hh is focused visually before talking to him or her
  - Most students who are d/hh can only focus on one thing at a time. Therefore, it is difficult for the student to watch, listen, and take notes at the same time. Note-taking assistance can be important when the pace of the class seems overwhelming to the student.
- Use facial expressions and gestures that are as normal as possible
- Do not exaggerate words because it makes speechreading more difficult
- Repeat the key words if the student does not understand
- Rephrase the statement if the student still does not understand
- Demonstrate the concept when necessary
- Remember that oral tests are difficult. Try to find ways that best suit the student's ability
- Ask the student to repeat himself if you do not understand
- Repeat what you understood and ask the student to resume
- Try other accommodations, if communication becomes difficult (e.g., writing, drawing, asking the student to show you)

Modifications to the Physical Environment

- Incorporate preferential seating:
  - Students (deaf or hard of hearing) should be seated so that they can see the class and what is written on the board at the same time
  - Students should have seating options that allow them to hear the teacher and see her or his face for visual cues
  - Students may need to move around during the day if the teacher moves around from station to station or the teacher may need to figure out how to stay in one central location
  - Students should be seated away from noise sources (e.g., doorways, pencil sharpeners, fans, and windows)

■ Remember classroom arrangement:
  ■ Seats should be arranged in a semicircle or full circle for group discussions in order for the student to better follow the discussion
  ■ Teachers should not stand in front of a window or a light

Modifications to the Acoustic Environment

■ Incorporate child's personal amplification:
  ■ The teacher should become familiar with a student's personal amplification
  ■ The teacher and student should complete a daily amplification check
  ■ Teachers should be aware that a student's personal amplification works best if they are within 3 feet of the student
  ■ Teachers should be aware that personal amplification devices amplify all sounds, including background noises. The student may experience difficulty identifying sounds during background noise
■ Incorporate personal FM devices:
  ■ Teachers should be aware that during whole group teaching, a personal FM system will allow a student to hear the teacher's voice better
■ Eliminate background noise when possible:
  ■ Close classroom doors to cut down on hallway and exterior noise
  ■ Use double-pane windows to cut down on outside noise (Audiologists and teachers do not get to give much input on this modification; however, this could be important to know)
■ Acoustically treat the classroom environment:
  ■ Cover the walls with posters and/or artwork (to absorb some of the reverberant sound)
  ■ Use drapes on the windows to mute sound
  ■ Add floor mats or carpeting to mute sound
■ Ensure appropriate lighting

Source: Adapted from: Meeting Educational Needs of Underserved Students-MENUS (2002). MENUS Manual: An educator's guide and practices to meet the needs of deaf and hard of hearing students in grades Pre-K to 12. California State University Northridge and the National Center on Deafness (U.S. Department of Education, Office of Special Education and Rehabilitative Services (H325N990017). Available from: http://menus .csun.edu

- adapting or simplifying texts
- modifying the expectation for areas, such as spelling or vocabulary (i.e., the student who is d/hh is only required to learn 10 of the 20 spelling words)
- modifying grading scales
- modifying assessments or tests

Accommodations are supports or services provided to help a student access the curriculum and demonstrate learning. Most teachers and school personnel make accommodations for every student at some point. For example, a teacher may realize that a particular class of students needs the material to be broken down into smaller components. The teacher does not change her expectation; the class will still have to learn all of the material. But the way that the material is presented will be different from class to class. In the same way, when accommodations are made for a student who is d/hh, the expectation for that student's academic performance is no different from the expectations for the student who has normal hearing. See the box on the previous page for a list of possible accommodations for students who are d/hh. Every student is an individual, and therefore, needed accommodations should be considered on a case-by-case basis.

ACADEMIC ISSUES FOR STUDENTS WITH HEARING IMPAIRMENT

Wide variations in academic performance make it difficult to predict which academic areas will give students who are d/hh problems. Age of onset of hearing loss, age of identification, age at amplifi-cation, type and frequency of appropriate intervention received, family support, and other child-specific issues are all part of the complete picture of a child with hearing impairment when it comes to learning. That said, there are general concepts that can be presented in this section that allow the school-based audiologist to be prepared to provide teachers with information about how to enhance learning for students who are hearing impaired.

The audiologist in the school setting is usually seen as the "expert" on all things hearing related, which means teachers will seek out the school-based audiologist when looking for appropriate educational strategies. Remember that, as an audiologist, you are the expert on hearing and amplification but, depending on your background, you may not be the expert on education and learning strategies. Respect the experience and knowledge that a classroom teacher is able to provide regarding the student. Your input regarding a specific child's hearing loss will help the teacher develop appropriate teaching strategies for that student's needs.

Perhaps the most difficult aspect of sharing information on teaching children with hearing impairment is the variability we see in academic performance from student to student. Given two children with the same degree and type of hearing loss, one may require no special services and do quite well in the mainstream, whereas the other may require assistance from a special educator, speech-language pathologist, and sign language interpreter. One useful tool that can provide a general overview of academic risks associated with hearing loss is a document entitled, "Relationship of Hearing Loss to Listening and Learning Needs" (which can be found at: http://www.kandersonaudconsulting .com/Listening_and_Learning.html).

This document has been modified to list accommodations and modifications that should be considered for students with varying degrees of hearing loss. Although every student with hearing loss will not display all the difficulties described, or need all the supports suggested, this information will allow a teacher to see the potential academic risks associated with even a mild degree of hearing loss.

SUBJECT AND CONTENT AREAS

Each school subject, or content area, provides its own unique challenge to students with hearing impairment. Although some academic difficulty encountered by students with hearing impairment has to do with general classroom structure (i.e., acoustics, seating, following directions, access to visual cues, listener fatigue), much of the difficulty comes from the nature of the subject matter, and how that subject matter is traditionally taught in schools. Teachers can modify some of their teaching methods once they know the specific challenges associated with each content area. The school-based audiologist can provide that type of information to teachers, thereby helping teachers maintain a proactive approach and address difficulties identified in students who are d/hh as soon as they arise

Reading and Language Instruction

Students who are d/hh sometimes enter school significantly behind other students in terms of preliteracy skills. Delays in identification, amplification, and remedia-tion usually mean that a student's "hearing age" is not commensurate with their hearing peers. Prereading skills taught in preschool and kindergarten are taught with the assumption that children are able to discriminate the sounds of English. Obviously, this is problematic for some children with hearing loss as they may or may not hear or perceive the sounds of the language correctly. To further compound the issue, printed English (i.e., reading material) is a representation of the spoken sounds of English. Therefore, when children with hearing loss struggle to learn the sounds of the spoken language, this translates into problems with learning to read.

Even when children are amplified early and appropriately, there are perceptual consequences of listening with an impaired auditory system (Moore, 1996). For students with hearing loss in the mild to moderate range, amplification provides access to phonological information needed in learning to read and write. Even for children with severe to profound degrees of hearing loss, improved amplification (i.e., cochlear implants and advanced signal processing in hearing aids) has made acoustical information accessible. This improvement in accessing acoustic information translates into the positive effects seen in research findings on reading and academic achievement in these children (Marschark, Rhoten, & Fabich, 2007). However, it is important for educators to understand that amplification alone cannot overcome the difficulties students with hearing impairment have with the auditory perception of speech (Kelly & Barac-Cikoha, 2007), or with the language skills necessary to become competent readers.

In general, students with severe to profound hearing loss lag far behind their hearing counterparts on measures of reading success. The Gallaudet Research Institute (GRI) assists in providing norms for the Stanford Achievement Tests (Harcourt Assessment, 2003) by measuring deaf readers' comprehension of a variety of reading passages. The most recent data, which included a sample of 3,800 readers, indicated the median score for a 10-year-old (i.e., a 4th to 5th grader) who is deaf was equivalent to the average hearing child in the 7th month of the 1st grade. By the time the student who is deaf reaches 12th grade, the median score is comparable to a hearing child in the 5th month of the 3rd grade. Similar results were obtained when measuring reading competence at the word level (i.e., reading vocabulary; GRI, 2004).

There are two patterns that have been well-documented in the literature for over 20 years regarding readers who are deaf:

> (1) average 18- to 19-year-old students with severe to profound hearing impairment are reading no better than average 9- to 10-year-old hearing students, and (2) there seems to be an annual growth rate of less than half a grade per year with a leveling off or plateau effect occurring at the third- or fourth-grade level for most [deaf] students. (Trezeck, Wang, & Paul, 2010, p. 7)

Although these results could be discouraging, it should be pointed out that in the 2004 study (GRI), 5% of the 12th grade group with deafness obtained levels equal to or better than the average hearing reader in the 12th grade (Kelly & Barac-Cikoja, 2007), indicating that reading success is possible for deaf readers.

As an educational audiologist, a discussion of how classroom acoustics, appropriate amplification, and access to visual information may affect reading development is important to have with regular educators teaching children who are d/hh. We know that students with hearing impairment may have both "processing" issues (perception and identification of phonemes, letters, and words) and "language" issues (semantic and syntactic deficits, limited background knowledge). Teachers can be guided in providing instruction that takes these weaknesses into account. Bringing in a reading specialist or deaf educator is often indicated in cases where reading fluency and/or comprehension is severely compromising a child's education. Alternative coding mechanisms, both morphologically based sign systems and phonologically based systems, may need to be considered for students who are d/hh and not making progress with a traditional phonics-based approach to reading. In addition, a consultation with a speech-language pathologist familiar with the language needs of students who are hearing impaired is usually necessary to help teachers understand the difficulties that children with hearing impairment have with semantics, syntax, figurative language, prior knowledge, and meta-cognition (refer to Chapter 3 for additional information).

Mathematics Instruction

In her autobiography, *To Talk of Many Things*, mathematician Dame Kathleen Timpson Ollerenshaw (2004), deaf since childhood, wrote, "[mathematics was] the one subject in which I was at no disadvantage. Nearly all equations are found in books or shown on the blackboard as the teacher speaks. Learning mathematics is rarely as dependent on the spoken word as are most lessons and lectures in other subjects." Although it is true that the achievement gap between students who are d/hh and students with typical hearing is smaller in math than in reading (GRI, 2004), challenges still remain for the student who is hearing impaired learning math in the regular classroom setting.

The National Council of Teachers of Mathematics' (NCTM) position statement reads: "Culture, background, and language must not be a barrier to full participation in mathematics programs preparing students for a full range of careers. All students, regardless of their language or cultural background, must study a core curriculum in mathematics based on the NCTM standards" (NCTM, 1994). Because math relies less on the spoken word, it may be an area where a student with hearing impairment feels on equal footing with other hearing peers.

By educating teachers about factors that could impede mathematics learning, the educational audiologist can support mathematics learning in students who are d/hh. For instance, classroom acoustics may make it difficult to perceive and process oral directions quickly (a skill critical to elementary oral math drills). The vocabulary of math may be daunting for a student already deficient in general vocabulary knowledge. Additionally, the syntactic complexity of written math problems may be responsible for a student with hearing impairment being unable to get to the math skills being targeted in the problem. Pagliaro (2006) discusses difficulties in translating written English math concepts to American Sign Language, stating, "no standardized signs exist for many math concepts." Signing, counting, and language differences "may limit the types of problems [deaf students] experience in their conceptual development of mathematics" (p. 34). The author also comments that teachers in deaf education often do not have math certification and recommends enhancing teacher preparation to augment student learning in this area.

Determining which areas of learning are causing difficulty for the student who is d/hh (e.g., auditory perception in the classroom, vocabulary, language differences, etc.) will guide the educational audiologist's degree of involvement in this academic area. Once audiological causes of difficulty are ruled out, a specialized educator may need to be consulted for further assistance. By sharing the possible barriers to mathematics learning with the classroom teacher before problems arise, the audiologist can set the stage for a quicker and more appropriate response to the difficulties experienced by the student.

Science and Social Studies Instruction

For students who are d/hh and who have difficulties with vocabulary and higher-level syntax, science and social studies may present another set of challenges. Success in these areas of learning depends a great deal on reading ability. As discussed above, as a group, the reading levels of students who are d/hh historically have lagged behind those of their hearing peers.

Textbooks increase in complexity quickly in the elementary school years. Once a student reaches middle school (4th through 6th grades), they are expected to be familiar with different types of texts, sentences of varying complexity, use of different voices in writing, and varying lexicons for each subject. Students who are d/hh may be putting so much energy into decoding the surface structure of the material that they never get to the deep structure, where meaning is understood.

The importance of preteaching cannot be overemphasized for students having these sorts of difficulties. How the act of "preteaching" is accomplished must be individualized to each student. Some students obtain success with a simple vocabulary list sent home a week ahead of each unit to become familiar with new vocabulary. Others might need a preview of the complete unit introduced in tutoring, resource, or speech-language therapy sessions. An educational audiologist can facilitate this type of additional support by educating teachers about the effect of limited "incidental learning" on language development, and how repeated exposure to new topics and vocabulary can support learning for these students.

Visual and Multisensory Learning

Perhaps the most common classroom accommodation listed for students who are d/hh is that course content be presented visually, or that teachers make use of multisensory teaching methods. This is an excellent recommendation, as it gives the student with hearing impairment the opportunity to use other, possibly stronger, modalities to enhance learning.

Most effective teachers realize the importance of visual aids and the use of multisensory activities for all students, but often teachers are unclear how the *use* of these techniques may be different for a student with hearing impairment. For instance, students who are d/hh are not able to simultaneously attend to the teacher's voice and other materials presented, whether that is a map on the wall or tracing letters in sand. If they focus only on the visual aid or activity, they miss

speechreading cues and facial expressions of the teacher. Similarly, if the students focus only on the teacher to ensure they are getting the important information, they miss out on the opportunity to use the teaching aid to enhance understanding. Students who are d/hh simply cannot multitask in this manner the way their hearing peers do.

It takes intentional planning to appropriately use visual aids or other sensory activities with a student who is hearing impaired (Dye, Hauser, & Bavelier, 2008). It may be that the teacher has to direct attention to visual aids between explanations, or that the student with hearing impairment be paired with another student during an activity. It may be as simple as allowing the student with hearing impairment to have a copy of the visual aid to take home and study. What works for each teacher and student will be different. However, a discussion of how methods may differ for students with hearing impairment is highly recommended when students who are d/hh are having difficulty in any of the content areas of an academic setting.

ASSESSMENT OF CLASSROOM PERFORMANCE

It is sometimes necessary to assess a child's performance in the classroom, going beyond clinical audiology testing and educational testing performed by school personnel. Generally, when an audiologist assesses a student's classroom performance, it is because an opinion is needed on how the child is functioning in the "real world." Test results that look good in the sound booth do not always equate to the child's ability to access meaningful auditory information in the classroom. Classroom acoustics, compatibility issues with existing educational technology, other medical and/or educational conditions the child exhibits, behavioral difficulties, and other factors can interfere with a student's ability to receive or use classroom information in a meaningful way. It is often up to the educational audiologist to sort out which classroom behaviors can be attributed to the student's hearing loss and which cannot. For educational audiologists, especially those with less experience in school settings, this may be a daunting task.

Fortunately, several tools that educational audiologists can use for assessing a student's level of functioning in the regular classroom setting are commercially available. Most are informal questionnaires that rely on educator's judgments regarding specific classroom behaviors using the student's classmates as comparisons. Although informal, many are standardized, allowing scores to be reported and possible changes to be noted across time. See the box below for a list of these questionnaires.

Informal classroom observations made by the school-based audiologist are useful for taking note of general classroom setup and acoustics, style of teaching used, level of participation of the student with hearing loss, and so forth. Observations are usually written in report form with suggestions and/or conclusions that the educational team will consider in future educational planning for the student in question. The audiologist observing a student in the classroom should keep in mind that one session of observation may be affected by many factors, one of which is the presence of the observer herself.

List of Questionnaires

Screening Instrument for Targeting Educational Risk (SIFTER)
http://www.kandersonaudconsulting.com/uploads/SIFTER.pdf

Preschool SIFTER
http://www.kandersonaudconsulting.com/uploads/Preschool_SIFTER.pdf

Secondary SIFTER
http://www.kandersonaudconsulting.com/uploads/Secondary_SIFTER.pdf

Listening Inventory For Education (LIFE)
http://www.kandersonaudconsulting.com/uploads/StudentLIFE.pdf
http://www.kandersonaudconsulting.com/uploads/TeacherLIFE.pdf

Children's Auditory Performance Scale (CHAPS)
Available from the EAA online store (http://www.edaud.org)

Functional Listening Evaluation
http://www.handsandvoices.org/pdf/func_eval.pdf

Rather than rely entirely on a classroom observation, the use of standardized checklists and questionnaires mentioned earlier, along with a review of written records, should add to the educational audiologist's understanding of how the child is functioning as a whole in the educational environment.

SOCIAL SKILLS AND ACADEMIC SUCCESS

"Blindness separates you from things, but deafness separates you from people," is a commonly repeated quote from Helen Keller, who lost both her sight and hearing in early childhood. There is no doubt that children with hearing impairment are at risk when it comes to developing social skills. Language and communication ability play a large role in developing social competencies, and language deficits are inherent in the disability of hearing loss and deafness.

A student's "success" in school should not only be measured by grades on a report card, but should also be measured by social and emotional integration with peers and teachers. As adults, social skills are important in many aspects of our lives, including our ability to maintain productive careers and personal relationships. Students learn how to work and live with others in school, but students who are d/hh may have more difficulty managing social relationships than their typical hearing peers do.

The ability to develop peer relationships is particularly important for school-age children as it provides many opportunities for social learning. Students who are d/hh in the mainstream setting often report feelings of isolation. Breakdowns in communication are inevitable, and often students with hearing impairment do not possess the strategies to repair the breakdown. Students with typical hearing pick up appropriate social behaviors by watching and listening to others (i.e., incidental learning), whereas students with hearing impairment miss out on many of these social and environmental cues.

Two important social competencies are particularly difficult for students with hearing impairment: functioning as part of a group and enjoying spontaneous humor. Groups, especially in social contexts, present unique challenges for several reasons. The communication structure is loose, the dialogue is fast paced, and the language used may be casual (slang, abbreviations, etc.). Students who are d/hh generally need to be explicitly taught strategies for assisting them with becoming a real part of a group. Spontaneous humor between peers can serve as a strong bonding experience, but can be a frustrating experience for the student with hearing loss. Jokes are usually told quickly, and often as an aside, meaning the speaker may drop the level of his voice, making perception even more difficult for a student with hearing loss. Both the student and his hearing peers need to be taught strategies to make group work successful. Strategies like announcing a change in topic, using an FM system, or spacing working groups far apart to reduce background noise can make a world of difference for the student with hearing loss. Teachers also need to be made aware of possible barriers to group work for the student who is d/hh. Teaching appropriate self-advocacy skills to students with hearing impairment can be a good first step in teaching other students to recognize the difficulties experienced by these students with hearing loss. John Anderson explains, "We are asking students to participate in the world of sound. Groups are a microcosm of that world. How a student does in groups has a lot to say about how he is doing in the world" (Anderson, 1999).

The need for an understanding of social language in school goes beyond developing peer relationships. Even comprehension of simple children's literature assumes the ability to understand that people may have different beliefs about the same event. Consider "Little Red Riding Hood" and the fact that the reader knows the wolf is not grandmother, but Little Red Riding Hood does not. Realizing that different perspectives are possible makes the reading more enjoyable, and lays the groundwork for higher level comprehension tasks. As students enter middle and high school, they are often asked to discuss opposite beliefs and attitudes surrounding an event or idea, particularly in their studies of history and politics. From a young age, different perspectives should be presented explicitly by teachers, making it a point to discuss what characters are thinking and feeling. This particular social language construct, or "theory of mind," is highly correlated to a child's overall language skills. Social language constructs hold true for students who are oral, as well as students who use any form of sign language (Schick, 2005).

Participation in extracurricular activities and clubs is one way students who are d/hh can enhance self-esteem by developing a sense of belonging. Unfortunately, many students with disabilities do not pursue these types of activities due to barriers presented by their disabilities. However, federal law is clear in recognizing the importance of students with disabilities being able to have meaningful participation in school-sponsored, extra-curricular activities.

Students with disabilities may not be excluded from participating in nonacademic services and extracurricular activities on the basis of disability. Persons with disabilities must be provided an opportunity to participate in nonacademic services that is equal to that provided to persons without disabilities. These services may include physical education and recreational athletics, transportation, health services, recreational activities, special interest groups or clubs sponsored by the school, and referrals to agencies that provide assistance to persons with disabilities and employment of students. (Requirements under Section 504 of the Rehabilitation Act of 1973)

Audiologists may have to be creative with developing plans for assistive technology and communication during extracurricular activities, especially athletics. Newer educational audiologists will obtain assistance and useful ideas from networking with other audiologists involved with professional organizations, such as the Educational Audiology Association. Also, researching strategies used by professional athletes with disabilities can be useful for obtaining assistance with developing plans. The important message, however, is that extracurricular activities are possible for students with hearing impairment, and can provide myriad opportunities for social interaction with peers.

The role that social learning plays in the education of children who are d/hh cannot be ignored. Parents and educators will better understand their student's classroom performance if they understand how social skills and social language affect students with hearing impairment. Working on these skills are as important as other educational skills targeted in remediation plans. As explained by Dr. Brenda Schick (2005), "If a child is isolated from peers and teachers by communication barriers and language delays, social issues must be addressed. It is completely appropriate to request IEP goals that focus on these issues" (p. 3).

> *"If a doctor, lawyer, or dentist had 40 people in his office at one time, all of whom had different needs, and some of whom didn't want to be there and were causing trouble, and the doctor, lawyer, or dentist, without assistance, had to treat them all with professional excellence for nine months, then he might have some conception of the classroom teacher's job."*
>
> —Donald D. Quinn

CONCLUSION

Professionals in the educational setting share a common wish for all students to have success in school, meet educational goals, and develop into contributing members of society. A successful school experience involves a host of factors, over many of which we, as audiologists, have no control. One way of meeting the needs of the students we serve is to share our knowledge of how hearing impairment affects the entire educational environment. However, many of the issues discussed in this chapter are what audiologists may consider "out of their comfort zone." Discussing educational issues affecting students who are d/hh with classroom teachers through a relationship of mutual professional respect will make you a more effective educational audiologist. Educational audiologists who provide technical support and expertise regarding hearing loss in a nonthreatening way will generally have a greater impact that those who take on the persona of "expert" on things we as audiologists may have no training in. Consider the quote in the box below when working with educators; it will serve you well.

REFERENCES

Anderson, J. (1999). *Navigating groups in family and school.* Presentation at the 2008 Alexander Graham Bell Association for the Deaf- Utah fall conference. Retrieved June 9, 2011 from http://agbell-utah-conf-2008 .eventbrite.com/

Bhasin, T., Brocksent, S., Avchen, R., & Braun, K. (2006). Prevalence of four development disabilities among children aged 8 years— Metropolitan Atlanta Development Disabilities Surveillance Program 1996 and 2000. In *Surveillance Summaries,* January 27, 2006. *MMWR; 55*(S S01), 1–9.

Cole, E., & Flexer, C. (2010). *Children with hearing loss: Developing listening and talking, birth to six* (2nd ed.). San Diego, CA: Plural.

Dye, M., Hauser, P., & Bavelier, D. (2008). Visual skills and cross-modal plasticity in deaf readers: Possible implication for acquiring meaning from print. *Annals of the New York Academy of Science, 1145,* 71–82.

Gallaudet Research Institute. (2004). *Stanford Achievement Test: Norms booklet for deaf and hard of hearing students.* Washington, DC: Author.

Harcourt Assessment. (2003). *Stanford Achievement Test: Tenth edition.* San Antonio, TX: Harcourt Assessment.

Individuals with Disabilities Education Improvement Act of 2004. 20 U.S.C. §1400 et seq. (2004).

Kelly, L., & Barac-Cikoja, D. (2007). The comprehension of skilled deaf readers. In K. Cain & J. Oakhill (Eds.), *Children's comprehension problems in oral and written language: A cognitive perspective*. New York, NY: Guilford Press.

Marschark, M., Rhoten, C., & Fabich, M. (2007). Effects of cochlear implants on children's reading and academic achievement. *Journal of Deaf Studies and Deaf Education, 12*(3), 269–282.

Moore, B. (1996). Perceptual consequences of cochlear hearing loss and their implications for the design of hearing aids. *Ear and Hearing, 17*(2), 133–161.

National Council of Teachers of Mathematics [NCTM]. (1994). In D. Geddes (Ed.), *Curriculum and evaluation standards for school mathematics*. Addenda Series, Grades 5–8. Reston, VA: Author.

National Dissemination Center for Children with Disabilities (NICHCY). *Building the legacy/Construyendo el legado: A training curriculum on IDEA 2004*. Retrieved from http://www.nichcy.org/Laws/IDEA/Pages/BuildingTheLegacy.aspx

Nittrouer, S. (2009). *Early development of children with hearing loss*. San Diego, CA: Plural.

Ollerenshaw, D. K. T. (2004). *To talk of many things: An autobiography*. Manchester, UK: Manchester University Press.

Pagliaro, C. (2006) Mathematics education and the deaf learner. In D. F. Moores & D. S. Martin, D. S. (Eds.), *Deaf learners: Developments in curriculum and instruction*. Washington DC: Gallaudet University Press.

Rebhorn, T., & Küpper, L. (2007). Content of the IEP (Module 13). *Building the legacy: IDEA 2004 training curriculum*. Washington, DC: National Dissemination Center for Children with Disabilities. Available from: http://www.nichcy.org/training/contents.asp

Rebhorn, T., & Smith, A. (2008). LRE decision making (Module 15). *Building the legacy: IDEA 2004 training curriculum*. Washington, DC: National Dissemination Center for Children with Disabilities. Available from: http://www.nichcy.org/training/contents.asp

Rhoades, E. A. (2006). Research outcomes of Auditory-Verbal intervention: Is the approach justified? *Deafness and Education International, 8*(3), 125–143.

Schick, B. (2005). Social cognition and theory of mind. Communication connections, *Hands and Voices*. Available at http://www.handsandvoices.org/comcon/articles/socCogTheorMind.htm

Trezeck, B, Wang, Y., & Paul, P. (2010). *Reading and deafness: Theory, research, and practice*. Clifton Park, NY: Delmar Cengage.

U.S. Department of Education, Office for Civil Rights, *Free Appropriate Public Education for Students with Disabilities: Requirements Under Section 504 of the Rehabilitation Act of 1973*, Washington, DC, 2010.

Educational Audiology in the Real World

Mike Macione, AuD
Educational Audiologist
Jackson County Intermediate School District
Jackson, Michigan

I have been an educational audiologist for nearly 23 years and honestly cannot imagine doing anything else. As an undergraduate student at the University of Connecticut in the early 1980s, I had no idea what I would major in until I met someone who was an audiologist. She inspired me to become an audiologist, and I soon discovered I really enjoyed pediatrics and the school-based aspects of audiology. Graduate school at the State University of New York-Plattsburgh prepared me well to become a competent, caring clinician. The first two positions I had were working in settings with developmentally disabled children and adults, first in New York State, then in southeastern Connecticut. These positions taught me the value of patience and understanding. In Connecticut, we provided services to several preschool and Head Start programs and this solidified my interest in working with preschool and school-age children.

When I moved to Michigan in the early 1990s, it was important for me to find a position that allowed me to work in educational audiology. I have been working for the Jackson County Intermediate School District for nearly 15 years, and I can enthusiastically say I am doing everything I love and wanted to do! I provide services to preschoolers and school-age students throughout the entire county. I am based in a center that also houses our early childhood programs, developmentally disabled students, and several Head Start programs. My responsibilities include complete diagnostic testing, auditory processing testing, and taking care of the equipment needs of the deaf/hard of hearing students in the entire county, as well as being an advocate for these students. I spend a fair amount of my time in classrooms outside the center my clinic is in. I truly enjoy being able to spend time in classrooms working closely with the students and their teachers.

In Michigan, we have approximately 50 educational audiologists and over the years we have become a fairly close-knit group. Most of us know one another and have worked together on various projects over the years. Getting to know all of these professionals has prompted me to become involved in various organizations, both statewide and nationally. I have served on the Executive Council of the Michigan Speech-Language-Hearing Association and been president of the Michigan Educational Audiology Association. I believe that being involved in your state associations is one of the single most important things you can do to "give back" to the profession. This is truly a way you can have an effect on legislative issues that are pertinent to the state in which you reside and work. Currently, I serve on the Board of Directors of the Educational Audiology Association. Serving on the EAA board has allowed me to develop professional relationships on a national level. I have met and worked with other educational audiologists from all over the country and even abroad. It has allowed me to become involved in issues that are very important to educational audiologists on a national and sometimes international level.

I earned my Doctor of Audiology through the University of Florida 10 years ago. I was a strong supporter of audiology moving to a doctoral-level profession. I believe that the AuD moves the profession forward. It allows audiologists to be the most important source of hearing health care in this country. I really cannot imagine doing anything else. I wake up thankful for the position I have. It has helped define me as a person and allowed me to be happy going to work every day.

9

Program Management

Donna F. Smiley, Cynthia M. Richburg, and
Susan J. Brannen

OBJECTIVES

By the end of this chapter, the reader will be able to:

1. Identify issues related to the establishment of school-based audiology programs or practices.
2. Discuss possible funding sources for school-based audiology programs or practices.
3. Discuss factors to consider when evaluating the effectiveness of school-based audiology programs or practices.

INTRODUCTION

This chapter elaborates on the unique characteristics of maintaining or establishing an audiology practice in the public school sector. Variations in how programs are started, as well as how they are managed, will exist depending on the service delivery model (e.g., district employed versus contract services). However, the goals of the program should be centered on student outcomes.

Establishing or maintaining a program that provides audiology services to a public school is indistinguishable in many ways from establishing and providing ser-

vices for a program in any facility. That is, "bottom lines" (e.g., costs and customer satisfaction) remain critical to the success of the practice. However, audiology services in the schools must demonstrate an impact on student outcomes and school performance, and the services must be in line with mandated legislation.

DEVELOPMENT

Data suggest that many school districts across the United States do not access school-based audiology services at the present time (Richburg & Smiley, 2009). For the audiologist interested in school-based practice, there are many potential opportunities for developing services in this sector. However, there are many issues to consider when developing a proposal for a school-based practice or program.

Justification

A crucial component for proposing the establishment of a school-based audiology practice or program is the *justification* for the services provided in that program. The individuals (e.g., principals, school board members, special education supervisors, etc.) who make decisions about hiring or contracting an audiologist need to be educated about why school-based audiology services are needed.

Unlike many other types of practices, public schools have legislation and regulations that open the door for audiology services and funding. The Individuals with Disabilities Education Act (IDEA) historically contained language that acknowledges the role of "audiology." IDEA, now Individuals with Disabilities Education Improvement Act (IDEIA), is a federal law that is mirrored in every state through state-level laws and regulations. States cannot lower any of the standards put forth in IDEA, or IDEIA, without risking the loss of funding. States may increase standards and services, but they may not decrease the services stated in the federal mandates. The language of IDEA and IDEIA suggests that all schools have audiology services in place; however, this is not always the case. School districts have managed to "get by" with using fragmented services and allowing other professionals to take on the respon-

sibilities delineated as the audiologist's. Many school districts view a child's managing (clinical) audiologist as someone who can appropriately cover the needs for this "related service." However, the related service roles described in special education regulations go beyond those of an audiologist in clinical practice. School-based audiologists connect diagnostic (clinical) information to the day-to-day reality and impact of hearing loss in the classroom (Educational Audiology Association, 2009a). The audiologist interested in developing a practice (or position) that provides services to schools should study special education regulation and be familiar with the manner in which school districts in a given state view audiology services. The authors believe that many school district personnel are simply unaware of school-based audiology services, the value of these services, or even the legislation mandating that these services be provided.

Other topics that need to be addressed during the justification process of developing school-based audiology services include: (1) the prevalence of hearing loss, (2) the educational impact of hearing loss, and (3) services a school-based audiologist is capable of providing. It is important to highlight the fact that school-based audiologists serve *all* students (e.g., through hearing screenings and addressing classroom acoustics) and are capable of providing technical assistance and professional development to the school district's staff.

Do not be mistaken, justifying new school-based audiology services is not easy, especially in the present economy. Persistence and consistency are two traits needed during the justification stage of building a school-based audiology program. Advocacy and marketing of school-based audiology services (two of the subsequent stages for program development) can act as part of the justification process and are discussed in more detail later in this chapter.

Budgeting

The justification for any new school-based program is built on a sound budget. In fact, any audiology practice has to develop a budget capable of supporting its needs. Therefore, a school district will need to preselect the services it needs, which will then allow the audiologist to realistically plan for costs.

Costs Associated with School-Based Audiology Services

The service delivery model provided by the school-based audiologist will have the most influence over the budget. A practice/program that conducts direct services within the school building utilizing portable instrumentation requires a budget quite different from the practice/program that provides services within a central location using less portable equipment. In addition, if the practice/program provides direct services using both delivery models, then that budget will also look different. When developing the budget for a school-based audiology practice or program, one must consider the following:

- **Staffing needs**—salary, as well as benefit costs;
- **Travel expenses**—these vary depending on the service delivery model and distances included in the school district(s): mileage, and travel expenses related to overnight

stays or continuing education requirements;
- **Audiological equipment needs**—these vary depending on the needs established by the service delivery model; equipment needs may include: audiometer, hearing aid analyzer, otoacoustic emissions, tympanometer with acoustic reflex capabilities, and an otoscope. Some school-based audiology services utilize a sound-treated booth also;
- **Technology**—these vary depending on the student population being served: personal FM systems, hearing aids (loaner or demonstration), spare parts for cochlear implants, classroom soundfield amplification systems, hearing aid stethoscopes, and variable batteries to support the technology;
- **Equipment and technology repairs and upkeep**—these vary depending on equipment, number of units being maintained, in-house versus contractual calibration costs, age of equipment, and updating capabilities (software) of the equipment; and
- **Office equipment and technology**—these vary depending on the size and needs of the school district, student population, support staff, and allocated space: desks, basic computer(s), printer(s), office supplies, and rental or mortgage costs for space.

The audiologist establishing a school-based practice/program must calculate what it will cost to provide the services initially, as well as over time. For example, the initial outlay for purchasing audiological equipment will be quite costly.

However, those costs would be spread out over many years (i.e., the life of the equipment) because the equipment would not have to be purchased every year. Therefore, revenue generated via third-party payment or by contractual fees should offset the initial costs of the practice/program and allow the program to be solvent and either break even or operate at a profit.

Possible Sources of Funding for School-Based Audiology Services

The final consideration in the area of budgeting is funding. Determining the potential funding sources for school-based audiology services is crucial for the establishment and survival of the practice/program. Funding from federal sources (i.e., IDEA and/or Medicaid) is filtered through state departments of education. There are many different funding formulas, and each state determines how the money will be divided. The audiologist interested in school-based practice would be advised to become familiar with local schools' funding sources and schemes.

Medicaid funds may be available to school districts providing school-based audiology services. The Centers for Medicare and Medicaid Services (CMS), although federal in scope, allows states to establish individual guidelines, known as the state Medicaid Plan. All Medicaid eligible children are allowed to obtain hearing aids and the appropriate evaluations for the fitting and selecting of such devices (see EPSDT Web site: https://www.cms.gov/Medicaid EarlyPeriodicScrn02_Benefits.asp). A child must meet the Medicaid eligibility criteria for hearing loss levels as established in each individual state's Medicaid plan. However, Medicaid may not always be a viable choice for school districts. A school

district's ability to access Medicaid funds for audiology services will be governed by state regulations. In some states, schools are not approved providers for audiology services under the state Medicaid plan. Nevertheless, a private practice audiologist who serves schools may be eligible to become a Medicaid provider. Audiologists are encouraged to determine if they meet their state's requirements.

There are some funds associated with the No Child Left Behind (NCLB) Act of 2001. However, these funds are often limited to, and designed for, very specific purposes or a very specific demographic. Again, the audiologist interested in obtaining funding to develop a school-based program is encouraged to look into NCLB requirements.

In 2009, the American Recovery and Reinvestment Act (ARRA) was signed into law. This law was intended to stimulate a slow economy, and it provided roughly $100 billion for America's public schools. Some of the money was added to existing programs (e.g., IDEA, Title 1); others funds were brand new (e.g., State Fiscal Stabilization Fund; Ellerson, 2009). ARRA funding was limited to a 3-year period, and school districts needed to apply for the funds by justifying their use and the expected outcomes. Assistive technology use across domains (with all students, regardless of hearing acuity) was an area often supported by these funds. For example, some schools purchased classroom soundfield amplification systems for general education classrooms using the justification that these systems would be a preventive measure.

Another funding source could be available within the school district itself. That is, local funding is available to schools through the taxation structure of the local school district. Obviously, the funding from this taxation structure varies tremendously, based on the affluence of the district and the economic times.

Finally, it is possible for an audiologist to consider grant funding to support the start-up of an audiology practice/program within the schools. Historically, there have not been long-standing grant programs to support audiology services rendered over time. Therefore, the audiologist providing services to schools should not expect grant funding to support the program on a long-term basis. Building time into one's schedule to look for, write, and submit applications for grants would be an important aspect of developing a successfully funded practice/program.

ADVOCACY AND MARKETING

School-based audiologists are the professionals uniquely qualified to ensure that all students have appropriate and adequate access to auditory information presented in the educational environment (Educational Audiology Association, 2009a). However, as has been mentioned several times throughout this text, many school districts across the United States still do not provide school-based audiology services.

Advocacy simply implies that one supports or recommends a specific program, group, or interest. Advocating for school-based audiology services is the responsibility of many groups of interested individuals. The entire profession of audiology needs to advocate for the inclusion of school-based audiology services in all schools. Clinical audiologists will be able to better serve the children in their practices if those children go out to

their school environment with a school-based audiologist there to ensure that the hearing technology is used appropriately. In addition, speech-language pathologists who practice in schools can help to advocate for the inclusion of school-based audiology services. Parents of children who are deaf or hard of hearing or who have other auditory disorders should also be advocates for school-based audiology services.

Advocacy needs to include educating others about the benefits of school-based audiology services. School district personnel (including administrators, teachers, and other staff), community partners, and parents should be educated about the value of school-based audiology services. Often, these constituencies need to understand what school-based audiology looks like for them on a personal level.

Exhibits and demonstrations that advocate *and* educate may prove to be valuable tools for the audiologist wanting to start a new program/practice. A portion of the education process can be focused toward marketing the school-based services that are to be provided. Marketing allows the audiologist to convince the administrators, educators, and parents that the services are needed, and marketing motivates those same constituents to act on providing those services to students who are deaf or hard of hearing. Therefore, marketing strategies and advocacy go hand in hand.

Even in school districts having long-standing audiology services, the audiologist must continue to advocate for the program. Newly employed teachers, school nurses, and administrators need to be made aware of the audiology services available to students. Otherwise, those professionals may not access the services, which could hurt the effectiveness of the program over time.

DAY-TO-DAY MANAGEMENT OF SCHOOL-BASED AUDIOLOGY PROGRAMS

It is beyond the scope of this textbook to cover every aspect of practice management. Many excellent texts that provide in-depth information in this area are available (Glaser & Traynor, 2008; Hosford-Dunn, Roeser, & Valente, 2008). There are, however, a few areas worth noting that may be specific to the practice of audiology in the school setting. These areas are discussed below in no particular order of importance.

Job Description

Any position needs a solid job description. Job descriptions provide a structure for the day-to-day functions of the employee, and thorough descriptions let the employee and employer know what is expected of each other. In addition, a good job description leads the way to a fair evaluation of the employee's work.

If the reader needs to develop a job description for a new practice/program, the Educational Audiology Association (EAA) has two documents that might be of assistance: *Minimum Competencies for Educational Audiologists* (n.d.) and *Recommended Professional Practices for Educational Audiology* (2009b). These documents provide good examples of the competencies and practices typically needed and performed by school-based audiologists.

Caseload Versus Workload

When building a new school-based audiology practice/program, it will be impor-

tant to determine how many audiologists are needed in any given school district. The recommended ratio for audiologists to students (i.e., all students, not just those with identified hearing losses) is 1:10,000 (ASHA, 2002; EAA, 2009b). Another way of expressing this ratio is to use the terminology Full-Time Equivalent, or FTE. That is, there should be one FTE audiologist for every 10,000 students. This recommendation would be an example of a "caseload" standard. However, when making decisions about how many audiologists it will take to provide a set of services in schools, a workload analysis might also be of benefit. A workload analysis would encompass all of the activities that a school-based audiologist would need to perform to deliver and maintain services within the school district. Some of the issues that may affect workload (and, therefore, dictate a need to reduce the caseload) include:

- The time required for travel between schools;
- The number of schools and local education agencies (LEA) served;
- The number of students with hearing loss or other auditory disorders;
- The number of students with other disabilities requiring audiologic evaluation and intervention services;
- The number of hearing aids, cochlear implants, bone-anchored implants (osseo-integrated devices), and hearing assistance technologies being used by the student population;
- The scope of the audiology services being provided;
- The amount of professional development being provided by the school-based audiologist;

- The amount of responsibilities being provided in the hearing loss prevention program; and
- Other duties assigned outside of audiology services (ASHA, 2002).

This list is in no way exhaustive, but it does provide information that must be taken into consideration when calculating the needed manpower for a school-based audiology program or practice.

Ethical Considerations

As with any audiology practice, audiologists working in schools have to adhere to ethical practice guidelines. The reader is encouraged to study the ASHA and the American Academy of Audiology Code of Ethics (American Academy of Audiology, 2009; American Speech-Language-Hearing Association, 2010). In addition, school-based audiologists need to become familiar with regulations that govern privacy of student records.

The Family Educational Rights and Privacy Act (FERPA; 1974) is a federal law that protects the privacy of student education records. Schools are subject to this law if they receive funding from applicable programs of the U.S. Department of Education. In general, FERPA gives parents or eligible students (i.e., 18 years of age and older) the right to inspect and review the student's education record. However, in most cases, schools must have written permission from the parent (or eligible student) to release any information from a student's education record.

Another document governing the privacy of student records is the Health Insurance Portability and Accountability Act of 1996 (HIPAA) Privacy Rule. In general, the HIPAA Privacy Rule establishes national standards for the protection of individuals'

medical records and other personal health information. HIPAA (1996) sets limits and conditions on the use and disclosure of personal health information.

Public school personnel understand that FERPA (1974) is applicable to their work. However, many school personnel may not know if public school districts have to comply with HIPAA (1996) or not, and the answer to this question is not straightforward. HIPAA (1996) applies to health plans, health care clearinghouses, and health care providers who conduct health care transactions electronically. If a school provides health care to students (e.g., in a health clinic), then the school is considered to be a "health care provider" as defined by HIPAA (U.S. Department of Health and Human Services, 2008). If the school conducts any covered transactions electronically in connection with that health care, the school would then be considered a covered entity under HIPAA. As a covered entity, the school would have to comply with the guidelines. However, many schools only maintain health records that are considered to be education records or treatment records under FERPA (1974), and education and treatment records are excluded from the HIPAA Privacy Rule. Conversely, if schools conduct electronic transactions for payment from third-party payers, then those schools may be considered health care clearinghouses. As clearinghouses, the schools would then be subject to the HIPAA Privacy Rule.

School-based audiologists can do several things to ensure that they are in compliance with FERPA and HIPAA regulations that affect their work in schools. Keep current releases on file that give the school-based audiologist permission from the parent or eligible student to communicate with other health care providers (i.e., clinical audiologist, ENT physician, and pediatrician) as needed. In addition, the audiologist may ask school districts to consult with legal advisors to determine if HIPAA applies to the district or to any functions that may occur in the district (i.e., third party billing conducted electronically). Ultimately, it is the responsibility of the school-based audiologist to make sure that applicable regulations are being following for the services that he or she provides.

Providing AuD Students with Practical Experience

School-based audiology practices/programs are excellent training grounds for graduate students in audiology. Graduate students who complete a rotation or externship in a school-based audiology practicum can receive experience not only in the diagnostic aspects of audiology, but also in the practice aspects of advocating for student rights, hearing assistance device fitting and testing, and collaborating with other school personnel. AuD students completing a rotation or externship get to see what happens when the "patient" leaves a clinical setting and enters into his or her real-world environment.

In addition to the typical audiological diagnostic evaluations, audiology graduate students experiencing a school-based externship may get to participate in some of the following activities:

- developing and/or implementing a school hearing screening program;
- creating and/or implementing professional development (continuing education) for educators, administrators, and other school personnel;
- explaining audiological test results to teachers and other school personnel; and

- discussing appropriate educational strategies for students with hearing loss (Benafield, Smiley, Richburg, & Serpente, 2011).

There are some challenges associated with having graduate students in audiology complete practical experiences in school settings, and we would be remiss if these challenges were not discussed here. Making productive use of the graduate student's time is of concern in settings where excessive travel occurs between schools. In some states, there are limited opportunities for these types of experiences due to the lack of schools utilizing school-based audiology services. Finally, graduate students in audiology may not be interested in obtaining experiences in schools because they do not see it as a viable option for future employment (Benafield et al., 2011).

School-based audiologists should partner with a university training program to provide practical experiences to graduate students in audiology. As the opportunities in school-based audiology grow, the future workforce will also need to grow to meet these new opportunities.

Clerical Support

Despite the implementation of technology that is purported to make life easier (i.e. computers, Smart phones, e-mail, texting, etc.), a busy school practice needs clerical support. The school-based audiologist spends a great deal of time in the schools and on the road between schools. Therefore, he or she may not be in the office on a daily basis. However, not being in the office on a daily basis makes contacting teachers, parents, and administrators difficult, especially when dedicated or protected time to accomplish clerical tasks is not available. Therefore, a staff person whose job description includes clerical responsibilities can make a great deal of difference in the school-based audiologist's ability to be productive and efficient.

Clerical support can be even more critical when there are multiple audiologists working from the same central office location. Scheduling access to the testing booth or portable instrumentation requires clerical staff members who handle the details. In districts where only one audiologist provides all of the services, it may be possible to share clerical support with other staff or other allied health providers (e.g., physical or occupational therapists, speech-language pathologists, or school psychologists).

Clerical support in the school-based audiology practice may be helpful in preparing reports and keeping track of documentation. In addition, clerical staff may assist the audiologist with keeping a database of students, as well as equipment. When equipment needs to be sent in for repair, clerical staff may be able to offer assistance with the task.

As a program or practice grows, the need for support services will also grow. The audiologist building a school-based practice or program should be sure to plan for these needs as the program develops.

Record Keeping

School-based audiologists need to keep appropriate documentation on the services they provide. This documentation may include audiological assessment information, as well as notes regarding communications with school personnel on a given student. As mentioned in the previous section, school-based audiologists may need to develop databases for students (type and severity of hearing loss, assistive technology used, classes with and without support mechanisms in place, etc.) and equipment (serial numbers, repair records, where the equipment is being used, etc.). Keeping these forms of documentation in a secure location is important for adhering to HIPAA (1996) and FERPA (1974) regulations, as well as ethical constraints that govern the practice of audiology.

EVALUATING THE EFFECTIVENESS OF THE PROGRAM

Managing an audiology program for services in schools requires focusing on several issues: student outcomes, cost effectiveness, and alignment with the regulations governing school practices. Education and its associated costs should be measured by student outcomes. However, in assessing the effectiveness of school-based audiology programs, it is difficult to simply draw a straight line from the services that have been provided to the student's level of achievement. Much of the work of the school-based audiologist has to be measured over time. The work of the audiologist cannot be evaluated solely by itself; it must be viewed in conjunction with all of the other educational efforts that are being conducted on behalf of the students. In other words, the whole picture has to be evaluated, not just a specific component.

Outcomes are measured in many different ways within a school setting. The U.S. Department of Education and state departments of education have embraced some level of standardized assessments that are used as "benchmarks." Unless severely disabled, children in public school programs are expected to meet these benchmarks. Audiology services and interventions must be contributing to the student's success in these arenas. Yet, it would be difficult to prove that a student's increase or decrease on a benchmark test score was directly related to the provision of school-based audiology services. Although the ultimate goal (outcome) is for students to be able to increase their knowledge base, it is not recommended that standardized test scores be used to document the effectiveness of school-based audiology services. Instead, broader measures across time should be employed to access the effectiveness of these services. For example, surveys provided to school personnel, students, and family members may provide some insight into the effectiveness of a program. Other methods for measuring the impact of audiology services include, but are not limited to:

- the ability of the audiology services to keep amplification working daily (thereby, accessing optimal auditory input);
- improving the teacher's attitudes for using a student's device by adjusting FM hearing assistance technologies to allow multiple students to use a single frequency for only one class a day;
- facilitating peer communication and improving discussions within a classroom by equipping the class with appropriate pass-around transmitters; and
- supporting the student in achieving self-advocacy skills to promote increased socialization.

The EAA Advocacy Committee is currently working on a set of outcomes and associated evidences that the school-based audiologist can use to define and measure critical components of educational audiology services. Refer to the EAA Web site (http://www.edaud.org) for updated information on this topic.

CONCLUSION

Managing an educational audiology practice requires many skills: expertise in the laws and regulations that govern schools, an excellent ability to communicate with different classroom-based personnel, budget acumen, and above all—flexibility. The opportunity to provide audiology services to students facing the daily challenges of learning in a primarily auditory classroom is an opportunity not to be missed. Managing the practice that allows this to happen is an opportunity for personal growth and development.

REFERENCES

American Academy of Audiology. (2009). *Code of ethics*. Available from the AAA Web site: http://www.audiology.org/resources/documentlibrary/Pages/ codeofethics.aspx

American Speech-Language-Hearing Association. (2002). *Guidelines for audiology service provision in and for schools*. Available from the ASHA Web site: http://www.asha.org/docs/pdf/GL2002-00005.pdf

American Speech-Language-Hearing Association. (2010). *Code of ethics*. Available from the ASHA Web site: http://www.asha.org/docs/pdf/ET2010-00309.pdf

Benafield, N. J., Smiley, D. F., Richburg, C. M., & Serpente, A. K. (2011, July). *Practicum for Au.D. students in school-based audiology settings*. Poster presented at the biennial meeting of the Educational Audiology Association, Nashville, TN.

Educational Audiology Association. (n.d.). *Minimum competencies for educational audiologists*. Available from the Educational Audiology Association Web site: http://www.edaud.org/associations/4846/files/Min.Comp09.pdf

Educational Audiology Association. (2009a). *School-based audiology services*. Available from the Educational Audiology Association Web site: http://www.edaud.org/associations/4846/files/AdvocacyStatement_1_core.pdf

Educational Audiology Association. (2009b). *Recommended professional practices for educational audiology*. Available from the Educational Audiology Association Web site: http://www.edaud.org/associations/4846/files/Professional%20Practices_pos09_REVISED.pdf

Ellerson, N. M. (2009). *Schools and the stimulus: How America's public school districts are using ARRA funds*. Available from the American Association of School Administrators Web site: http://www.aasa.org/uploadedFiles/ Policy_and_Advocacy/files/AASAStimulusSurveyAug09.pdf

Family Educational Rights and Privacy (FERPA), Act 20 U.S.C. § 1232g; 34 CFR Part 99 (1974).

Glaser, R. G., & Traynor, R. M. (2008). *Strategic practice management: A patient-centric approach*. San Diego, CA: Plural.

Health Insurance Portability and Accountability Act, Pub. L. No. 104-191, 45 CFR, Parts 160–164. (1996).

Hosford-Dunn, H., Roeser, R., & Valente, M. (2008). *Audiology practice management*. New York, NY: Thieme.

No Child Left Behind Act of 2001, Pub. L. 107-110, 20 U.S.C. §6301 et seq. (2001).

Richburg, C. M., & Smiley, D. F. (2009). The "state" of educational audiology revisited. *Journal of Educational Audiology, 15*, 63–73.

U.S. Department of Health and Human Services and U.S. Department of Education. (2008). *Joint guidance on the application of the Family Educational Rights and Privacy Act (FERPA) and the Health Insurance Portability and Accountability Act of 1996 (HIPAA) to student health records*. Available from the U.S. Department of Health and Human Services Web site: http://www.hhs.gov/ocr/privacy/hipaa/understanding/coveredentities/hipaaferpajointguide.pdf

Educational Audiology in the Real World

Robin Gaschler, MA
Educational Audiologist
The Multi-District Deaf/Hard of Hearing Program
Blue Springs, Missouri

I received my Master of Arts degree in audiology from the University of Kansas Medical Center (KUMC) in 1993. At that time, the Master's was the entry-level requirement for the profession. As part of the program, I wrote and published a thesis and completed a minimum of 350 clock hours of supervised clinical experience. I was in my final practicum site with the Multi-District Hearing Impaired Program (now Multi-District Deaf/Hard of Hearing Program) in the Blue Springs, Missouri School District when this job opening presented itself. I applied for the position and am still here 17 years later. The requirements for this position include audiology licensure from the State of Missouri and ASHA certification. A separate "hearing instrument dispensing" license requirement has since been discontinued and is now recognized as part of the scope of practice under the audiology license.

The Multi-District Deaf/Hard of Hearing Program (MDDHHP) provides audiological and educational services to students aged 3 through 21 years, and the staff work in school districts in northwest Missouri on an annually renewable contractual basis. At present there are 29 participating districts. Our staff includes two full-time audiologists (one 9-month position and my 10-month position) and an educational consultant. Administrative and clerical support is provided by the district's Department of Special Education. Students may attend school in their home district when appropriate, or may be contracted to attend school in Blue Springs where the services of MDDHHP staff, teachers of the deaf, interpreters, speech-language pathologists, and a counselor for the deaf are included. Our students have varying degrees of hearing loss, may wear hearing aids or cochlear implants, and may use FM amplification. Some students use sign language, some use total communication, and some are auditory/oral. Given our location near Kansas City, our students have access to many dispensing audiologists (including a children's hospital and KUMC) and two cochlear implant mapping sites.

MDDHHP audiologists provide comprehensive audiological evaluations to students in all participating districts in a sound booth located in a Blue Springs elementary school. We schedule both audiologists to work with the very young or difficult-to-test students and have equipment to perform otoacoustic emissions screenings, air/bone/speech/soundfield audiometry, diagnostic tympanometry, acoustic reflexes and reflex decay, electroacoustic analysis of hearing aids and FM equipment, and real-ear measures. We have a few "loaner" hearing aids for demonstration, FM troubleshooting, or temporary student use. We make ear impressions per district request, re-tube earmolds, and troubleshoot hearing aids. We provide FM equipment for trials, troubleshooting, or use with students in Blue Springs schools. The other districts may choose to purchase FM equipment per our recommendation or access equipment through the state rental program at the Missouri School for the Deaf. We do not perform auditory processing evaluations; that diagnosis does not qualify students in Missouri for special education services.

Our primary responsibility is to provide diagnostic audiological evaluations and educational related recommendations and follow-up, as opposed to conducting the hearing/middle ear screening programs. Rather, we train the staff in our participating districts through an annual workshop and ongoing consultation regarding screening and referral procedures. Students who do not pass the screenings may come to Blue Springs for follow-up testing, or access other medical or audiological services in the community. We write our results and recommendations in report format and disseminate the information to the schools. Other duties may include traveling for hearing aid or FM in-services, trouble-shooting equipment, classroom observations, or attending IEP meetings. We also host an annual transition workshop for all students who are deaf or hard of hearing within our service area. My 20-day extended contract is for FM maintenance and inventory. Much of my time is spent in collaboration by phone or E-mail (to ensure access to classroom information) with dispensing and mapping audiologists in the community, hearing aid and FM manufacturers, and school staff. Our program also offers annual "calibration checks" for the screening audiometers used by our participating districts.

MDDHHP continues to be a practicum site for students in the KUMC audiology program, so student supervision is part of our work. Perhaps, one day, one of our students will be fortunate to become part of a staff working at the interesting and diverse job of an educational audiologist!

SECTION IV

Additional Aspects of School-Based Audiology

10

Collaboration Among School-Based Professionals

Cynthia M. Richburg and Donna F. Smiley

OBJECTIVES

By the end of this chapter, the reader will be able to:

1. Define and describe collaboration as it relates to professionals working with students who are deaf or hard of hearing (d/hh).
2. Determine what collaborative efforts need to take place so that students can succeed.
3. Describe possible barriers to collaboration.
4. Discuss possible solutions for these barriers.
5. Discuss efforts that encourage, support, and promote collaboration among professionals working with students who are d/hh.

INTRODUCTION

Collaboration among professionals working with children who are deaf or hard of hearing (d/hh) is just as important as the actual knowledge and skills possessed by each professional. A role of the school-based audiologist is to act as a link between services provided at school and services provided by physicians, clinical audiologists, therapists, educators (regular and special), administrators, and parents. Collaboration functions to prevent duplication of services provided to a student or improve services that have already been provided. The sharing of information, knowledge, and skills is an absolute must for any educational audiology program providing services to students who are d/hh.

171

COLLABORATION DEFINED AND DESCRIBED

Webster's definition of *collaborate* is, "to work jointly with others or together especially in an intellectual endeavor" or "to cooperate with an agency or instrumentality with which one is not immediately connected" (http://www.merriam-webster.com/dictionary/collaboration). Synonyms of collaboration include partnership, alliance, teamwork, relationship, group effort, and cooperation. Collaboration among professionals can refer to the notion of sharing expertise and relying on others on an ongoing basis. It also implies that individuals with differing expertise and skill levels work together to maximize each person's strengths and build on each person's knowledge base. However, the definition of collaboration as it applies to professionals working with students who are d/hh is not as succinct or clear cut. Those of us in the area of school-based audiology like to use a definition, or description, that we feel applies to the *chaos* of the reality of working with students and families of students who are d/hh. That definition includes "the act or process of ensuring that a student has a working amplification device, is listening in an acoustically friendly environment, is working on age- and level-appropriate studies, is capable of producing speech intelligibly, is being monitored routinely, is living up to family expectations, *and* fits in with his/her peers." In all seriousness, any definition of collaboration that applies to professionals working with students who are d/hh should include something about benefiting those students and allowing them to obtain the best services possible.

There are many instances in which collaborative efforts should be completed to benefit not only students, but also the professionals involved. School-based collaboration can be described as: (a) many professionals working together for a student's, or students', benefit, (b) two professionals working on a specific program to improve learning outcomes in the classroom setting, (c) two or three professionals giving feedback to each other (known as "peer coaching"), or (d) active participation in decisions that affect a group of educational professionals (known as "teacher empowerment"). Community collaboration can be described as: (a) many professionals working within a community to establish services for students who are d/hh, (b) professionals, community leaders, and parents working on establishing funding sources for developing service delivery models, or (c) professionals, students, and local service organizations (i.e., Quota International, Optimist International, fraternities and sororities) working together to establish funding sources and learning opportunities for school districts. Students studying school-based audiology are recommended to read more about community collaboration and developing community needs assessments in Johnson, Benson, and Seaton (1997, pp. 131–140), where discussion on collaborations with professionals involved in hearing screenings, child-find programs, and service organizations is covered more fully.

In general, three terms are routinely used within the profession of audiology to describe collaborative efforts: multidisciplinary, interdisciplinary, and transdisciplinary. To briefly illustrate these terms, *multidisciplinary collaboration* can be described as members acknowledging the importance and contributions of several disciplines; however, service provision remains independent. *Interdisciplinary collaboration* can be described as members sharing responsibility for service delivery; however, individual professionals remain primarily responsible for their specific discipline. Finally, *transdisciplinary collaboration* can be described as members committing to teaching, learning, and working across disciplines for planning and providing integrated services (Friend & Cook, 2007). Multidisciplinary efforts have the least amount of collaboration, interdisciplinary teams have a bit more collaboration, and transdisciplinary teams have the most collaboration. Transdisciplinary collaboration should be the goal of all school-based audiologists. Be aware that in the literature on collaboration, there is a distinction between collaboration, consultation, and teamwork (co-teaching and teaming), although many people will use the terms collaboration and teamwork interchangeably. Although many audiologists will be brought in as consultants for other professions, this chapter focuses on collaboration as a means of effective communication, cooperation, and coordination of efforts among various professionals.

PERSONS INVOLVED IN COLLABORATION

Professionals trained specifically to work with students who are d/hh include audiologists, speech-language pathologists (SLPs), teachers of children who are d/hh (deaf educators), educational interpreters, and special educators. The school-based audiologist will likely be part of a team of professionals working both within the school system and within the medical setting. Audiological services within the schools are considered to be a "related service" according to special education law. Other related services may include, for example, nursing, speech and language therapy, orientation and mobility, occupational therapy, physical therapy, and low vision services. The school-based audiologist will experience the need for collaborating with one or more of these professionals throughout her or his career.

There are also ancillary professionals who come in contact with students who are d/hh, such as social workers, school psychologists, counselors, aides/assistants, regular classroom teachers, administrators, school nurses, physicians/pediatricians, school coaches, art teachers, librarians, computer teachers, and even disability services office staff for students at the post-secondary level. But the other important players who often are not involved enough in the collaborative process are the parents, grandparents, foster parents, and the students themselves.

We would be remiss if we did not include organizations whose members could act as part of a collaborative team. For instance, parent support groups, advocacy groups, child care or after-school care agencies, sign language clubs, and churches could all be part of a collaborative process, depending on what activities are needed to build an alliance.

BENEFITS OF COLLABORATION

Collaboration, if done well, can be very valuable to all involved in the process. It can lead to professionals being more productive, more efficient, less fatigued, and more creative. In addition, working with other professionals in the schools and in the community can make service provision less redundant and more cost effective. Ultimately, collaboration can result in a feeling of "ownership" by those who serve students with special needs.

Professionals who work together in a collaborative manner provide services and support for students in the classroom setting, but they also provide an entire range of benefits to those who are involved with that student. For instance, when a school-based audiologist works with a student's regular classroom teacher, the audiologist is able to help the teacher develop a repertoire of course materials and instructional strategies for assisting the student with learning new information and hearing better in the classroom environment. Ultimately, the student gets more out of the learning experience, the teacher gets help for a student with special needs, and the audiologist is able to move on to another student knowing that the first student will be taken care of and will have appropriate classroom instruction. Likewise, when a school-based audiologist works with a student's clinical audiologist to get hearing aids that can be fit appropriately with a personal FM device, the student is able to hear better in the poor signal-to-noise ratio of the school's gymnasium, the student's coach is able to communicate strategic moves more efficiently, the audiologists are able to feel good about their successful fitting, and who knows—the student may be drafted by a college recruiter and earn a scholarship toward a four-year degree. But realistically, benefits of collaboration can include an increase in the effectiveness of instruction to the student, decreases in the redundancy of services provided for a student, and the number of students requiring grade retention may decrease.

BARRIERS TO COLLABORATION

Audiology students may wonder why a discussion on collaboration is necessary, especially when they have witnessed a good amount of collaboration from faculty, clinical supervisors, and preceptors during their academic experience. However, once a professional gets out into the "real world" and starts seeing clients, the ability to collaborate often takes a back seat or becomes unworkable, no matter how much a professional desires to collaborate with others.

Montgomery (1990) listed several reasons why professionals are not able to collaborate easily. The first reason is the fact that the collaboration idea may be new and different to one or more of the professionals involved in the collaborative activity. If a person is not familiar with the idea of working with others, sharing ideas, or cooperating on projects as a team, or if the person has never been asked or required to do these things, there may be some hesitancy on the part of that person to be involved in the process. Along the same lines, a professional may be unwilling to change the way he or she has always done something. Motivation is a necessary component for collaboration among all professionals involved.

Another reason collaboration may not occur readily, according to Montgomery (1990), is because an administrator may believe that the collaborative efforts will be expensive, or that money will be mismanaged because too many professionals are involved in the collaboration. Entire administrations may be unwilling to change, and may even direct employees to make no changes. For example, if various professionals decide to work together to change a service delivery model currently used for students who are d/hh in their schools, a school district may not support the collaborative efforts.

Some professionals do not feel that they need help from other professionals. These professionals believe that they know what their students need, and they may even feel that their education and training provided them with enough knowledge and skills to provide services independently. In addition, many professionals have strong personalities that conflict with other professionals' personalities to the point that relationships are not able to be established or maintained for collaborative purposes.

Another barrier to collaboration lies in the fact that many professionals who work with children who are d/hh are not fully prepared in their training programs, or through continuing education, to work with these children. Similarly, barriers exist because these professionals do not have access to an educational audiologist and do not know what an audiologist is or what an audiologist does.

In surveys distributed to 87 teachers of children who are d/hh, 209 speech-language pathologists, and 110 special educators (Knickelbein & Richburg, in press; Richburg, 2007; Richburg & Knickelbein, in press) concerning their knowledge of basic audiological concepts (i.e., interpreting audiograms and tympanograms) and their preparedness for helping their students with hearing aid, FM system, and cochlear implant problems, several of these barriers were identified. As seen in Table 10–1, the majority of

Table 10–1. Percentages of Teachers of Children Who Are Deaf/Hard of Hearing (Teachers), Speech-Language Pathologists (SLPs), and Special Educators (Spec educ) Who Responded to Survey Questions Concerning Their Knowledge of Basic Audiological Concepts and Preparedness to Help Their Students with Problems with Their Hearing Aids, FM Systems, and Cochlear Implants.

Survey Question	Professionals	Percentage of Responses
Knowledge of basic audiological concepts	Teachers	**78.2% high** (10.2% low)
	SLPs	**70.2% high** (16.6% low)
	Spec Educ	9.6% high (**83.7% low**)
Preparedness for helping with hearing aids	Teachers	**71.2% high** (16.1% low)
	SLPs	27.3% high (**60.5% low**)
	Spec educ	15.4% high (**74.0% low**)
Preparedness for helping with FM systems	Teachers	Question not on survey
	SLPs	25.9% high (**60.5% low**)
	Spec educ	10.6% high (**85.6% low**)
Preparedness for helping with cochlear implants	Teachers	22.1% high (**66.3% low**)
	SLPs	22.1% high (**89.3% low**)
	Spec educ	4.8% high (**93.3% low**)

Responses were ranked on a Likert scale of 1 to 9, with 1 to 4 being "low" and 6 to 9 being "high."

the teachers and SLPs felt confident with their audiological knowledge. Only the teachers felt really confident with the preparedness to help students with hearing aid problems, but the majority of the members in these professional groups felt ill-prepared to help their students with FM system or cochlear implant problems. These data help to build the case that collaboration among professionals is necessary for providing the best service delivery for students with hearing impairments.

Similarly, the professionals in these studies (Knickelbein & Richburg, in press; Richburg, 2007; Richburg & Knickelbein, in press) were asked if they had access to educational or contractual audiologists in their schools. Only 69.3% of the teachers, 61.5% of the SLPs, and 58.6% of the special educators reported having access to an audiologist in their current work setting. These low numbers support the idea that collaboration is hindered as some professionals do not even have access to an audiologist in their schools.

Finally, some answers provided by these professional groups indicated that the professionals had limited knowledge about the audiological services offered in their school districts, and many teachers, SLPs, and some special educators indicated that they have additional responsibilities placed on them because they do not having access to an audiologist. The concerns created by these findings are ethical in nature. That is, some of the added responsibilities (services) that these professionals are expected to provide are clearly out of the scope of practice for their professions. The ethics of collaboration is discussed later in this chapter.

Along with the human aspects that bar collaboration from occurring, scheduling conflicts, time availability, physical location concerns, and lack of resources can band together to decrease collaborative efforts. That is, most professionals working in educational environments (and medical settings) have little time in their weekly schedules to set aside for working on collaborative processes. Differences in planning schedules (e.g., 30 minutes versus 1 hour, first thing in the morning versus last thing before the end of the work day, etc.), differences in school schedules versus clinic schedules, time limits within those schedules, and "emergency" changes within a professional's daily schedule (which may result from equipment failure or identification of hearing loss in a student) all play roles in barring collaboration. It is difficult to schedule multiple professionals to have available time at the *same* time in any day or week. Additionally, when one professional has an office in one school and the other professional has an office in a different place, the distance and time it takes to travel to another location may hinder efforts for collaboration.

Lack of resources also hinders collaboration. For instance, there may not be a large enough space set aside for groups to work together, and there may not be equipment or technologies to support collaboration. Due to funding issues and/or policies for technology use, a school district may not allow its therapy materials, computers, projectors, or other instructional materials to be used at a different location.

Lack of support, in general, from administrators, family members, and students may also deal the final blow to collaborative efforts. Administrators may lack knowledge regarding the resources needed for educating students with hearing impairment. Administrators may not be willing to allow the professionals time/

space/resources for collaboration. Or, family members and students themselves may not be willing to participate in collaborative efforts. If parents, caregivers, or students are members of a minority group, educational professionals must be aware of the family's perceptions of the student's hearing loss and provide a collaborative atmosphere in which the family feels comfortable. Also, historical, attitudinal, and perceptual factors regarding the educational system and/or educators may keep parents or students from being willing to collaborate. That is, some parents or caregivers may be suspicious, fearful, or even distrusting of school personnel due to their own negative experiences as students. To a lesser degree, some parents and students simply may not have the ability to leave work or class for a meeting with hearing professionals. They also may not have access to transportation to attend that meeting. Whatever the circumstance may be, collaborative efforts are not as effective without participation from the students and their family members.

OVERCOMING BARRIERS TO COLLABORATION

There are several means by which professionals can overcome the barriers mentioned above. Some means will be harder to implement than others, and some may or may not be necessary for every situation. For instance, building professional respect, parity, and mentorship may seem simple and obvious; however, these necessary components of collegiality and collaboration are often overlooked or ignored.

Professional respect centers around truly caring about colleagues and respecting the educational training they have had. One needs to remain open-minded about other professionals' viewpoints and experiences on specific topics. Respecting the services that other professionals provide for students with hearing impairments and the work that they accomplish is imperative for forming collaborative relationships.

With respect to parity, Friend and Cook (1990) state that, "one of the most difficult barriers to establishing collaborative programs" is creating the environment, sense, and belief that each participant (each collaborator) is *equally* valuable. The belief that there is no superior-subordinate relationship should exist among members in any collaborative effort. That is, no one professional (no matter what their degree may be, no matter how long they may have been practicing, no matter what their training may be) should act as the superior, or person in charge. All activities should be equally shared, which leads to the concept of mentorship as a means of improving collaboration among professionals. Sharing information, activities, therapies, ideas, and resources allows one professional to mentor and, thereby, form a relationship with other professionals.

Other means by which barriers to collaboration can be overcome, and which appear to be fairly effortless (if not obvious), include establishing volunteer participation, mutual goals, shared responsibility for decision-making, and shared accountability. It seems unnecessary to say that no one should be forced to participate or collaborate in a program; however, forced participation is often experienced within school systems. In order for collaboration to be successful, each participant must *choose* to engage in a collaborative activity, not be expected or instructed to participate. If a professional is told about the expectation of collaboration in the job description or during the interview, then that person can decide whether or not to take the job. Choosing to participate in a collaborative effort gives each participant a feeling of empowerment and self-worth. If you plan to implement a collaborative program in your setting, keep in mind that it may take anywhere from 1 to 2 years for a person to become comfortable with the expectations and role responsibilities involved in collaboration (Friend & Cook, 1990).

Another seemingly obvious component of collaboration is the establishment of mutual goals. Again, although this sounds overly simplistic as a "fix" for barred collaboration, not having mutual goals is often a source of conflict among professionals trying to collaborate. This contention is mainly due to miscommunication among participants, especially if the participants represent different professions and different areas of expertise. It is recommended that collaborators discuss in clear, concrete terms what the collaborative program or situation is to include. It is also recommended that collaborators confirm with administrators that the agreed upon goals of collaboration will be permitted, given local, state, and federal mandates. Finally, collaborators should set specific times to assess the goals, and to determine if the goals have been met or if they need to be changed.

Along the lines stated earlier about professional parity, sharing responsibility for decision-making can eliminate some of the barriers to collaboration and smooth the way for collaborative relationships. All collaborators must abide by the concept that all participants are equal; therefore, each person has equal responsibility for all the decisions made during the collaboration. Also, shared responsibility for decision-making contributes to identifying mutual goals. If the decisions are not shared, the goals are not likely to be identified or met. It is recommended that specific time (before, during, or after school) be set aside to discuss decisions to be made.

Shared accountability for outcomes can also eliminate collaborative hurdles. That is, all participants in collaborative programs should be accountable for the outcomes—good or bad—of a program. Sharing accountability ensures that all participants maintain a sense of "ownership" in the program. For example, it is recommended that decision-making, which is part of determining program strengths and weaknesses, should be shared.

All participants should be expected to provide input regarding their insights of the program's outcomes. Every collaborator should be congratulated for good outcomes, and every collaborator should be held accountable for poor outcomes. Every collaborator should then be expected to provide suggestions for the source(s) of the problem and come up with solutions to those problems.

Getting to know administrators, policy makers, and school board members can help to eliminate some of the barriers to collaboration. Introducing yourself and subtly teaching these officials about the roles and responsibilities of school-based audiologists, speech-language pathologists, psychologists, and other professionals can help to build bridges for communication, and ultimately help serve students with hearing impairments. A good way to introduce yourself is simply by attending meetings, dinners, or banquets in which these officials are present. Using letters that are original (not form) and having many people (not just one or two) sign them is a way of introducing a group's efforts towards collaboration and joint program achievements. Providing examples of students' achievements or positive outcomes resulting from collaborative efforts is an excellent way of introducing the group's efforts and educating officials about those efforts. Officials should be educated about the scope of practice of the educational audiologist, IDEA regulations and updates, and the effects of hearing loss, background noise, and classroom acoustics. Finally, the value of multidisciplinary collaboration for each child with hearing loss, and the methods used for communication between other professionals and educational audiologists, should be shared with administrators and school officials.

Ultimately, the most difficult barriers to overcome with respect to collaboration are the lack of time and support needed for establishing and building collaborative relationships. Although it is easier said than done, making collaboration with other professionals a high priority in your work setting is really the most effective way of dealing with these obstacles. Scheduling very specific times each week and growing relationships with other professionals who also have established collaboration as a priority, will help to gain success in this area.

SPECIFIC EXAMPLES FOR FACILITATING COLLABORATION

Change is never accepted easily or without some controversy. However, developing collaborative programs, or delivering collaborative services, can often result in change. If your collaborative efforts will *change* a service delivery model or school-based program, Montgomery (1990, p. 78) recommends the following:

- Alert the principal well in advance, even if only a few students will be affected;
- Emphasize that this approach will increase productivity for the professionals and improve student outcomes;
- Communicate the essence of the collaborative effort in a one-page description, no longer;
- Ask for presentation time at "Parents' Night" or during teacher trainings or in-services. Tell them about the collaboration; and
- Write a short article for the school newspaper to publish.

When building classroom collaboration, Kooper (2003) suggests offering a brief in-service meeting at the beginning of the school year (breakfast meetings are usually well attended). At this meeting, select the appropriate professional(s) who will be responsible for performing the daily listening checks of the hearing aids and FM systems.

In addition, review ways to improve the acoustics in the classroom. The meeting should highlight the auditory challenges faced by students with hearing impairment. Providing a simulated aided and unaided hearing loss example may help to get classroom teachers "on board" when it comes to offering excellent service delivery. Kooper (2003) also recommends demonstrating the student's personal FM system by allowing the teachers to listen through the system, in the HA-only mode, then in the FM mode.

Although Kooper (2003) provided an example in which the audiologist supplies the majority of the information to a group providing services to students with hearing impairments, it is recommended that the school-based audiologist expect more from the other professionals at the meeting. The audiologist should construct meetings so that participants can provide input from their professional experience. Asking a classroom teacher for input concerning the use of a personal FM system would illustrate how the audiologist values the teacher's professional opinion and recognizes the importance of that teacher's experience in the classroom/with that specific child. Also, asking the teacher about her concerns for the student and/or the equipment would provide you with much-needed information. This would keep the situation from being too much like a superior-subordinate relationship, and the effort of collaboration would be more evident.

THE ETHICS OF COLLABORATION

Audiologists should also not forget the ethical issues associated with collaboration. According to Dettmer, Thurston, and Dyck (2005), there are five principles to ethical behavior of collaboration. These five principles include competencies of the service provider(s), protecting the welfare of students, maintaining confidentiality, responsibilities associated with making public statements (political correctness), and relationships with other consultants. The potential for ethical dilemmas exists in collaborative practice. For example, confidentiality must be maintained to develop a trusting relationship with colleagues and other professionals. The feasibility of collaboration may be impeded by lack of time and resources (as mentioned earlier in this chapter), and school-based

audiologists need to be aware of the possibility of these setting up a dilemma. The other two possibilities for ethical dilemmas include accountability and conflicting ideas among professionals. That is, working with other professionals who may not have the same priorities or service delivery expectations, or who may not agree with your way of thinking, can lend itself to concerns of ethics.

FURTHER LITERATURE ON THE TOPIC OF COLLABORATION

Educational audiology and the fields associated with Communication Sciences and Disorders are not the only groups of professionals who are interested in, or have had problems with, collaboration. There are many interesting studies and books written on the topic of collaboration, from different perspectives and using different models. If you find yourself in a position where you are expected to collaborate with other professionals, but are having problems setting up positive, effective relationships, it is recommended that you read more on this topic. A good place to begin your search would include the textbooks referenced throughout this chapter (Dettmer, Thurston, & Dyck, 2005; Friend & Cook, 2007) and issues of the *Journal of Educational and Psychological Consultation* and *Remedial and Special Education* focusing on school consultation and collaboration.

REFERENCES

Collaboration. (n.d.). In Merriam-Webster's online dictionary. Retrieved from http://

www.merriam-webster.com/dictionary/collaboration

Dettmer, P., Thurston, L., & Dyck, N. (2005). *Consultation, collaboration, and teamwork for students with special needs* (5th ed.). Boston, MA: Allyn & Bacon.

Friend, M., & Cook, L. (1990). Assessing the climate for collaboration. In W. A. Secord & E. H. Wigg (Eds.), *Best practices in school speech-language pathology* (pp. 67–73). San Antonio, TX: Psychological Corporation.

Friend, M., & Cook, L. (2007). *Interactions: Collaboration skills for school professionals* (5th ed.). Boston, MA: Allyn & Bacon.

Johnson, C. D., Benson, P. V., & Seaton, J. B. (1997). *Educational audiology handbook.* San Diego, CA: Singular.

Knickelbein, B. A., & Richburg, C. M. (in press). Special educators' perspectives on the services and benefits of educational audiologists. *Communication Disorders Quarterly.*

Kooper, R. (2003, September). Educational audiology: Building classroom collaboration. *ASHA Leader.*

Montgomery, J. (1990). Building administrative support for collaboration. In W. A. Secord & E. H. Wigg (Eds.), *Best practices in school speech-language pathology* (pp. 49–56). San Antonio, TX: Psychological Corporation.

Richburg, C. M. (2007). *Can educational audiologists assist teachers of children who are deaf or hard-of-hearing?* Oral presentation at the summer conference for the Educational Audiology Association, Reno, NV.

Richburg, C. M., & Knickelbein, B. A. (in press). Educational audiologists: Their access, benefit, and collaborative assistance to speech-language pathologists based in schools. *Language, Speech, and Hearing Services in Schools.*

Educational Audiology in the Real World

Charlean Raymond, MS
Educational Audiologist
Rio Rancho Public Schools
Rio Rancho, New Mexico

Everyone has to figure out what they want to be when they grow up. For some, it takes longer than others. I was fortunate that my life circumstances helped lead me to my profession as an educational audiologist. My story begins as a young child in the Los Angeles Public Schools with chronic ear infections, to the point I don't remember not having an ear infection. Every year I was screened by the audiologist, and every year I failed. Every year a note went home to my parents, and I am not so sure my parents or my teachers at the time understood the impact my hearing loss might have on my ability to learn. I now also see how my hearing loss impacted my social skills. By the time I got to high school, my hearing loss had progressed to a mild to moderate hearing loss, and I had become one of the best speech readers ever. I was working harder and harder to get information in the classroom. Because I continued to perform above average in my classes, no one was too concerned. I am thankful that a nurse at my high school followed through and gave my parents a referral to the House Ear Institute so that I could begin to get the help I needed. There I was seen by an audiologist who, against protocol, took the time to explain my hearing loss to me. I was then fit with a bone-conduction hearing aid at 16 years of age. I was so happy to hear that I didn't care about the fact that I had this headband and a cord coming down to a box (the receiver), which I wore in my bra (vanity has never been one of my downfalls). I was so thankful that I could hear what was happening in the classroom. I didn't have to nod my head pretending I knew what was being said and what was going on any more. So, it was in high school when I knew that I wanted to be able to help students like me get the help they needed. I knew how important it was to help parents and teachers understand the impact hearing loss has on learning in the classroom and developing social skills. I wanted to be a part of that. I wanted to be an educational audiologist.

When I was in graduate school at the University of New Mexico, my Professor asked me what kind of setting I wanted to work in when I graduated. That was easy; I knew exactly what I wanted to do. My desire was to work in a setting where I would be identifying children who, because of chronic ear infections, had experienced conductive hearing losses. I wanted to help parents understand the impact hearing loss would have on their child's communication development and education. I got my wish. I had the privilege of working 13 years for the Albuquerque Area Indian Health Board Otitis Media Project. We provided audiology services for seven different Indian Reservations in New Mexico and Southern Colorado. I learned quickly that my priorities were not necessarily the same as everyone else's. I wasn't going to change the world, but I could make a difference in the education of those children with hearing loss.

Move ahead 35 years from my first bone-conduction hearing aid. Now I am doing exactly what I wanted. I am the District Audiologist for the Rio Rancho Public School in

New Mexico serving 19 schools. I have the privilege of helping parents, educators, and students understand and accept hearing loss. It is exciting to see the advances that have been made in technology that give my students a greater access to instruction and communication with their hearing peers. I think I have the best job in the District because of the variety of situations and work that I get to do. No day is ever the same. One day I may evaluate some preschool children for our Child Find Program, and then the next day help write a transition plan for one of our Deaf and Hard of Hearing high school students. I truly am an educational audiologist; educating administrators about the need for classroom amplification systems, educating teachers about how to use their students' equipment in the classroom, and working with students who are struggling daily with their hearing loss. I do miss having other audiologist's in my office. I sometimes feel like the Lone Ranger, which is why I am always thankful whenever I have the opportunity to network with other educational audiologists.

11

School-Based Audiology in Schools for the Deaf

Kathryn Tonkovich, Cynthia M. Richburg, and
Donna F. Smiley

OBJECTIVES

By the end of this chapter, the reader will be able to:

1. Identify the roles, knowledge, and skills an audiologist based in a school for the deaf must possess.
2. Identify how audiological services are provided to children in schools for the deaf.
3. Identify how early identification and advances in technology have impacted deaf education.
4. Identify how the programs in schools for the deaf differ from regular schools.

INTRODUCTION

The landscape of Deaf Education has changed considerably over the past century. Parents are now presented with a variety of communication options within the first months of their child's life, or as soon as a hearing loss is identified. Early Intervention (EI) programs (for children ages birth to 3 years) employ specialists who assist parents in creating communication-rich environments for their children. Creating these rich environments ensures that children are ready to begin school with communication systems intact, rather than having them start from scratch upon entering the classroom. Advances in cochlear implant and hearing aid technology provide access to spoken language from infancy, and provisions within Federal law ensure that children have access to educational curricula needed to be successful in school and beyond. These advances in technology have provided children with hearing loss better quality and earlier access to a world of sound. Therefore, traditional state-supported segregated schools for the deaf may find they have to re-think and re-vamp their models of service delivery.

Working as an audiologist in a school for the deaf has its own unique challenges and rewards. The typical skill-set for this audiologist, like other school-based audiologists, must be expanded beyond simply performing evaluations and providing recommendations. That is, an audiologist who works in this type of setting not only needs to have the core skills for audiological assessment and management, but might also need to demonstrate proficiency in American Sign Language (ASL) or be familiar with the tenets of an auditory-oral philosophy, which stresses more of a listening and spoken language option.

Some schools for the deaf utilize ASL, some use total communication, and others use listening and spoken language options. It should be stressed that communication methodologies and educational philosophies vary from school to school, and program to program. Families who choose to enroll their children in a "deaf school" may find that there has been a movement from sign language to auditory-oral communication at their state school for the deaf, whereas a school in a neighboring state may emphasize ASL as the primary language for their students. Regardless of the setting and/or placement options chosen, individualization within that setting must occur in order for a child's hearing, educational, and social needs to be met (Chaffo, 2008).

This chapter discusses some program options not available in regular education school systems, and introduces vocabulary terms needed to navigate the world of deaf education. The audiologist employed in a school for the deaf must be knowledgeable about aspects of Deaf Culture in order to be sensitive to the desires and communication needs of the family of a child who is deaf. Likewise, the audiologist employed in a school utilizing an auditory-oral or auditory-verbal approach to communication should be familiar with aural habilitation for a variety of age groups, as well as listening skills and communication skills hierarchies. No two audiologists employed in schools for the deaf will have exactly the same experience, which is also true for school-based audiologists employed in regular education settings.

Deaf Versus deaf

Although various terms are used to refer to people with sensorineural hearing loss (SNHL), the most common term used by the lay public is deaf (with a lowercase "d"). The term Deaf (with an uppercase "D") defines a cultural group of people united by distinct traditions and strengths arising from the use of sign language as a communication form. Most people who communicate primarily by sign language have congenital SNHL, and many are the children of Deaf parents. People who acquire SNHL in later childhood, or adulthood, generally continue to use oral communication, and few see themselves as members of the Deaf community.

A BRIEF HISTORY OF DEAF SCHOOLS IN AMERICA

An audiologist working at a school for the deaf should be familiar with deaf education, past and present. From an historical perspective, the education of deaf students in America is rooted in emotional and political controversy, stemming from clashes between two main camps; the "manualists," who use sign language to communicate, and the "oralists," who use spoken language to communicate (Cerney, 2007).

Schools Using Manual Communication

The oldest existing school for the deaf in America, the American School for the Deaf, opened in 1817 in Hartford, Connecticut and was founded by Thomas Hopkins Gallaudet and Laurent Clerc. The school became the first recipient of state aid to education in America in 1819. Instruction in this school at that time was delivered in sign language. The school's current educational and communication philosophy is Total Communication.

In 1864 the Columbia Institution for the Deaf at Washington, DC was established. The school is now called Gallaudet University, and it is the only liberal arts college for the deaf in the world. However, many universities and institutions currently offer college and postgraduate degrees to students who are deaf or hard of hearing.

Schools Using Oral Communication

In 1869, the Horace Mann School was established in Boston and became the first public day school for deaf students. In 1906, Junior High School No. 47 was founded in New York City and became the largest day school in the country. Both of these schools emphasized an oral education approach (Delaney, 2004). Another prominent oral school was the Clarke School for the Deaf in Northampton, Massachusetts. The Clarke School, established in 1867, still exists and has been expanded to include multiple campuses across the country. In 2010, the Clarke School changed its name to "Clarke Schools for Hearing and Speech," to reflect their mission to teach children to listen and speak using current advances in technology (http://www.clarkeschools.org/about/welcome).

The education of children who are deaf or hard of hearing changed dramatically within the last century, both in population size and in school curriculum. By 1867, 24 state residential schools for the deaf had been established (Delaney, 2004). From 1850 to 1950, enrollment in residential schools for the deaf rose from 1,100 to over 20,000 students. A rubella epidemic in the 1960s caused this number to triple by the early 1970s. At that time, more than one third of children who were deaf attended residential schools, with another third attending special school programs (Marschark, 2007).

More recently, enrollment at residential schools has decreased, particularly at the elementary grade level (Marschark, 2007). The 2003 Annual Survey of Deaf and Hard of Hearing Children and Youth, conducted by the Gallaudet Research Institute (GRI), found that, out of 40,000 children who are deaf or hard of hearing in the United States, 27% of the children attended a special school or center, and 46% were fully mainstreamed in regular public schools (GRI, 2003). The remaining numbers of students were either in self-contained classrooms, resource classrooms, home schools, or "other" settings. Furthermore, data released from the United States Office of Special Education Programs in 2004 showed that, of the students ages 6 to 21 years who are served under IDEA due to hearing loss, over 85% attended regular public schools for at least part of the school day (Marschark, 2007).

The significant changes that have occurred since 1970 are mostly the result of state and federal laws that mandate children who qualify for special education be educated in the "least restrictive environment." Additionally, these changes are a result of the emergence of *mainstreaming* and *inclusion* environments. The focus on the education of children who are deaf or hard of hearing has shifted away from a vocational focus to a more academic one. Some schools for the deaf have been closed, due to decreased enrollment, the advent of the rubella vaccination, greater access to technology, and the increase in popularity of mainstream settings (Marschark, 2007).

THE ROLES OF AUDIOLOGISTS BASED IN SCHOOLS FOR THE DEAF

The roles of an audiologist based in a school for the deaf are no different than the roles described in Chapter 4; however, some roles may be added, due to the population of children served in a school for the deaf. For example, audiologists based in schools for the deaf may also have to:

■ Perform audiological evaluations for children of any age (0–21 years);

if early intervention services are provided through the school for the deaf, this could include children from birth to 3 years of age;

■ Counsel parents who are themselves deaf about their child's hearing loss and technology options;

■ Possess an ability to perform audiological assessments for special populations (multisensory impaired, for example);

■ Have a familiarity with deaf-blindness and its educational impact;

■ Have proficiency in ASL, as well as familiarity with other communication methodologies;

■ Be familiar with current philosophies and terminologies that are unique to the deaf school environment (e.g., bimodal bilingualism);

■ Provide in-service trainings to staff, including staff who are themselves deaf or hard of hearing;

■ Be prepared to travel to students who live in outlying areas, if the school for the deaf provides statewide services to any student with a sensory impairment;

■ Establish hearing assessment clinics to provide audiological services to students in outlying areas; and

■ Program and fit loaner hearing aids and HAT; maintain a loaner hearing aid bank for the school.

Therefore, audiologists based in schools for the deaf must possess the same skills and perform the same roles as audiologists based in regular education, public school facilities. However, they also must acquire specialized knowledge pertaining to their particular program and possess unique skills to perform their jobs effectively.

PRIVATE PROGRAMS VERSUS PUBLIC PROGRAMS FOR THE DEAF AND HARD OF HEARING

As with any school, there are private and public options for parents of children with hearing loss. Private schools typically charge tuition and are often funded by donations from private sources. Publicly funded schools receive funding from the state and federal government, in addition to local tax dollars. Tuition for private schools is paid out of pocket by parents (Cheffo, 2008). Publicly funded programs are free for students to attend; however, they must qualify for services based on special education criteria.

Private oral schools, called OPTION schools, for children with hearing loss are located in various cities across the country. These programs include comprehensive audiologic management within their programs because ensuring access to technology is a crucial component of learning spoken language. Students in these programs are exposed to intensive speech and language early in their preschool years, and these intense services may be extended through elementary grades to establish reading skills (Cheffo, 2008).

RESIDENTIAL PROGRAMS IN SCHOOLS FOR THE DEAF

For some students, a *residential* program at a school for the deaf is the only educational option in which the child can receive direct instruction in the family's chosen communication option. In a residential program, the student attends school during the week and resides in dormitories on campus, returning home on the weekends, if possible. State schools that exclusively educate students who are deaf and hard of hearing traditionally have been residential schools. Students who live in the immediate area have been allowed to commute to the school as day students (Cerney, 2007). This option is still available in many states and may be chosen when the student resides in an area that lacks the type of educational environment needed (Maxon & Brackett, 1992).

A residential program can provide the structure and supportive atmosphere a student needs to be more successful. One of the benefits of a residential placement is a nurturing, protective environment and an affiliation with other students and adults who are hard of hearing or deaf (Cheffo, 2008). Residential students attend classes with other students who are deaf or hard of hearing and are able to benefit from the socialization process of interacting with the same students after hours. One of the challenges of residential placement is, however, that students have to be away from family at least during the week.

OUTREACH PROGRAMS AT SCHOOLS FOR THE DEAF

Outreach is the informal term used to describe services to students who may live great distances from self-contained classes or residential programs. Publically funded state schools for the deaf may provide services to students across an entire state, and these services may be provided by an itinerant teacher or an educational consultant. These consultants provide services to students who are mainstreamed in their neighborhood districts, and these services may include: (1) working individually with students to address speech, language, and/or listening goals as outlined by the student's IEP; (2) collaborating with the classroom teacher, staff, and parents; and (3) providing technical assistance to students with classroom soundfield or personal FM systems.

The audiologist may be expected to travel to provide audiologic management to students in outreach areas. For example, in the state of Utah, audiological services are offered statewide by the Utah School for the Deaf and Blind. The audiologists collaborate with the itinerant teachers of the deaf and with specialists from early intervention agencies to perform follow-up audiological testing and provide amplification recommendations and fittings in areas where there is limited access to outside audiological services.

BILINGUAL PROGRAMS IN SCHOOLS FOR THE DEAF

Programs that offer instruction in both ASL and English were once called "bilingual-bicultural" programs, or "Bi-Bi" programs. Some programs have since become "ASL-English Bilingual" programs. Typically, in an ASL-English Bilingual program, American Sign Language and English are considered to be separate languages of equal importance and value. These programs advocate the initial use of ASL to provide early access to language. This use of ASL is followed by a combination of ASL and written English to promote literacy, followed by a combination of ASL, written English, and spoken language (Marschark, 2007). An audiologist work-

ing in a school for the deaf may need to be familiar with these and other communication methodologies depending on their school's philosophy and the communication options provided for students. Petitto and colleagues (Petitto, Katerelos, Levy, Guana, & Ferraro, 2001; Pettito & Kovelman, 2003) and Grosjean (2008) provide more information on this subject.

DUAL-SENSORY IMPAIRMENT (DEAF-BLINDNESS) IN SCHOOLS FOR THE DEAF

Children who are deaf-blind attending schools for the deaf typically have more severe disabilities than children who have only deafness or only blindness. The parents of these children have chosen these deaf-blind schools for cultural or communication reasons (Cheffo, 2008). Many of the children who attend these programs require a more restrictive environment and additional educational support, such as intervenors for deaf-blind persons. The audiologist working in this setting will also need to be familiar with blindness, low vision, and the impact of multisensory impairment in the educational setting.

DIFFERING PERSPECTIVES ON EDUCATION FOR STUDENTS WHO ARE DEAF OR HARD OF HEARING

A difference in perspectives exists in the arena of deafness/Deafness. Audiologists tend to see deafness from the "medical" or "pathological" model, whereas some individuals who are Deaf view deafness from the "cultural" model. Audiologists are trained to diagnose and treat deafness and, as a result, some audiologists view deafness as a disability.

The cultural model, however, looks at embracing deafness and diminishing the idea of deafness as a disability. The cultural model emphasizes sign language as the natural language of people with hearing loss. Therefore, some audiologists who work in schools for the deaf that utilize the ASL or Bi-Bi methodology struggle to overcome what might be considered a conflict of interest. That is, they are the hearing health care professional in a program that might not consider the ability to hear a priority. However, with the influx of more students with cochlear implants, this attitude is beginning to change.

CHANGES AND CHALLENGES IN EDUCATION OF THE DEAF

Many changes have occurred in the traditional service delivery provided by schools for the deaf. In recent years, schools for the deaf that have traditionally used sign language have developed equally successful auditory-oral programs for their students. In fact, some state-supported schools for the deaf have created auditory-oral infant and preschool programs in response to the implementation of Early Hearing Detection and Intervention (EHDI) programs. Some schools now provide integrative models whereby typical peers attend classes at the school for the deaf (also called *reverse mainstreaming*), and students who are deaf or hard of hearing attend regular schools for part of the day (Cheffo, 2008).

With changes come challenges. Some challenges that schools for the deaf are currently encountering include the necessity of providing staff with new skills to meet the needs of students who have had access to better technology (e.g., cochlear implants) earlier in their lives. Additionally, becoming a statewide resource center on deafness (rather than just a school for the deaf) could be the best way for these schools to meet the different demands being placed on them. Traditional schools for the deaf need to continue to refine their methods for delivering services in order to keep up with current technology, philosophies, and parent choice options.

As with all aspects of today's economy, many schools for the deaf have funding challenges that may affect their capacity to function as they have in the past. Several state-supported schools for the deaf have been closed due to budgetary shortfalls. Along the same lines, some universities are closing their deaf education programs and are no longer offering degrees in that specialty area, due to funding issues in higher education. This is affecting, and will continue to affect, administrators' ability to hire certified teachers of the deaf to teach in schools for the deaf. Finding ways to evolve with the times while maintaining fiscal responsibility could be the only way some schools for the deaf will be able to keep their doors open.

CONCLUSION

An audiologist who works within a school for the deaf will have a unique opportunity to meet and work with children of all ages, with varying backgrounds, and varying degrees and etiologies of hearing loss. This audiologist will work with children who can communicate in different ways and who have the potential to achieve success, regardless of their educational program and communication methodology. The type of audiological services provided by the audiologist in a school for the deaf will depend on the school setting and the services outlined in a child's IEP.

The audiologist at a school for the deaf is typically responsible for providing routine diagnostic assessments, technological troubleshooting and support, and may also fit and program hearing aids, cochlear implants, and personal FM systems. A working knowledge of communication methodologies, educational placement settings, and special education law will positively boost the audiologist's skill set and make him or her a crucial member of the IEP team.

REFERENCES

Cerney, J. (2007). *Deaf education in America: Voices of children from inclusion settings.* Washington, DC: Gallaudet University Press.

Cheffo, S. (2008). Educational placement options for school-aged children with hearing loss. In J. Madell & C. Flexer (Eds.), *Pediatric audiology, diagnosis, technology, and management* (pp. 250–261). New York, NY: Thieme.

Delaney, M. (2004).The history of teacher education for the deaf in the United States. In R. K. Rittenhouse (Ed.), *Deaf education at the dawn of the 21st century: Old challenges, new directions* (p. 2). Hillsboro, OR: Butte Publications.

Gallaudet Research Institute. (2003). *Regional and national summary report of data from the 2002-2003 Annual Survey of Deaf and Hard of Hearing Children and Youth.* Washington, DC: GRI Gallaudet University.

Grosjean, F. (2008). The bilingualism and biculturalism of the deaf. *Studying bilinguals* (pp. 221–240). Oxford, UK: Oxford University Press.

Marschark, M. (2007). *Raising and educating a deaf child: A comprehensive guide to the choices, controversies, and decisions faced by parents and educators* (2nd ed.). New York, NY: Oxford University Press.

Maxon, A., & Brackett, D. (1992). *The hearing impaired child: Infancy through high-school years.* Boston, MA: Andover Medical Publishers.

Petitto, L. A., Katerelos, M., Levy, B., Gauna, K., & Ferraro, V. (2001). Bilingual signed and spoken language acquisition from birth: Implications for mechanisms underlying bilingual language acquisition. *Journal of Child Language, 28*(2), 1–44.

Petitto, L. A., & Kovelman, I. (2003). The bilingual paradox: How signing-speaking bilingual children help us to resolve it and teach us about the brain's mechanisms underlying all language acquisition. *Learning Languages, 8*(3), 5–18.

Educational Audiology in the Real World

Susan J. Brannen, AuD
Chair, Department of Audiology
Monroe 2 Board of Cooperative Educational Services (BOCES)
Spencerport, New York

Audiology was not my first career, but working in the schools was my first choice. Since finishing my Master's degree, I knew that working with children in an educational setting was a matched set. I came to audiology via a degree in English literature and Russian language. Working at a school for the blind and deaf/blind introduced me to speech-language pathology and audiology. It was only a matter of a few years before I found myself licensed and credentialed and working at a school for the Deaf. From there, I worked at the National Technical Institute for the Deaf at Rochester Institute of Technology, and although these were older students, it was still an educational facility. Then 26 years ago the opportunity to start a program for public schools was offered. I have since worked at a Board of Cooperative Educational Services (BOCES), a collaborative that provides services to 13 different school districts. Initially, I provided services from birth to 21 years, more recently just 3 to 21 years. I see students from preschool classrooms designed for children 3 to 5 years old with developmental disabilities, from classrooms for school-age children with a variety of disabilities, and from our district-based general education classrooms for children with hearing loss, a central auditory processing delay, or other auditory-type deficit.

The program has evolved, and now our working environment allows us to practice a full range of audiological services. We have full diagnostic facilities to include two channel audiometers, middle ear analyzers, OAEs, ABRs, video-otoscopy, and real-ear and verification instrumentation for fitting of FM hearing assistive technology and hearing aids. It started as just me, and three other audiologists and an audiometric technician have joined me. Collectively we follow 400 to 500 children directly and manage a hearing screening program for another 1000 children.

I see all of the students on my caseload with their parents at these facilities for purposes of evaluation. I team with all of the teachers, related service providers, and administrators within the schools themselves. I also have open communication with our community audiologists who are dispensing hearing aids or fitting cochlear implants. As follow-up to the evaluation, I am able to go out to the student's school and provide in-service training to the classroom team to facilitate a better understanding of the student with hearing loss or an auditory processing delay. I am also able to engage the student's peers, allowing them the opportunity to "experience" a hearing loss or listen through a hearing aid or FM hearing assistive technology device.

Our facilities are on the campus where the career and technical education classes are held. Shortly after receiving my AuD degree and updating my skills in industrial audiometry, I offered a hearing loss conservation/prevention program to our Career and Technical Education Center to educate and screen the students within these programs. Currently, we are in 10 different vocational areas seeing more than 700 high school students enrolled in these technical classes. Additionally, using the Dangerous Decibel initiative and some of their interactive materials, we offer our districts this program for their 5th through 7th graders. Personally, I have been fortunate to be involved professionally at the state and national levels. This continued networking with colleagues has enriched the audiology program here at BOCES, as well as provided much support and information to me.

Where else could I do all of this? I work collaboratively with parents, speech-language pathologists, teachers of the deaf and hard of hearing, classroom teachers, school psychologists, other related services providers (as required), and administrators. This is done in the context of the student's academic needs and expectations based on the curriculum. It could take the shape of designing an auditory training program, speechreading program, or remedial program for auditory processing deficits. It could be within the classroom and with the student's peers. I attend IEP meetings where goals are set and accommodations are determined. I conduct comprehensive audiological evaluations, as well as full batteries of tests to determine an auditory processing delay. I verify personal amplification and fit students with FM hearing assistive technology. I consult with districts that are prepared to install soundfield systems, taking noise and reverberation measurements to be sure that this type of amplification system is appropriate, as well as compatible, with personal systems. I work directly with the students to help them better acclimate to their hearing loss and amplification and to learn to advocate for their own needs. I follow them from preschool through high school. I have knowledge of legislation and regulations to better assist everyone in meeting the needs of the student. I go into vocational education classrooms and provide instruction/activities on the impact of noise, not only in their vocational choice, but in their personal lives.

I have made two choices: to be an audiologist and to work in the schools. What could be better?

12

Cochlear Implants in the Classroom

Erin C. Schafer and Jace Wolfe

OBJECTIVES

After reading this chapter, the reader should be able to:

1. Describe the separate and collaborative roles and responsibilities of the school-based audiologist and cochlear implant audiologist for children with cochlear implants.
2. Provide information on troubleshooting external sound processors that may be conducted in the school settings.
3. Recommend the most appropriate types of frequency modulated (FM) systems for children with cochlear implants and review troubleshooting techniques for those devices.

INTRODUCTION

Almost all educational audiologists serve children who use cochlear implants. These children range in age from 3 to 21 years and use unilateral implants, bilateral implants, or an implant in combination with a hearing aid on the non-implanted ear (bimodal stimulation). Cochlear implants are manufactured and distributed by three corporations in the United States: Advanced Bionics, Cochlear, and MED-EL. These manufacturers release new implants and sound processors every few years. An overview of cochlear implant sound processors is provided in Table 12–1. If the child wears a hearing aid on the unimplanted ear, the manufacturer of that aid varies, and the aid may be fit by a clinical audiologist rather than the cochlear implant audiologist.

Children with cochlear implants are educated in mainstream, self-contained, or

Table 12–1. Contemporary and Previous Generation Cochlear Implant Sound Processors

Advanced Bionics	Cochlear Corporation	MED-EL
Harmony: BTE	CP810: BTE	OPUS 2: BTE
Auria: BTE	Freedom: BTE or body worn	OPUS 1: BTE
CII and Platinum: BTE	ESPrit3G: BTE	TEMPO+: BTE
Platinum Series Sound Processor (PSP): body worn	SPrint: body worn	CIS PRO+: body worn

inclusion-based classrooms (i.e., educated within a classroom of normal-hearing students), whereas some will be taught in a combination of these educational models. No matter which model is deemed most appropriate by the child's management committee, the child is guaranteed the opportunity to learn in the least restrictive environment (LRE) according to the federal laws discussed in Chapter 1 (Special Education Law Library, 2004). Unfortunately, the least restrictive environment (LRE) for most children with cochlear implants, the typical general education classroom, is plagued with poor acoustics, inappropriate unoccupied noise levels, and unavoidable distance from the teacher (Knecht, Nelson, Whitelaw, & Feth, 2002; see Chapter 2 for a review).

As a result of the poor acoustic environment seen in classrooms, careful management of children with cochlear implants is absolutely imperative for academic success. This need for support and management is evident in the child's degraded speech understanding in any environment with noise and reverberation (Schafer & Thibodeau, 2003, 2006; Schafer & Wolfe, 2008). For example, speech-recognition scores of children may decrease by an average of 35% when listening in a noisy versus quiet listening condition (Schafer & Thibodeau, 2003). Therefore,

management of the poor signal-to-noise ratio with hearing assistance technology (HAT; e.g., frequency modulated [FM] system) is of utmost importance for children with cochlear implants. Children who are good candidates, and implanted at an early age, will often have good speech perception performance in ideal listening situations (i.e., quiet). Because of this good performance, which is often evident in the classroom, audiologists often have to remind school personnel that these children still have an impaired auditory system and severe-to-profound sensorineural hearing loss. The success of a child with a cochlear implant in a school environment will depend heavily on cooperation between school-based and cochlear implant audiologists to ensure consistently functioning external cochlear implant equipment.

ROLES OF THE COCHLEAR IMPLANT VERSUS EDUCATIONAL AUDIOLOGISTS

Occasionally, a cochlear implant team will include an educational consultant to facilitate communication between a cochlear implant team and school personnel.

These consultants are often audiologists, speech-language pathologists, or social workers. Despite the presence of an educational consultant, it is also imperative for the child's primary cochlear implant audiologist and educational audiologist to communicate directly about the child's performance, recommended equipment settings, changes in programming (i.e., mapping), processor programming for use with an FM system, and troubleshooting techniques. This communication is particularly important for young children who may not be able to report equipment problems or changes in hearing status with the implant. To aid in this communication, there is a published Team Tracking Form to help audiologists, therapists, and teachers assimilate information as they work together to serve children with cochlear implants (http://www.moogcen ter.org/Bookstorenbspnbspnbspnbspn bsp/tabid/149/Default.aspx; The Moog Center for Deaf Education, n.d.). The specific and combined roles of the two audiologists are described in the following paragraphs and outlined in Table 12–2.

Roles of the Cochlear Implant Audiologist

Following implantation, the cochlear implant audiologist conducts regular audiological assessments and programming (i.e., mapping) of the cochlear implant sound processor. Optimization of the child's program is crucial for audibility of low-level sounds, comfort of high-level sounds, clarity of speech and environmental signals, and provision of a range of loudness experiences (i.e., soft to loud).

Table 12–2. Roles of the Cochlear Implant and Educational Audiologist

Cochlear Implant Audiologist	Educational Audiologist
• Regular training & continuing education on programming	• Monitor function of sound processor
• Facilitate communication among cochlear-implant team	• Fit and monitor FM systems
• Conduct implant-activation appointment	• Attend IEP meetings
• Refer patient to LSLS	• In-service training for school personnel
• Conduct postactivation programming and audiological testing appointments (every 3–6 months):	• Recommend classroom modifications
– Track listening progress	• Update testing: auditory impairment intelligibility
– Fine-tune programming	• Instruct others on how to perform daily listening checks
– Explain care and use of the device	• Facilitate communication among school personnel, parents, and the cochlear implant team
– Recommend follow-up appointments	• Collaborate with the cochlear implant audiologist for special programming of the sound processor
• Collaborate with educational audiologist to provide necessary programming for FM system & train on device troubleshooting	• Train school personnel on connecting, charging, and troubleshooting minor problems with the FM system

Cochlear implant audiologists are highly specialized and trained for working with these devices due to their experience with regular programming of cochlear implants, attendance at manufacturer training sessions, and sometimes special certification (i.e., American Board of Audiology). As a result, only the cochlear implant audiologist should program the cochlear implant.

Although the timing of appointments varies across implant centers, during the first year of implant use, children are typically seen for a 2-day activation session and follow-up sessions at 1 week, 1 month, 3 months, and 6 months. If the child is not already receiving audition-based therapy, the audiologist should refer the child and family to a Listening and Spoken Language Specialist (LSLS) or a speech-language pathologist to seek habilitation or rehabilitation to support speech and language development. After these initial appointments, children are usually seen every 3 to 6 months. During each session, the audiologist tracks the child's listening progress, fine-tunes programming, provides information about the care and use of the device, and recommends follow-up appointments. Prior to and following implantation, the audiologist facilitates communication among the cochlear implant team members, family, and school personnel.

Roles of the Educational Audiologist for Children with Cochlear Implants

The needs and independence of a child with a cochlear implant at school will vary depending on his or her age and success in using the cochlear implant. This success is highly correlated with a host of factors, including implantation at an earlier age, having a shorter duration of deafness, and the lack of additional disabilities. Unfortunately, up to 40% of these children will have additional disabilities or conditions other than hearing loss (Gallaudet Research Institute, 2008). As a result, children who are younger, those who are newly implanted, and those with additional disabilities will likely require more assistance from an educational audiologist than will older children who have several years of implant experience.

Educational audiologists provide a variety of services for children with cochlear implants, including monitoring of sound processor function, fitting and monitoring of FM systems, attendance and advocacy at school meetings, conducting professional development training for school personnel, recommending classroom modifications (i.e., preferential seating, acoustical modifications, etc.), providing updated testing and paperwork for the auditory impairment eligibility, and facilitating communication among school personnel, parents, and the cochlear implant team regarding the child's needs and progress. The primary role of the educational audiologist in working with children using cochlear implants is monitoring the function of the cochlear implant sound processor and fitting and monitoring FM systems. If a child is not able to indicate sound processor malfunction, the audiologist needs to instruct school personnel about procedures for performing daily listening checks (see Troubleshooting section that follows). In addition, most children with cochlear implants will require an FM system to achieve optimal speech recognition in the typically noisy and reverberant school classroom. When coupling to a personal FM system, the child's sound processor may require special programming; therefore, collaboration with the cochlear implant audiologist is essential. School personnel will also need to be trained on connecting, charging, and troubleshooting minor problems with the FM system.

TROUBLESHOOTING THE COCHLEAR IMPLANT SOUND PROCESSOR

There are several simple and efficient techniques to verify the functioning of a child's sound processor at school. The audiologist should equip school personnel with a working knowledge of basic troubleshooting skills; more advanced troubleshooting should be the responsibility of the educational audiologist.

At least two people at the child's school should be trained on the general use and function of the sound processor. In our experience, the best professionals for this role include the classroom or special education teacher, school-based speech-language pathologist, or school nurse. The educational audiologist should provide an in-service training for these professionals and include the parent and child, when appropriate. It is beneficial to provide handouts with labeled diagrams of the sound processor components, buttons, and functions, as well as any external troubleshooting equipment (e.g., signal check wand). These types of diagrams can usually be found on the cochlear implant manufacturer's Web site along with good resources for school personnel (Table 12–3 provides some excellent resources). Once the professional is familiar with the general function of the implant, the audiologist should review ways to verify sound processor functioning (Table 12–4).

Table 12–3. Online Cochlear Implant Resources for School Personnel

Manufacturer	Description	Web Site
Advanced Bionics Corporation	Tools for Schools. Includes product information, educational support, and rehabilitation resources.	http://www.advancedbionics.com/Support_Center/Educational_Support/Tools_for_Schools.cfm?langid=1
Cochlear Corporation	Educator's Guide to Cochlear Implants. Information regarding classroom preparation, children's needs at school, basic troubleshooting, accessories, and, hearing assistance technology.	http://www.cochlearamericas.com/Support/2156.asp
MED-EL	BRIDGE to better communication. Includes a product catalog of rehabilitation tools, loudness scale charts, and interactive listening activities.	http://www.medel.at/english/50_Rehabilitation/index.php?navid=54
Alexander Graham Bell Association for the Deaf and Hard of Hearing	A basic overview of the function of cochlear implants.	http://www.agbell.org/DesktopDefault.aspx?p=Cochlear_Implants

Table 12–4. Ways to Verify Cochlear Implant Sound Processor Functioning at School

Technique	Procedure	Processor
• Behavioral listening check	• Child repeats auditory-only sounds or words	• Any sound processor
• Transmission signal indicator/lights on • Processor or Remote	• Check processor LCD display or lights	• ABC: Auria, Harmony • CC: Freedom, CP810 • ME: Opus 1, Opus 2
• Monitor/ Mic test earphones or amplifier speaker	• Plug into processor to listen to microphone output	• ABC: Auria, Harmony • CC: Freedom, CP810
• Signal check	• Hold the wand over transmitting coil while processor on child's head	• CC: Freedom, CP810

A behavioral listening check may be performed to ensure adequate audibility and detection for sounds across the speech frequency range using the Ling Six-Sound Test (/ah/, /oo/, /ee/, /s/, /sh/, and /m/; Ling, 1976, 1989). These six phonemes encompass the typical range of speech frequencies, and after a period of implant use, children should be able to detect or repeat them when spoken at a conversational level at a distance of approximately 15 feet. A behavioral listening check may also be performed using simple words (e.g., spondees) or commands (e.g., touch your nose).

Indicator lights and codes are available on many sound processors to help the audiologist, parent, and school personnel identify problems. The LED lights may be disabled or enabled in the programming software to indicate several different parameters or problems (e.g., the selected program, a weak battery, the external processor is not transmitting a signal to the internal device, etc.). Because the exact function of the indicator light varies with each manufacturer, the educational audiologist should consult the processor's user manual for specific information regarding the function of the indicator light.

For some sound processors, listening earphones can be connected to the sound processor to monitor the signal from the sound processor microphone. When this is possible, the audiologist should ensure that the child's parents or educators evaluate the integrity of the signal from the sound processor microphone on a regular basis (i.e., ideally, on a daily basis). It is important to keep in mind that the signal from the monitoring earphones represents the signal from the sound processor microphone and, therefore, does not indicate exactly what the child perceives (i.e., does not represent the processed signal). With that in mind, the monitoring earphone check is probably best described as an assessment of the function of the sound processor microphone, or FM receiver, if the earphones can also detect the signal from an FM receiver.

All manufacturers provide additional tools to evaluate the status and integrity of the cochlear implant sound processor. For instance, Cochlear and Advanced Bionics use signal wands to assess whether a radio frequency (RF) signal is being transmitted from the transmitting cable, MED-EL uses Speech Processor Test Devices to detect the most common sound processor faults, and Cochlear uses a "screening check" via remote control to make certain that the sound processor is fully functional.

Educational audiologists should be encouraged to use the aforementioned troubleshooting/evaluation tools to assess the function of a child's cochlear implant sound processor. Ideally, the educational audiologist would visually inspect the external hardware with particular attention to the integrity of the cables, the microphones, and the battery contacts. In many cases, the transmitting cables are the most susceptible component to failure. Also, any place in which two or more parts of the sound processor connect to one another should be evaluated. When a faulty component must be replaced, the educational audiologist will need to contact the parent and the cochlear implant audiologist. Ideally, the educational audiologist would have extra cables and replacement equipment, but realistically, this is often not possible given budget constraints and the wide variety of sound processors used by children in the schools. When possible, listening earphones should be used to evaluate the integrity of the sound processor microphone. Furthermore, the school-based audiologist should be familiar with the use of specialized troubleshooting tools offered by each manufacturer. These checks would preferably take place on a daily basis, but at the very least, should be performed on a weekly basis.

RECOMMENDING AND TROUBLESHOOTING FM SYSTEMS FOR CHILDREN WITH COCHLEAR IMPLANTS

Children with cochlear implants may use the same FM transmitters as those used by children with hearing aids, and over the past few years, the development of miniaturized FM receivers and improved sound processor audio-input capabilities has greatly simplified the coupling of FM receivers to cochlear implants. As shown in Figure 12–1, several personal FM receivers are designed for use with cochlear implants and include receivers that are: (1) body worn; (2) dedicated, where the receiver is compatible with one case design; and (3) universal, which can be connected to most sound processors regardless of manufacturer. Body-worn receivers may be more cumbersome because they must be connected with impedance-matched cords or cables or with a neck-loop. A neckloop may only be used when the user has a telecoil in his or her sound processor, but telecoils are built into all contemporary processors. At this time, there is only one dedicated receiver, the Phonak Freedom MicroLink, which is shown in Figure 12–1. Universal receivers are miniaturized and cost effective because, with the correct adaptor, they can be coupled to most cochlear implant sound processors and hearing aids.

When a child is using a cochlear implant and an FM system, it is imperative that audibility is maintained for signals from the FM system and the environment (e.g., speech from classmates). All contemporary sound processors allow for mixing of these two signals, and many of the current FM receivers are programmable to allow for adjustments to the FM gain or strength of the signal delivered from the receiver to the implant sound processor.

Research to Support Personal FM Systems for Children with Cochlear Implants

According to previous research, personal body-worn (i.e., electrical coupling with

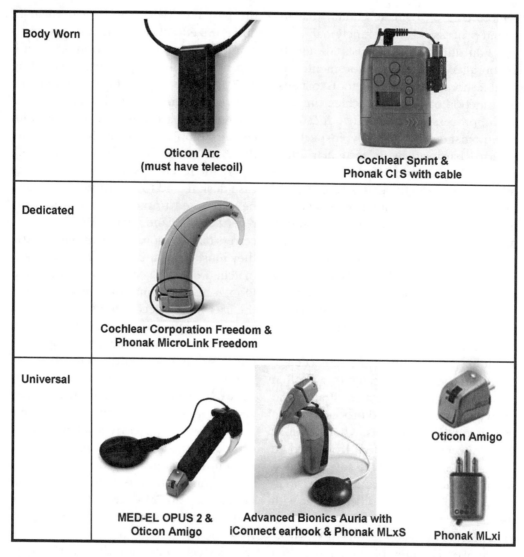

Body Worn	Oticon Arc (must have telecoil)	Cochlear Sprint & Phonak CI S with cable
Dedicated	Cochlear Corporation Freedom & Phonak MicroLink Freedom	
Universal	MED-EL OPUS 2 & Oticon Amigo Advanced Bionics Auria with iConnect earhook & Phonak MLxS	Oticon Amigo Phonak MLxi

Figure 12–1. Personal FM receivers that may be used with cochlear implants. *Note:* Body-worn receiver with neckloop may only be used with processors having telecoils.

cords), dedicated, or universal FM receivers provide the greatest improvements in speech recognition in noise for users of cochlear implants as compared to classroom mounted (i.e., multiple loudspeakers) and personal (i.e., small desktop speaker) soundfield FM systems (Schafer & Kleineck, 2009). At this time, there is no research to support the use of body-worn receivers with neckloops for cochlear implants. As a result, personal body-worn or universal FM receivers that electrically couple to the sound processor with a cord, cable, adaptor, or earhook, as well as dedicated receivers, should be recommended for these children. When children are using bilateral cochlear implants or bimodal stimulation, FM input should be provided to both ears to allow for potential binaural benefits (i.e., summation; Schafer & Thibodeau, 2006). With the exception of body-worn receivers, providing input to both ears will require the use of two FM receivers.

Assistance with ordering the most appropriate devices and connections for FM systems to contemporary sound processors is easily accessible from most cochlear implant and FM manufacturer representatives and Web sites. When selecting a specific FM device, the primary goals are to: (1) provide a direct, impedance-matched electrical connection to the sound processor that it not overly cumbersome, (2) provide input to both ears, when appropriate, and (3) allow for flexibility with programmability (see following section).

Troubleshooting the Cochlear Implant-Personal FM System Interface

Prior to troubleshooting potential issues with the FM system, the school-based audiologist or school personnel should make every attempt to rule out a problem with the sound processor. After confirming the sound processor is functioning properly, the FM system may be verified using several techniques. First, a behavioral listening check, similar to the one described previously, may be performed by asking the child to repeat words or sounds that she hears as the school professional speaks into the transmitter microphone. As shown in Figure 12–2, the signal may also be verified by speaking into the transmitter microphone and listening to the output of the FM receiver when plugged into an inexpensive ampli-

fier speaker or into a hearing aid with the appropriate audio shoe (approximately $30.00 to $50.00). The latter option is feasible for most children with cochlear implants because many still have behind-the-ear hearing aids that were used prior to the implant or wear a hearing aid on the nonimplanted ear. In addition to having the hearing aid, the school or parent would need to purchase the audio shoe and a simple listening tube. Once the FM receiver, audio shoe, and listening tube are connected, the functioning and output of the FM receiver through the hearing aid may be verified. One FM system manufacturer (Phonak) sells a MicroLink Checker that allows for a direct connection between the miniaturized FM receiver and headphones (see Figure 12–2). A person with normal-hearing sensitivity can listen to the output of the FM receiver through the earphones while speaking into the FM transmitter microphone. The only means to simultaneously verify the signals from the speech processor microphone and FM transmitter microphone is through the use of monitor earphones (see Figure 12–2). These specialized earphones plug directly into the speech processor. They do not provide the processed signal, but do allow for verification of the signal from the microphone just prior to entering the speech processor. The sensitivity on the sound processor may be reduced or turned all the way down to verify the FM signal. Conversely, when checking the signal from the processor microphone, the FM transmitter may be muted and the sensitivity of the sound processor may be increased. Monitor earphones are available for most speech processors manufactured by Cochlear Corporation; however, the child may require special sound processor programming to enable the use of monitor earphones.

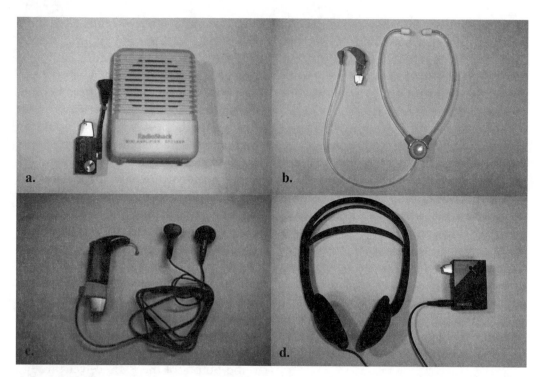

Figure 12–2. The signal from the FM system may be verified using the following equipment: (*a*) Phonak CI S and cable plugged into Radio Shack Mini Amplifier Speaker, (*b*) Phonak hearing aid, audio shoe, and MicroLink MLxS receiver coupled to listening tube, (*c*) Cochlear Corporation ESPrit 3G, MicroLink Adaptor, and Monitor Earphones, and (*d*) Phonak Micro-Link Checker.

If the school-based audiologist has exhausted all possible troubleshooting techniques to address an FM signal that is distorted, intermittent, or absent, the cochlear implant audiologist will need to be contacted. The implant audiologist may ask the school professional to try several troubleshooting approaches, such as replacing the FM and sound processor batteries, recharging the system, and checking the connections. If these approaches do not resolve the problem, the school-based audiologist should begin the assessment by verifying the function of the sound processor (see Table 12–4). Assuming the sound processor is functioning properly, the school-based or implant audiologist should troubleshoot the FM system by systematically replacing each component, including the transmitter microphone, transmitter, coupling conduits (i.e., FM cords, cables, neckloops, adaptors, and earhooks), and receiver. A backup system, as well as extra cords, cables, and adaptors, are necessary for successful troubleshooting of FM systems coupled to cochlear implant sound processors. Once the faulty component is identified, it should be replaced and another listening check should be conducted.

PROGRAMMING CONSIDERATIONS FOR COCHLEAR IMPLANTS AND PERSONAL FM SYSTEMS

There are several programming consider-ations for the FM receiver and the cochlear implant sound processor that may signifi-cantly influence the child's performance. These parameters include FM gain of the FM receiver and audio-mixing ratio, input dynamic range (IDR), and sensitivity of the sound processor.

Programming for the FM Receiver

According to previous research (Schafer & Wolfe, 2008; Schafer, Wolfe, Lawless, & Stout, 2009), higher gain settings (e.g., +14 dB) on the FM receiver may provide significantly better speech recognition performance in noise than lower gain settings (e.g., +6). The results of these studies show optimal performance and comfort for nine adults and five children using Advanced Bionics implants when using receiver gain of +14 and +16 dB. Conversely, eight users of Cochlear Cor-poration sound processors did not ben-efit from increased receiver-gain settings. The performance differences between the users of Advanced Bionics and Cochlear Corporation were likely related to sound processor settings, which were explored in another study and are explained in a later section. There are no published stud-ies on the effects of receiver gain for users of MED-EL cochlear implants, but ben-efits of increased receiver-gain settings are expected.

Recent research suggests that use of Dynamic FM from Phonak Hearing Systems results in significantly better speech recognition in noise than tradi-tional FM systems programmed to the default gain setting (+10 dB) for users of Advanced Bionics and Cochlear Corpo-ration devices (Wolfe, Schafer, Heldner, Mülder, Ward, & Vincent, 2009). To utilize Dynamic FM, the Phonak inspiro trans-mitter and companion FM receiver (i.e., MLxi) are required. This technology auto-matically adjusts the FM-receiver gain according to the noise level in the envi-ronment with more noise (i.e., exceeding 57 dB SPL), resulting in higher FM gain than the default +10 dB setting. The goal of Dynamic FM is to maintain a favor-able signal-to-noise ratio at the listener's ear. In the initial experiment, users of Cochlear Corporation's Freedom did not show significant benefit from either type of FM system. However, when a certain parameter in the Freedom programming was adjusted (i.e., Autosensitivity [ASC]), speech recognition results were similar to those using Advanced Bionics implants. According to the results of this study, Dynamic FM may provide even greater benefit to users of cochlear implants than traditional FM systems.

The results of the studies on receiver gain and Dynamic FM provide evidence for the following recommendations: (1) with fixed-gain receivers, gain should be pro-grammed for +14 or +16 dB, (2) Dynamic FM may provide superior performance over a fixed-gain receiver, and (3) users of Cochlear Corporation Freedom implants will receive more benefit from FM sys-tems when ASC is activated in the sound processor programming.

Programming for the Sound Processor

In the sound processor, three parameters may particularly influence performance with an FM system: the audio-mixing ratio, IDR, and sensitivity. The educational audiologist will need to work closely with the cochlear implant audiologist to ensure that the most appropriate audio-mixing and sensitivity settings are used with the FM system. In most cases, educational audiologists will not make programming changes to the sound processor.

Audio-Mixing Ratio

The audio-mixing ratio is similar to the FM gain in that it controls the relative inputs from the sound processor and the FM system. However, rather than affecting the signal from the FM receiver, the mixing ratio modifies the signal from the sound processor microphone. The Auria and Harmony Advanced Bionics sound processors allow for programming of several audio-mixing ratios: (1) 30/70: processor microphone attenuated by 10 dB, (2) 50/50: equal emphasis, (3) auxiliary only attenuated: processor microphone attenuated by 20 dB, (4) auxiliary only: no processor microphone, and (5) microphone only, no auxiliary input. The 50/50 setting is the default, but the 30/70 and the 50/50 ratios are commonly used. The audio-mixing ratio is programmed by the cochlear implant audiologist during mapping and is then available in one or more of the multiple program slots on the sound processor. The Cochlear Corporation CP810 and Freedom sound processors also provide several mixing ratios: (1) 1:1-equal emphasis, (2) 2:1-processor microphone attenuated by 6 dB,

(3) 3:1-processor microphone attenuated by 9.5 dB, and (4) 10:1-processor microphone attenuated by 20 dB. In the CP810, the mixing ratios are adjusted with the CR110 wireless remote control, whereas mixing ratios for the Freedom are set by the cochlear implant audiologist in the programming software. A 1:1 audio-mixing ratio is enabled automatically in the MED-EL TEMPO+, OPUS 1, and OPUS 2 sound processors.

Previous research with Advanced Bionics users suggests no significant differences in speech perception or subjective benefit with a 30/70 or 50/50 audio-mixing ratio (Wolfe & Schafer, 2008). However, speech perception of low-level stimuli in quiet presented to the sound processor microphone (i.e., not to the FM transmitter) was significantly poorer when using the 30/70 mixing ratio. Pilot data collected in our laboratories show similar results for adults using Cochlear Corporation Freedom sound processors for the 3:1 and 1:1 ratios. As a result of these findings, a 50/50 or 1:1 mixing ratio is recommended for users of Auria and CP810/Freedom processors, respectively, to ensure audibility of both FM and environmental signals.

In summary, a 50/50 or 1:1 mixing ratio is recommended for users of Auria and CP810/Freedom processors, respectively, to ensure audibility of both FM and environmental signals. Access to the sensitivity knob may be helpful for users of the Cochlear Corporation ESPrit 3G processor because lower settings may improve performance in noise with the FM system. There are no published data to support the benefits of personal FM systems for users of MED-EL cochlear implants, but our experience suggests that these users also receive substantial benefit from FM systems.

Input Dynamic Range (IDR)

The IDR is the range of acoustic inputs coded by the sound processor within the person's electrical dynamic range (i.e., threshold to comfort level). Signal levels that exceed the upper end of the IDR are compressed. When using a narrow IDR (i.e., 30 to 40 dB for Cochlear Corporation), inputs from 25/35 to 65 dB SPL will be mapped into a person's electrical dynamic range, and with a wider IDR (60 dB SPL for Advanced Bionics; 55 dB SPL for MED-EL) inputs ranging from 25 to 85 dB SPL are normally mapped into the electrical dynamic range. Previous studies on the effects of FM gain showed greater FM benefit for users of Advanced Bionics versus Cochlear Corporation processors (Schafer et al., 2009; Wolfe et al., 2009). These performance differences were likely related to the IDR of the sound processor for the upper range of inputs.

The signal from the FM system may be affected by IDR because it influences the signals coded at the upper end of the dynamic range, and signals from the FM system are typically high intensity (i.e., 75 dB SPL). A narrower IDR with an upper end of 65 dB SPL will likely result in FM signal compression. As a result, increases in FM gain (e.g., from +10 to +16 dB) will not be coded or perceived due to the compression. Conversely, a wider IDR with an upper end of 85 dB SPL will allow for processor coding and perception of increases in receiver gain. Although it is interesting to identify the cause of the differences between manufacturers, at this time, the IDR parameter is not easily adjustable for FM use.

Processor Sensitivity

Although IDR may not be directly adjusted by an educational audiologist, changes to the microphone sensitivity on Cochlear Corporation implants may address the effects of a narrow IDR on FM performance. The sensitivity parameter controls the gain of the sound processor microphone. Increases in sensitivity result in mapping of lower intensity sounds from a distance, while decreases in sensitivity reduce the user's perception of soft and distant speech. Previous research with users of Cochlear Corporation devices suggests that lower sensitivity settings result in significantly better speech recognition in noise with an FM system than higher sensitivity settings (Aaron, Sonneveldt, Arcaroli, & Holstad, 2003). However, lower settings could also reduce the ability to hear environmental sounds. Behavioral testing, or a good reporter, will help the audiologist find an optimal sensitivity setting that will allow for audibility with environmental and FM signals. For young children, it may be best to disable the sensitivity knob, as it has significant control over audibility of signals. Instead, the sensitivity can be fixed at the typical user setting in the sound processor programming software.

The sensitivity control has different effects for the Cochlear Corporation CP810 and Freedom sound processors. For the Freedom, sensitivity influences only the sound processor input, not the FM input. Therefore, greater salience of the FM signal may be achieved with lower sensitivity settings; however, high-level signals from the FM system will be compressed. On the other hand, sensitivity in the CP810 influences the gain for the sound processor microphone and the FM system with lower settings, preventing compression of both signals. At a lower setting, an increase in FM-receiver gain, through manual adjustments or with Dynamic FM, should allow for coding and perception of a more intense signal from the FM system (unlike previous studies). In MED-EL processors, changes to sensitivity only influence the signal at the processor microphone, with reductions allowing for greater emphasis of the FM signal. A sensitivity setting of zero on the Freedom and to the off position on MED-EL processors deactivates the processor microphone and results in an FM-only condition.

Another option on Cochlear Corporation sound processors is Autosensitivity (ASC). This preprocessing feature automatically reduces the sensitivity of the processor microphone with increases to the environmental noise level and decreases to the signal-to-noise ratio at the microphone. As mentioned in the section on FM-receiver gain, previous research shows that ASC significantly improves speech recognition noise with a Freedom processor and FM system relative to no ASC (Wolfe et al., 2009). This finding is also expected for the CP810 sound processor. When using ASC and Dynamic FM, speech recognition was not significantly different for users of Advanced Bionics and Cochlear Corporation implants. Conversely, differences between the two groups were found when ASC was not used by the Cochlear Corporation recipients. The ASC improves performance because it reduces the effects of the narrower IDR in the Cochlear Corporation implants, which results in improved speech recognition performance in noise with increased receiver-gain settings. The ASC also significantly improved speech perception for signals presented to the sound processor microphone (not to the FM transmitter).

The information in this section highlights the use of the sensitivity parameter for improving performance with FM systems for users of Cochlear Corporation implants. Sensitivity may be controlled manually with a processor control or it may be controlled automatically with ASC. Given the findings of the studies cited in this chapter, the ASC preprocessing features should be enabled for users of Cochlear Corporation with and without the use of a personal FM system.

SUMMARY

Children with cochlear implants require careful management by educational audiologists to address their listening challenges with a cochlear implant, especially in the presence of consistently poor classroom acoustics and unfavorable signal-to-noise ratios. To provide these children with the best opportunity for academic success, the key facts discussed in this chapter should be considered:

- It is important that the child's primary cochlear implant audiologist and educational audiologist communicate directly about the child's performance, changes in programming (i.e., mapping), processor programming for use of an FM system, and troubleshooting techniques to facilitate a collaborative approach to ensuring the child's success at school;
- School personnel, such as the classroom teacher, special education teacher, speech-language pathologist, or the school nurse should be trained on the general use, function, and basic troubleshooting of the sound processor;
- Indicator lights and codes are available on all of the most recent sound processors to help the audiologist, parent, and school personnel identify problems. For some sound processors, listening

earphones can be connected to the sound processor to monitor the signal from the sound processor microphone;

- Management of the poor signal-to-noise ratio often found in typical classrooms through hearing assistance technology is of utmost importance for children with cochlear implants;

- Personal FM receivers include body worn, dedicated, and universal designs and can be connected to most sound processors regardless of manufacturer. Research indicates that personal FM receivers provide the greatest improvements in speech recognition in noise compared to classroom or personal soundfield FM systems;

- When a child is using a cochlear implant and an FM system, it is imperative that audibility is maintained for signals from the FM system and the environment; and

- There are several programming considerations for the FM receiver and the cochlear implant sound processor that may significantly influence performance, and the school-based and implant audiologist will need to work together to ensure optimal settings for both devices. These parameters include FM gain of the receiver and audiomixing ratio, input dynamic range (IDR), and sensitivity of the sound processor.

REFERENCES

Aaron, R., Sonneveldt, V., Arcaroli, J., & Holstad, B. (2003). *Optimizing microphone sensitivitysettings of pediatric Nucleus 24 cochlear implant patients using Phonak MicroLink CI+ FM system.* Poster presented at ACCESS: Achieving Clear Communications Employing Sound Solutions: Proceedings of the First International Conference, Chicago, IL.

Gallaudet Research Institute. (2008, November). *Regional and national summary report of data from the 2007–2008 annual survey of deaf and hard of hearing children and youth.* Washington, DC: GRI, Gallaudet University.

Ling, D. (1976). *Speech and the hearing-impaired child: Theory and practice.* Washington, DC: Alexander Graham Bell Association for the Deaf.

Ling, D. (1989). *Foundations of spoken language for the hearing-impaired child.* Washington, DC: Alexander Graham Bell Association for the Deaf.

Knecht, H. A., Nelson, P. B., Whitelaw, G. M., & Feth, L. L. (2002). Background noise levels and reverberation times in unoccupied classrooms: predictions and measurements. *American Journal of Audiology, 11,* 65–71.

Schafer, E. C., & Kleineck, M. P. (2009). Improvements in speech-recognition performance using cochlear implants and three types of FM systems: A meta-analytic approach. *Journal of Educational Audiology, 15,* 4–14.

Schafer, E. C., & Thibodeau, L. M. (2003). Speech recognition performance of children using cochlear implants and FM systems. *Journal of Educational Audiology, 11,* 15–26.

Schafer, E. C., & Thibodeau L. M. (2006). Speech recognition in noise in children with cochlear implants while listening in bilateral, bimodal, and FM-system arrangements. *American Journal of Audiology, 15,* 114–126.

Schafer, E. C., & Wolfe, J. (2008). Optimizing FM systems for the Auria speech processor. *Advanced Auditory Research Bulletin: 2007 Biennial Edition* (pp. 120–121). Valencia, CA: Advanced Bionics Corporation.

Schafer, E. C., Wolfe, J., Lawless, T., & Stout, B. (2009). Effects of FM-receiver gain on speech-recognition performance of adults with cochlear implants. *International Journal of Audiology, 48*(4), 196–203.

Special Education Law Library: Individuals with Disabilities Education Act of 2004 (IDEA 2004).

The Moog Center for Deaf Education. (n.d.). *Team tracking form*. Retrieved November 4, 2009, from http://www.moogcenter.org

Wolfe, J., & Schafer, E. C. (2008). Optimizing the benefits of Auria sound processors cou-pled to personal FM systems with iConnect adaptors. *Journal of the American Academy of Audiology, 19*(8), 585–594.

Wolfe, J., Schafer, E. C., Heldner, B., Mülder, H., Ward, E., & Vincent, B. (2009). Evaluation of speech recognition in noise with cochlear implants and dynamic FM. *Journal of the American Academy of Audiology, 20*(7), 409–421.

Educational Audiology in the Real World

Johnnie Sexton, AuD
President, John E. Sexton & Associates, Inc.
Executive Director, The CARE Project, Inc.
Greensboro, North Carolina

My name is Johnnie Sexton, and I have worked with children who have hearing challenges for 33 years, 30 as an educational audiologist. I received my BS degree in Speech, Language, and Auditory Pathology and, for a short time, worked as a school speech therapist. This experience, combined with my interest in children with hearing loss, allowed me to develop a keen interest in the school environment. After completing my MS in Audiology, I was fortunate to be hired as an audiologist for a federal grant to establish the statewide model for audiology in the schools of North Carolina. I was so very fortunate to have this opportunity—until the program lost its federal funding! I found myself unemployed.

I took a job in sales and consulting in the schools and retooled a bit for the job. I found it to be another wonderful experience that would lead to opening my own practice. The schools that were served by the federal grant really wanted the educational audiology services to continue, so many of the counties contacted me and asked if I would contract educational services with them/for them. Soon, I had started my own audiology practice specializing in providing school services. The practice has grown over the years, and today it serves 35 schools districts with 12 audiologists on staff.

Over the years, I delivered educational audiology services to various school districts, even though I had hired staff to work with me to fulfill the contracts. In recent years, I started expanding my work to take on new and different development projects and to devote my time and energy to the management of the practice. However, I do still take the time to visit the school districts where my staff members are working, and I make myself available to school-employed staff in all counties for consultation via phone and/ or e-mail, and even in person, if needed.

My average week is a bit unusual when compared to most educational audiologists. My day-to-day work includes the development, management, and implementation of an ongoing marketing plan to continue to grow my business. With the use of computer technology now, I am able to do E-mail blasts to all school directors (and any other group) to keep them updated and aware of the services my practice provides. I use this mechanism to also inform these people of changes in services; state and federal laws, policies, and procedures that would impact them; and so forth. In addition, I maintain contact with all of my staff. I check in on them to make sure they are doing well and to address any questions or issues, should they arise. For example, last week, three different staff audiologists had diagnostic equipment problems. I had to step in to make sure they had backup equipment and could manage the repairs. Fortunately, I have a very able office manager who works with me on these details.

I have devoted myself to an ongoing involvement with both professional organizations, as well as state licensure boards. At least weekly, I am involved in discussions regarding the laws that govern the practice of audiology and the dispensing of hearing aids. I have found over the years that I have been the only person with a background in school audiology to have a presence and a voice in state licensure in North Carolina. At times, this has been important when decisions are made regarding the delivery of services that may impact the school setting.

I also spent time this past week working on my new counseling program for children and families, ultimately headed for the school environment. So, I spent time this week meeting with the film editor and caption writer. I researched packaging ideas for the materials for this new program, meeting with vendors and art directors. I also visited with area agencies that work with the hearing-impaired population to get their input on the new program and the packaging ideas.

My time was also spent working on a grant proposal to expand my counseling program and to incorporate it as a nonprofit agency. This caused me to be in touch with a foundation in Denmark that had flown me there last fall to discuss my new program and how we could work on it together. I spent time submitting proposals on the new program to professional organizations and agencies in order to present the information at their respective upcoming conferences in 2010.

So, how do I spend my time? I am a public relations, marketing, development, financial, sales agent for my practice with a total focus on services in the schools. I love every minute of every day that I get to do this work, even after all these years.

One last thing . . . I took the time recently to complete my AuD degree. Although I didn't need it to continue to work, I felt it necessary to demonstrate my support for the newly required level of education in my chosen profession. I do feel that I have been lucky to have had my cake and eaten it, too!

13

Auditory Processing Disorders in the School-Age Population

Jeffrey Weihing and Frank E. Musiek

OBJECTIVES

By the end of this chapter, the reader will be able to:

1. Define the roles of the school-based audiologist and speech-language pathologist with respect to screening, assessing, and managing students for (C)APD.
2. Describe screening measures typically used by audiologists and speech-language pathologists to determine if further diagnostic investigation for (C)APD is warranted.
3. Describe the three categories of recommendations for classroom modifications in cases of (C)APD, including physically modifying the environment, encouraging behavioral changes and listening strategies in students, and using amplification or assistive listening devices on students.
4. Describe current management strategies used for students with (C)APD in the classroom and in the home.

INTRODUCTION

Initial suspicions of central auditory processing disorders ([C]APD) in school-age children typically arise from the children's observed academic and hearing difficulties. These difficulties are due to the findings that classroom learning is, in large part, auditorily based (Au & Lovegrove, 2001; Parviainen, Helenius, Poskiparta, Niemi, & Salmelin, 2006; Tallal, 1980), and hearing must occur in an environment that is negatively affected by noise and reverberation (Knecht, Nelson, Whitelaw, & Feth, 2002). Although the normal central auditory nervous system (CANS) maintains a mechanism for squelching the negative effects of these less than optimal listening conditions (see Akeroyd [2006] for a review), children with (C)APD seem to be unable to do so effectively (Cameron & Dillon, 2008; Chermak, Somers, & Seikel, 1998). Therefore, these children's deficits become evident in the classroom environment. Given the importance of having children meet academic milestones, addressing these deficits is crucial and calls for swift identification of processing difficulties.

Proper treatment of (C)APD must take into account many different aspects of the school system. For instance, efforts to increase the audibility of the signal relative to the noise must address the limitations of the classroom environment and make it more favorable for listening (Knecht et al., 2002). Likewise, educators must be made aware of how to communicate more effectively with the child who has (C)APD (American Academy of Audiology (AAA), 2010; Baran, 1998). Finally, direct services provided to the child for long term remediation of the disorder will occur in the school and, therefore, guidelines for treatment must be given to those who frequently provide the service, such as the speech-language pathologist (SLP).

Since many different professionals are responsible for meeting the needs of the child with (C)APD, the process of identification and treatment is an exceedingly multidisciplinary effort (AAA, 2010; American Speech-Language-Hearing Association (ASHA), 2005; Chermak, 2002; Katz & Tillery, 2005; Witton, 2010). Foremost in this team of professionals are

the audiologist and SLP. It is the audiologist who will play an integral role in the accurate diagnosis of the disorder and in determining the necessary treatments; however, it is generally the SLP who will screen for the disorder to determine if a diagnostic referral is necessary. The SLP is also the professional who ultimately administers the prescribed remediation, in most instances. It is the interaction of these two professionals, the audiologist and the SLP, as they aim to screen, diagnose, and "treat" (C)APD in the school system that is the focus of this chapter.

AN OVERVIEW OF (C)APD IN THE SCHOOL-AGE POPULATION

(C)APD, by definition, is a hearing disorder that generally occurs in the presence of normal peripheral hearing and arises from abnormalities in specific regions of the central auditory nervous system, including portions of the brainstem, cerebrum, and/or associated sub-cortical regions. Much of what is known about the physiological underpinnings of the disorder and their relationship to (C)APD tests arose from neurological studies in adults, where investigators examined the patients' performance knowing the site of lesion in the CANS. In these patients, auditory deficits were shown during more complex listening tasks, despite normal performance on peripheral measures (e.g., Baran, Bothfeldt, & Musiek, 2004; Hurley & Musiek, 1997; Musiek, 1983a; Musiek & Pinheiro, 1987). Other researchers have investigated this lesion model in pediatric patients and indicated a similar pattern of deficits as witnessed in adults (Bamiou,

Musiek, & Luxon, 2001; Boscariol, Garcia, Guimaraes, Hage, Montenegro, Cendes, & Guerreiro, 2009; Boscariol, Garcia, Guimaraes, Montenegro, Hage, Cendes, & Guerreiro, 2010; Hannay, Walker, Dennis, Kramer, Blaser, & Fletcher, 2008; Iliadou, Bamiou, Kaprinis, Kandylis, Vlaikidis, Apalla, et al., 2008; Jerger, 1987; Jerger, Johnson, & Loiselle, 1988).

The actual causes of (C)APD in school-age children are thought to be somewhat different from those observed in adults (Figure 13–1). However, overlap between these two groups is encountered in some neurologic and acquired aspects of the disorder, such as seizures and head injury, respectively. Other aspects are more age specific; for instance, unlike adults, children may encounter symptoms of (C)APD that are the result of maturational factors, such as delays in the development of myelin (Schmithorst, Holland, & Plante, 2010; for additional review, see Weihing & Musiek, 2007). Negative contributions due to maturational delay may dissipate

with time (Schochat & Musiek, 2006), possibly making the prognosis of the untreated pediatric patient somewhat more optimistic than the typical adult case. Additional causes of (C)APD in some children include microgyri, which are thought to contribute to reduced auditory function in important cortical regions (Boscariol et al., 2010), as well as possible genetic predispositions (Bamiou, Campbell, Musiek, Taylor, Chong, Moore, et al., 2007a; Bamiou, Free, Sisodiya, Chong, Musiek, Williamson, et al., 2007b; Jerger, Chmiel, Tonini, Murphy, & Kent, 1999).

Functions encompassed under the label of central auditory processing include, though are not exclusive to, dichotic processing, temporal processing, auditory closure, binaural processing, and localization. Tests of (C)APD often measure one or more of these processes in an attempt to assess the integrity of the CANS. Since improvements in (C)APD assessment are continually emerging, it is expected that no one test will be considered indicative

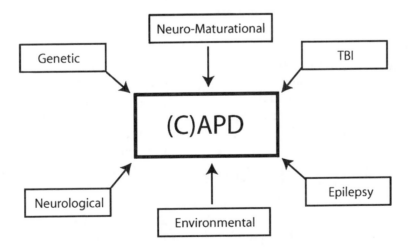

Figure 13–1. Some suspected causes of (C)APD in children, including generic (e.g., PAX6 mutation), neuro-maturational (e.g., myelin delay), traumatic brain injury, neurological (e.g., ectopic cells), environmental (e.g., mercury poisoning), and epilepsy.

of the presence of the disorder. Test effectiveness in diagnosis of the disorder is guided by clinical decision analysis using subjects with confirmed lesions of the CANS, which is considered the best, although an imperfect, gold standard for the disorder (AAA, 2010; ASHA, 2005).

Deficits in auditory processing generally contribute to at least two commonly reported symptoms associated with (C)APD. The first symptom is the report of difficulties hearing in noise, which are symptoms found most persistently in the classroom setting where ideal acoustics and signal-to-noise ratios may be difficult to maintain. A breakdown in nearly any auditory process can contribute to this difficulty of hearing in noise, as all processes benefit the listener during the extraction of meaningful speech information from background noise or competing signals in some way. This breakdown causes what some informally have termed the "funnel effect," which indicates that many unique types of auditory processing deficits contribute to, or are funneled into, a single symptom.

The second symptom frequently encountered in the pediatric patient diagnosed with (C)APD is some degree of academic difficulty, typically also related to a speech-language or reading issue. The relationship between central auditory processing (CAP) and academic performance is much more tenuous, and it is mentioned here merely in an attempt to describe the typical symptoms of school-age children with (C)APD. Although CAP has been linked to phonemic and/or phonological awareness skills (Corriveau, Goswami, & Thomson, 2010; Moore, Rosenberg, & Coleman, 2005; Norrelgen, Lacerda, & Forssberg, 2001; Richardson, Thomson, Scott, & Goswami, 2004; Sharma, Purdy, & Kelly, 2009; Walker, Hall, Klein, & Phil-

lips, 2006), which themselves have been linked to reading ability (Friend & Olson, 2010; Wayland, Eckhouse, Lombardino, & Roberts, 2010; Wood, Hill, Meyer, & Flower, 2005), the relationship between these three variables is complicated and we do not mean to imply a causal role to CAP. Rather, children with (C)APD seem to be more likely to encounter these academic issues than those without (C)APD, making it a relevant component of the profile of the pediatric CAP patient. Indeed, academic difficulties are frequently the primary factor motivating the parents and school systems to pursue CAP evaluations.

There are a host of additional symptoms that tend to occur in cases of (C)APD, including difficulty following multistep directions, requests for frequent repetitions, trouble understanding compromised speech, and difficulty locating the source of sounds. These symptoms overlap to some degree with other disorders. Chermak and colleagues (1998) have noted that the primacy, and not just presence, of certain symptoms may actually be a distinguishing factor of (C)APD. For instance, physicians frequently report hearing-in-noise difficulties as more problematic than other symptoms for children who are eventually diagnosed with (C)APD. This contrasts sharply with children who have a diagnosis of ADHD who do not tend to present with this issue as the primary symptom.

An attempt to identify (C)APD based on the patient case history has yielded conflicting findings. For instance, some studies have indicated that a history of otitis media increases the risk of (C)APD (Gravel, Wallace, & Ruben, 1996; Hall & Grose, 1993; Hall, Grose, Dev, & Ghiassi, 1998; Hall, Grose, & Pillsbury, 1995; Moore, Hutchings, & Meyer, 1991; Pillsbury, Grose, & Hall, 1991), whereas others have found no increase in risk based on this factor (Dawes, Bishop, Sirimanna, & Bamiou, 2008; Hoffman-Lawless, Keith, & Cotton, 1981). Likewise, other risk factors, such as birth and pregnancy history, have proven to be equally ambiguous because conflicting reports have been generated (Dawes et al., 2008; Iliadou et al., 2008). Much of the ambiguity surrounding these risk factors may be attributed to the manner in which (C)APD is diagnosed. Although there are numerous professional recommendations regarding how to approach making this diagnosis, the number of tests available and differing philosophies on what defines (C)APD makes it difficult to maintain a consistent definition of the disorder across different research facilities and clinics.

This chapter's authors generally utilize a diagnostic battery that incorporates processes recommended by ASHA (2005) and AAA (2010) and has been shown to be relatively sensitive and specific to CANS dysfunction. This battery includes the dichotic digits (Musiek, 1983b), competing sentences (Willeford & Burleigh, 1994), frequency patterns (Musiek & Pinheiro, 1987), gaps-in-noise (GIN) test (Musiek, Shinn, Jirsa, Bamiou, Baran, & Zaida, 2005), and masking level difference (Wilson, 1994). Respectively, these measures assess binaural integration, binaural separation, temporal sequencing, temporal discrimination, and binaural processing/localization. Additionally, a measure of auditory closure is typically incorporated and includes either the words-in-noise (Wilson, Farmer, Gandhi, Shelburne, & Weaver, 2010), filtered speech (Willeford, 1976), or NU-6 test (Tillman & Carhart, 1966) in speech babble. In this battery, performance below two standard deviations is considered below normal limits on the test, and at least two tests must

be failed for the diagnosis of (C)APD to be made (AAA, 2010; ASHA, 2005). Failure of one test would also indicate (C)APD if the listener's performance was below three standard deviations (AAA, 2010; ASHA, 2005).

Electrophysiological measures, such as the speech evoked auditory brainstem response (Johnson, Nicol, & Kraus, 2005; King, Warrier, Hayes, & Kraus, 2002), the middle latency response (Musiek & Lee, 1997; Schochat & Musiek, 2006), and the late cortical response (Gilley, Sharma, Dorman, & Martin, 2006; Sussman, Steinschneider, Gumenyuk, Grushko, & Larson, 2008) are also increasingly being used in the diagnosis of CAP. These measures have an added advantage over purely behavioral test batteries in that they generally are not greatly influenced by supramodal factors, such as severe comorbid speech-language and/or neuropsychological deficits (AAA, 2010; ASHA, 2005). Likewise, recent research has suggested that in some cases, even patients who have normal behavioral CAP performance can still be diagnosed with a significant CAP deficit through electrophysiological measures alone (Billiet & Bellis, 2011). Electrophysiological correlates of behavioral tests are also emerging, including evoked potential measures of signal in noise processing (Anderson, Skoe, Chandrasekaran, & Kraus, 2010), interaural differences in processing of signal intensity (Wambacq, Koehnke, Shea-Miller, Besing, Toth, & Abubakr, 2007), and gap detection ability (Atcherson, Gould, Mendel, & Ethington, 2009) among others. It should be noted that electrophysiological measures require instrumentation typically not available in school settings; therefore, assessments utilizing this technology will generally need to take place in the audiology clinic.

(CENTRAL) AUDITORY PROCESSING DISORDERS AND CO-MORBIDITIES

In children, (C)APD is frequently co-morbid with other disorders. Recent studies have shown that pediatric (C)APD tends to occur in isolation in approximately only 5% of cases and that, more often, the disorder occurs with a speech-language issue or reading disability (Sharma et al., 2009). This finding has several important implications. The first implication is that the child newly diagnosed with (C)APD is at risk for being diagnosed with other developmental disorders. This emphasizes the importance of having (C)APD patients also evaluated for speech-language and neuropsychological issues. Additionally, it highlights the strength of utilizing a team approach in the diagnosis and management of (C)APD. As other disorders are likely to be present, it is frequently more efficient for the audiologist to coordinate his or her efforts with other professionals. As such, diagnosis and management of (C)APD and related disorders is very much a team effort.

A second important implication related to the overlap of these disorders is that the diagnostic audiologist must be cautious not to attribute symptoms entirely to a CAP issue when the primary deficit may actually be in another domain. For instance, CAP may be overshadowed by a more primary neuropsychological deficit in an area, such as attention. It would be inappropriate to focus primary treatment efforts on the CAP issue in this scenario. Consensus committees have advocated in this regard for establishing the primacy of the deficit in the auditory domain (AAA, 2010; ASHA, 2005). There are a variety of ways that modality specificity can be established, including a neuropsychological assessment. If intelligence, cognition, memory, attention, and other factors are established to be within normal limits, then an existing CAP deficit becomes more central to remediation efforts. Similar attention should be paid to comorbid speech-language issues.

Conversely, it should not be overlooked that (C)APD may be a critical underlying factor in observed "co-morbid" issues. For instance, deficits in very basic auditory processes have been shown to be related to more complex speech-language issues (Benasich & Tallal, 2002; Hill, Hogben, & Bishop, 2005; Mengler, Hogben, Michie, & Bishop, 2005; Tallal, Stark, & Mellits, 1985). Likewise, short latency auditory evoked potential abnormalities have been noted in children diagnosed as having learning disabilities (Arehole, Augustine, & Simhadri, 1995; Banai, Abrams, & Kraus, 2007; Billiet & Bellis, 2011; Purdy, Kelly, & Davies, 2002).

SCREENING FOR (CENTRAL) AUDITORY PROCESSING DISORDERS

Screening for CAP issues can yield useful information in two situations: (1) determining to whom to refer students for a more comprehensive diagnostic evaluation, and (2) monitoring treatment effects over time in students who have already been diagnosed with the disorder. There are several options for the educational professional who would like to administer a screening test. The simplest method is often to excise a single test from a diagnostic test battery and to use performance on this measure as an indication of whether or not to pursue further testing, as has been suggested with tests such as the dichotic digits (Musiek, 1983b). Such an approach has the potential advantage of being relatively quick and reliable if the test selected shares those qualities.

A more comprehensive screening approach is to deliver a small battery of measures that assesses different auditory processes, thereby potentially increasing the ability of the battery to detect those at risk for the disorder. Such an approach was followed in construction of the popular screening battery, the Screening Test for Auditory Processing Disorders (SCAN; Keith, 2000). The SCAN has been published in separate versions for both younger children and older children/adults, and in several different languages. The screening battery is made up of four subtests, including filtered speech with a 500-Hz low-pass cutoff, speech in noise with a +8 signal-to-noise ratio (e.g., auditory figure-ground), competing words, and competing sentences. The latter two are dichotic tests, with the competing words subtest being administered in a binaural integration response mode (i.e., attend and repeat back both words) and the competing sentences subtest being administered in a binaural separation response mode (i.e., attend to one ear and repeat back the sentence heard). More recent versions of the SCAN also include subtests for gap detection and time compressed speech.

The SCAN has several strengths in its administration as a screener. The test has been standardized for a variety of ages, and performance can be compared to other standardized tests (Keith, 2000). Additionally, some reliability indices have shown it to be a relatively consistent performance measure (Amos & Humes, 1998). By design, the SCAN is easy to administer even for professionals not formally trained in the assessment of (C)APD. Normative values have been obtained at

a most comfortable loudness (MCL) level which, although introducing variance by differences in presentation level, makes it easier to determine a starting intensity for the test. Test guidelines also suggest it is appropriate for classroom environments with low levels of ambient noise (Keith, 2000), although this conclusion is dependent on the specific classroom under consideration.

In a diagnostic capacity, the SCAN has several very significant limitations and special consideration must be taken not to overinterpret the test results. These limitations arise from a variety of sources and a lengthy consideration of them here is beyond the scope of this chapter. In brief, encouraging clinicians to select their own cutoff criteria for normalcy, lack of supporting clinical decision analysis research, and certain conventions assumed for administration and scoring limit the diagnostic capabilities of this screening battery.

Another battery approach to screening, the Differential Screening Test for Processing (DSTP), has been developed by Richard and Ferre (2006). In this screening protocol, three CAP subtests are administered and include auditory discrimination, dichotic processing, and temporal patterning. Two other groups of subtests include processes in which, first, only language skills are measured and, second, both CAP and language skills overlap. Comparison of performance on the CAP measures to the other two subtest groups provides the professional with some estimate of the degree in which language skills are involved in the potential CAP issues.

There are several advantages of the DSTP over other screeners. Foremost among these advantages is the inclusion of a temporal patterning test in screening for CAP deficits. In adults, these types of tests have been shown to be some of the most sensitive to the presence of auditory cortex lesions (Chermak & Musiek, 1997), which suggests they may be highly sensitive to CANS pathology, in general. Another advantage of this screener is that it does not rely on separate, auxiliary speech-language tests in order to perform differential assessment. Standardization on both CAP and speech-language tests have been performed on the same group of subjects. As with the SCAN, however, there are several disadvantages to the battery, with the primary disadvantage being the audibility of the tests when administered at MCL outside of a sound booth.

Questionnaires that can be used to screen for (C)APD also exist. These include the Children's Auditory Performance Scale (CHAPS; Smoski, Brunt, & Tannahill, 1998) and Fisher's Auditory Problems Checklist (Fisher, 1976). The CHAPS is composed of questions that address the child's ability to listen in a variety of acoustic environments, auditory attention, and auditory memory. The approach to Fisher's checklist is somewhat different. Multiple behaviors consistent with (C)APD are provided in a list format and the responder is instructed to indicate which of the behaviors are exhibited by the child. Both questionnaires have been shown to be only slightly related to (C)APD (Wilson et al., 2010), but would likely serve well as an initial at-risk indicator of the disorder in some cases.

Although it is certainly beyond the audiologist's scope of practice to administer diagnostic tests of neuropsychological factors, there are several brief, useful screening measures that can be administered to assist with the interpretation of CAP batteries. These screening measures are only useful in the absence of a formal neuropsychological evaluation, as the latter is a significantly more comprehensive assessment of the same domains. For attention screening, the Auditory Continuous Performance Test (ACPT; Keith & Engineer, 1991; Riccio, Cohen, Hynd, & Keith, 1996) is a standardized measure of auditory attention that is normed through adolescence and can be administered through any audiometer equipped for CAP testing. For memory, the forward and backward digit span of the Wechsler Intelligence Scale for Children (WISC-IV; Wechsler, 2003) can also be administered informally and only requires that the child repeat back a series of numbers. Although certainly no substitute for a comprehensive neuropsychological evaluation, these screening measures can provide the audiologist with some idea as to whether supramodal factors (i.e., contaminating factors from other modalities) need to be incorporated into interpreting poor CAP test performance.

Taken as a whole, there are many potential screeners that can be used by audiologists and SLPs in the school system to identify children who may be at risk for (C)APD. Although research is still needed to determine which screener best meets the needs of the professional, the present tests and questionnaires discussed here provide a good starting point for classroom screening and further diagnostic investigation.

CLASSROOM MODIFICATIONS AND (CENTRAL) AUDITORY PROCESSING DISORDERS

A comprehensive discussion of classroom acoustics is considered elsewhere in this book (see Chapter 2). However, a brief consideration of the impact of classroom acoustics on CAP, and a description of modifications that can be applied to help reduce the impact, is highly relevant for the management of these disorders. Classroom considerations include any barrier to effective transmission of the auditory signal, whether that barrier is specific to the acoustic features of the classroom or to the manner in which information is presented and obtained by the child in the environment. Generally speaking, accommodations that increase the signal-to-noise ratio and/or provide the child with behavioral compensatory strategies for obtaining necessary auditory information can play a large role in the success of an intervention plan.

The impact of noise and reverberation on speech understanding in normal hearing pediatrics is well documented (see Chapter 2), with both variables showing a negative influence on speech understanding (Hodgson & Nosal, 2002). There tends to be a small maturational effect on hearing in noise ability (Bradley & Sato, 2008; Elliot, Connors, Kille, Levin, Ball, & Katz, 1979) with much of the change occurring between 6 and 7 years of age (Wilson et al., 2010). To achieve an 80% word recognition score, a 15 to 20 dB signal-to-noise ratio is needed for children ranging in age from 6 to 11 years; however, in actual teaching situations, only 20 to 60% of children receive these levels (Bradley & Sato, 2008).

The detrimental effects of noise are known to have long-term consequences, as reading in the presence of noise is known to negatively influence recall of information as long as 1 week later (Hygge, 1993). The addition of reverberation to the classroom is also known to have a negative impact on listening, although very short reverberation times can actually enhance speech understanding (Hodgson

& Nosal, 2002). As mentioned in Chapter 2, increasing the reverberation time from 0.4 to a 1.2 msec yields a decrement in word recognition of about 18% (Finitzo-Hieber & Tillman, 1978). The influence of reverberation also tends to vary by age with performance peaking around the age of 13 years (Neuman & Hochberg, 1983). Binaural hearing appears to combat the negative influence of reverberation somewhat, with younger children showing greater benefits from this listening mode (Neuman & Hochberg, 1983). Further complicating the classroom listening environment is the fact that the combined negative effect of noise and reverberation tends to be greater than would be predicted by the additive effect of both components (Finitzo-Hieber & Tillman, 1978).

Given the negative consequences of noise and reverberation in normal hearing children, it is not surprising that the impact of these variables is even greater in children with (C)APD. Research indicates that children with learning disabilities show poorer speech-in-noise performance than normal hearing cohorts (Elliot et al., 1979). Auditory and speech perception abilities also tend to be related to literacy at the end of the first year of school, perhaps to a larger degree than nonsensory psychological variables (Shapiro, Hurry, Masterson, Taeko, Doctor, & Doctor, 2009). Additionally, auditory pathology has been specifically related to poorer reading and phonological ability in cases of children who experienced early-onset otitis media which continued into the early school years (Shapiro et al., 2009). Although physiologic mechanisms for this effect have been proposed (Xu, Kotak, & Sanes, 2007), the observation that children with potential auditory processing issues require a better signal-to-noise ratio and lower reverberation times when compared to the normal hearing child is of utmost importance here.

Recommendations for classroom modifications in cases of (C)APD generally fall into one of three categories: (1) physical modification of the environment, (2) improving listening conditions by encouraging beneficial behavioral changes, and (3) adding amplification/ assistive listening devices. The first two modifications are considered here; the third modification is considered in the next section of this chapter. These classroom modifications, in general, were discussed thoroughly in Chapters 2 and 8, specifically, as they relate to children with hearing impairment. However, explicit attention to classroom modification in cases of (C)APD is addressed below.

With respect to physical modifications, the following changes have been recommended to improve classroom acoustics (Knecht, Nelson, Whitelaw, & Feth, 2002):

- The addition of drop ceilings to decrease classroom height to 10 feet can greatly reduce reverberation times;
- The addition of carpeting and wall dampers can also provide means for reducing reverberation times, although the former can be expensive and might possibly increase the risk of mold allergies;
- The installation of newer windows tends to be associated with better signal-to-noise ratios and lower reverberation times, particularly installations that are made with double panes of glass; and
- The installation of central air conditioning. Generally, only a central air conditioning system allows a classroom to meet ANSI guidelines, although adding this type of unit is an unrealistic modification in most

cases. As an alternative to changing existing HVAC equipment, the child with (C)APD should be seated as far from the window air conditioner as possible while still being close to the sound source.

With respect to improving listening conditions behaviorally, recommendations can be made for both the student and teacher. Many listening difficulties can be reduced in severity by allowing the child to have preferential seating in a location of the classroom that serves to optimize the signal-to-noise ratio. Generally, this location is in the front of the classroom, close to the teacher, and away from any significant sources of noise. This recommendation becomes less applicable, however, in nontraditional classrooms. For instance, if the classroom size is small and the teacher frequently moves between the students, alternatives (such as relying on an FM system to increase the signal-to-noise ratio) may be preferable. Another excellent approach to providing students with an improved acoustic environment is to offer a quiet study area where students can go to complete their work after instruction. This distraction-free environment will likely make it easier for the student with (C)APD to focus on work with improved concentration.

The classroom teacher may employ a variety of different teaching techniques to increase the degree of auditory information retained by the child with (C)APD (Baran, 1998). For instance, calling on the child periodically to draw his attention back to the topic at hand may provide benefit. As a general rule, it will help to speak slowly, although not too slowly, and clearly. The message being conveyed should be kept relatively short and concise, with little ambiguity. If something needs to be repeated, it should be rephrased when restated to increase the degree of redundancy in the auditory message. The addition of visual information to classroom instruction may also help to increase the amount of information retained by the student. This can include visual aids, written instructions, and lists with key details regarding classroom topics (e.g., vocabulary lists) being distributed prior to the day they are introduced in class.

Students with (C)APD should be encouraged to advocate for themselves and take responsibility for aspects of their remediation (Baran, 1998). For instance, a child with (C)APD should be instructed to ask the teacher to repeat details if he does not understand. The child should also be taught to use compensatory strategies to accommodate his listening difficulties. This strategy might include putting in extra effort the night before to prelearn material being taught the next day. Likewise, the strategy may be to teach the child to take advantage of other accommodations provided, such as preferential seating and visual instructions. Regardless of the strategy, the child with (C)APD needs to learn to approach the disorder as a challenge in which he or she is an active participant in remediation.

ASSISTIVE LISTENING DEVICES AND AMPLIFICATION AS A FORM OF REMEDIATION FOR (CENTRAL) AUDITORY PROCESSING DISORDERS

As previously stated, the most common symptom reported by professionals dealing with children who have (C)APD is that their patients have difficulty hearing in noise (Chermak et al., 1998). Indeed, all types of auditory processing issues (e.g., temporal processing, dichotic processing) are thought to contribute in some way to the ability to hear in background noise. Given the aforementioned less than optimal acoustic environments found in classrooms, obtaining an ideal signal-to-noise ratio can often be challenging. Yet, the use of assistive listening devices (which significantly improve the signal-to-noise ratio for the listener) is an extremely effective and immediate remediation for difficulties hearing in noise. These devices include noncustomized, ear-level and classroom equipment (known as hearing assistance technology, or HAT) and custom hearing aids.

Two forms of HAT include personal FM systems and soundfield classroom amplification systems. Personal FM systems are composed of a microphone and transmitter worn by the teacher and a receiver worn by the child with (C)APD. When the teacher speaks, the microphone receives the speech signal and transmits it wirelessly via FM signals to the child's receiver. In this way, the FM system overcomes the negative influence of poor classroom acoustics and background noise by sending speech directly to the ear of the child. Soundfield classroom amplification systems also exist to improve the signal-to-noise ratio for all students in the classroom at the same time. (For a more comprehensive discussion of the types of HAT, see Chapter 6.)

The purpose of HAT is to provide an immediate improvement in speech understanding in noise, which can help facilitate other forms of (C)APD remediation. Research studies have indicated that FM systems can increase the signal-to-noise ratio by as much as 11 dB (Larsen & Blair, 2008), and this improvement can greatly increase the amount of information available to the student with (C)APD when in noisy environments (Arnold & Canning, 1999). However, the use of any HAT should always be considered a relatively short term solution. Large magnitude improvements in speech understanding obtained from HAT generally do not remain once the amplification system is no longer used (Johnston, John, Kreisman, Hall, & Crandell, 2009; Lemos, Jacob, Gejao, Bevilacqua, Feniman, & Ferrari, 2009). Therefore, although the system can benefit speech understanding for the short term, it is the duty of other treatments (i.e., auditory training) to institute long-term CANS changes and make the use of HAT unnecessary.

Some research has also suggested that custom-fit amplification with speech-in-noise processing may help to benefit the child with (C)APD. Kuk and colleagues (2008) fit 14 children with a diagnosis of (C)APD with mild-gain open-fit hearing aids with speech-in-noise processing. The researchers then examined the children's performance longitudinally on several different speech-in-noise measures. Results showed that, when tested with the hearing aid in directional mode, these patients showed significantly better speech-in-noise processing. Using amplification as a remediation approach (rather than an FM system) has advantages in the sense that it can be more seamlessly integrated into the child's life, both in and out of the classroom. However, this approach also has limitations. For example, the expense of binaural amplification and possible long-term dependency on the amplification units would certainly be viewed in a negative light. Additionally, school systems currently purchasing FM systems for use with multiple students might not readily implement an approach that provides children with individual listening devices. Nevertheless, using amplification in this context poses an interesting avenue of research for future consideration in the treatment of (C)APD.

AUDITORY TRAINING AS A PRIMARY REHABILITATION APPROACH FOR (CENTRAL) AUDITORY PROCESSING DISORDERS

Auditory training remains an integral component of any remediation strategy for (C)APD. Although research demonstrating the efficacy of these procedures is still ongoing (Loo, Bamiou, Campbell, & Luxon, 2010), conclusions that consistent participation in training protocols can improve performance on auditory processing measures in the general pediatric population are emerging (Amitay, Irwin, & Moore, 2006; Moore, Halliday, & Amitay, 2009). Unlike classroom modifications and amplification approaches (which act as short-term solutions), auditory training is thought to be a service approach upon which significant long-term changes in processing ability can be instituted clinically.

Most of the research evidence supporting auditory training has come from computer-based protocols applied in normal listeners. Although research is far from conclusive in this area (Loo et al., 2010), this treatment option has been shown to yield improvements in *auditory discrimination* (Amitay et al., 2006; Delhommeau, Micheyl, & Jouvent, 2005; Delhommeau, Micheyl, Jouvent, & Collet, 2002; Jancke, Gaab, Wustenberg, Scheich, & Heinze, 2001; Kraus, 1999; Kraus, Mc-

Gee, Carrell, & King, 1995; Tremblay & Kraus, 2002; Tremblay, Kraus, Carrell, & McGee, 1997; Tremblay, Kraus, & McGee, 1998; Moore et al., 2005; Moore et al., 2009; Tremblay, Kraus, McGee, Ponton, & Otis, 2001), *temporal processing* (Agnew, Dorn, & Eden, 2004; Foxton, Brown, Chambers, & Griffiths, 2004; Kujala, Karma, Ceponiene, Belitz, Turkkila, Tervaniemi, et al., 2001; Kujala, Myllyviita, Tervaniemi, Alho, Kalliom, & Naatanen, 2000; Merzenich, Jenkins, & Johnston, 1996; Tallal, Merzenich, Miller, & Jenkins, 1998; Tallal, Miller, Bedi, Byma, Wang, Nagarajan, et al., 1996; Temple, Deutsch, Poldrack, Miller, Tallal, Merzenich, et al., 2003), and *dichotic processing* (Alonso & Schochat, 2009; Moncrieff & Wertz, 2008; Musiek, unpublished; Musiek, Baran, & Shinn, 2004; Schochat, Musiek, Alonso, & Ogata, 2010; Weihing & Musiek, 2007). From these studies, in general, several preliminary trends about computer-based auditory training can be drawn:

- Training effects (if they emerge) tend to occur relatively quickly, within the first several sessions (Moore et al., 2009);
- Training effects do not generally arise if the task is made too easy, while tasks that are impossible to complete correctly can still yield significant training effects (Amitay et al., 2006);
- Top-down processes (such as attention and arousal level) contribute significantly to the effectiveness of the intervention, although bottom-up auditory stimulation also plays a critical role (Amitay et al., 2006);
- General cognitive level seems to play an important role in effectiveness of the treatment, as children who are younger and/or have

a lower IQ tend to receive less benefit from training (Moore et al., 2009);

- Training effects tend to generalize to stimuli continua not used in the initial training protocol (Tremblay et al., 1997), although effects that generalize are weaker than those witnessed on the stimuli used in the actual training (Delhommeau et al., 2002; Delhommeau et al., 2005) and generalization tends to occur only after learning occurs with the initial stimuli (Wright, Wilson, & Sabin, 2010);
- Improvements can be noted electrophysiologically before they emerge in behavioral performance (Kraus et al., 1995); and
- Functional magnetic resonance imaging (fMRI) evidence of underlying training-induced activation changes suggests that there is not a single, simple pattern to be observed. In some cases, activation tends to decrease following training, consistent with more efficient recruitment of neural circuits (Jancke et al., 2001). In other cases, activation tends to increase and become more widespread (Temple et al., 2003).

Although computer-based auditory training is the form of remediation for (C)APD that shows the most support in the research literature, informal auditory training is often most easily instituted into the Individualized Education Plan (IEP) within the school setting. Reasons for this are varied, but often arise from the fact that the student is already receiving therapist-directed services, and informal one-on-one auditory processing training can be more seamlessly integrated with the existing IEP. As such, informal training exercises that mimic tasks found in computer-based programs can be delivered directly by an educational audiologist, speech-language pathologist, or other school professional. The informal aspects of training sacrifice the control and standardization of a computer-based procedure, although formal and informal tasks are generally similar enough that benefits with the latter can still be expected. Informal training is, therefore, the primary focus of the remainder of this section. These exercises will likely be most relevant to the professional working in the education system.

INFORMAL AUDITORY TRAINING WITH (CENTRAL) AUDITORY PROCESSING DISORDERS

An informal auditory training paradigm is selected based on the type of auditory processing deficit the child exhibits. For temporal sequencing deficits, the therapist can have the patient complete ordering and labeling tasks with nonspeech stimuli (Musiek, Chermak, & Weihing, 2007). This can be accomplished by using sounds recorded on a computer, a keyboard, or any electronic memory game, such as Simon®. A tonal sequence is played to the child without any visual cues and the child must repeat back the sequence heard. For instance, high-pitch and low-pitch tones might be played in a three-tone sequence and the child should repeat back the order of the tones he heard. As the child becomes more proficient at this task, a new tone can be added to the sequence, or the sequence length can be increased.

Another form of temporal sequencing training can be used to incorporate speech. This therapy is similar in approach to the sequencing training described above; however, it uses phonemes as the unit to be ordered instead of nonspeech stimuli. In short, the child is presented with a series of Consonant-Vowel-Consonant (CVC) words (e.g., "pan" and "cat") on flash cards, asked to say each word out loud, and then, without looking at the card, asked to substitute a phoneme in one word for a phoneme in the second word. For instance, the child might be asked to substitute the first sound in "pan" with the first sound in "cat" to produce the word "pat." This speech-based approach to auditory processing remediation tends to be more difficult than the nonspeech approach described above and is likely to be more heavily dependent on memory. However, it contains a level of ecological validity not obtained by traditional informal temporal processing training.

Temporal processing can also be targeted by addressing auditory discrimination ability. For example, vowel discrimination training may improve the ability of the CANS to identify frequency differences which contain meaningful information for communication (Musiek, Baran, & Schochat, 1999). Discrimination of subtle frequency cues, such as those which distinguish vowels, can become challenging in difficult listening situations for children with (C)APD. This informal training aims to improve detection of these cues under ideal listening conditions with the expectation that learning will be transferred to more complex listening environments. With this exercise, children are first asked to discriminate vowels in isolation. The vowels may be written by the therapist for purposes of identification, or the child may write down the vowel produced by the therapist. Once the child is able to complete this task with relative ease, the therapist should produce sequences of three vowels, CVs, or CVCs for the patient, depending on the desired level of difficulty. The therapist should then ask the patient which vowel was different from the other two. For example, the therapist might say "bo," "ko," and "ka." The patient would then need to correctly identify the third vowel as different from the first two. Sequences can also be lengthened beyond three tokens to further increase the task's difficulty.

For dichotic processing deficits, the therapist can have the patient complete an informal version of the Dichotic Interaural Intensity Difference (DIID) training (Moncrieff & Wertz, 2008; Musiek, 2004; Musiek & Schochat, 1998; Weihing & Musiek, 2007). This procedure is designed to address dichotic processing issues that are more severe in one ear. The therapist should present a continuous dialogue to the ear that performs better on dichotic tasks (e.g., the "stronger" ear). This dialogue can be presented over headphones from a DVD, audio-book, or any other type of media, as long as it is unfamiliar to the child. The ear that performs more poorly on dichotic tasks (e.g., the "weaker" ear) should be exposed to a different dialogue over headphones arising from a second media source also unfamiliar to the child. The dialogue in the weaker ear should be set to a conversational level, while the dialogue in the stronger ear should be set to a level at which 50% of the speech in the weaker can be understood (Figure 13–2). Once this level is established, both dialogues should be played while the child attends to the weaker ear in training blocks that are approximately 5 minutes in duration. Fol-

lowing this 5-minute interval, the child should be asked questions about the content of the dialogue in the poorer ear to ensure that he has understood it. The level of the dialogue in the stronger ear should be increased gradually over a period of weeks until the child is eventually able to follow the dialogue in the poorer ear when the interaural intensity level between the ears is approximately 0 dB.

For auditory closure deficits, there are several informal treatment options. First, speech-in-noise desensitization training will allow the patient to get practice detecting important speech information in difficult listening situations. Setup and administration of this procedure is relatively straightforward. A CD with a stereo speech babble track is used to present noise to the patient. Relatively nonoccluding ear buds should be used, similar to the style sold with iPods. The therapist reads some text to the child and the intensity of the babble is set to the lowest level at which 100% speech recognition performance can be obtained. Following determination of this level, the therapist continues to read an unfamiliar text to the child in training blocks lasting approximately 5 minutes. At the end of each block, the therapist asks the child specific questions about the text to ensure that he has been able to follow the auditory message. As with the DIID, the level of this competing stimulus should be gradually increased over a period of weeks until the child is able to follow the read message in a fairly difficult signal-to-noise ratio.

Several other compensatory training paradigms which aim to strengthen language and memory skills that support CAP can be utilized. With regard to language, building a child's vocabulary so that there is a greater degree of intrinsic

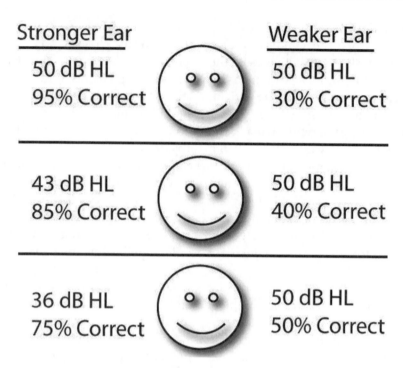

Stronger Ear

50 dB HL
95% Correct

Weaker Ear

50 dB HL
30% Correct

43 dB HL
85% Correct

50 dB HL
40% Correct

36 dB HL
75% Correct

50 dB HL
50% Correct

Figure 13–2. Establishing starting levels for the informal Dichotic Interaural Intensity Difference (DIID) procedure. At 30 dB HL in the right ear and 50 dB HL in the left ear, the patient obtains about 50% correct in the left ear, while still maintaining good right ear performance. Performance, therefore, indicates that this is a good starting level for the informal DIID procedure.

redundancy in the speech signal can often benefit the child. As discussed earlier in the classroom modifications section, if the child is provided with class-relevant vocabulary ahead of time, he can learn words before they are used in class, and CAP of the speech signal can occur in the context of existing language-related knowledge of the vocabulary word. These vocabulary building exercises would be expected to take considerable strain off the bottom-up CAP mechanism by enhancing top-down abilities.

It should be noted that auditory training, whether formal or informal, aims to improve the auditory processing ability alone. The link between auditory training and speech-language or reading improvements is much more tenuous. At best, it can be said that auditory processing may benefit the phonemic and phonological processing of the patient (Loo et al., 2010; Moore et al., 2005), and because this processing is known to be related to important speech-language and reading abilities, indirect benefits may be observed outside the auditory domain. Research is still inconclusive for defining the magnitude of the degree of observed benefits, however, and because of this, parents and teachers should always be cautioned that observable academic benefits, although possible, may be limited. Appendix 13-A gives step-by-step instructions for some informal auditory training exercises.

FORMAL MUSICAL TRAINING AS A (CENTRAL) AUDITORY PROCESSING DISORDERS THERAPY

Although not necessarily an option for all patients, formal training with a musical instrument conducted outside of school may provide additional therapeutic advantages for those diagnosed with (C)APD (for a thorough review, see Kraus & Chandrasekaran [2010] and Chermak [2010]). This therapy approach places obvious economic and time demands on the patient and patient's family, which may not occur with other treatment strategies. However, for many children, it offers a structured and engaging type of auditory training in which auditory events are discriminated, sequenced, and related to a visual representation of the perceived sound. This is thought to benefit not only temporal processing of auditory information, but the ability of the CANS to extract speech from background noise utilizing beneficial top-down mechanisms (Parbery-Clark, Skoe, & Kraus, 2009a; Parbery-Clark, Skoe, Lam, & Kraus, 2009b; Soncini & Costa, 2006; Strait, Kraus, Parbery-Clark, & Ashley, 2009).

As with many current forms of (C)APD remediation, evidence for the efficacy of formal musical training is still emerging. In pediatric samples, formal training predicted performance on measures of temporal processing (such as auditory discrimination), and some measures of speech-language abilities (Forgeard, Win-

ner, Norton, & Schlaug, 2008; Jentschke & Koelsch, 2009; Marin, 2009; Moreno, Marques, Santos, Castro, & Besson, 2009). It has been suggested that one potential reason for the transfer of benefits to speech-language functions is that musical training enhances the ability of the child to detect pitch contour changes inherent to speech (Schon, Magne, & Besson, 2004).

Studies have also shown that subjects with formal musical training have detectable electrophysiological differences in cortical and/or subcortical temporal processing of auditory information (Fujioka, Ross, Kakigi, Pantev, & Trainor, 2006; Moreno et al., 2009; Musacchia, Sams, Skoe, & Kraus, 2007; Musacchia, Striat, & Kraus, 2008; Trainor, Shahin, & Roberts, 2003; Wang Staffaroni, Reid, Steinschneider, & Sussman, 2009). Interestingly, some variance in electrophysiological indices is also explained by the age at which musicians started their training and the number of years they had been practicing (Trainor et al., 2003; Musacchia et al, 2008), although differences were still noted with as little as six months (Moreno et al., 2009) to one year of training (Fujioka et al., 2006).

Relatively direct assessment of auditory regions of the central nervous system has indicated some areas that might be involved with this beneficial training effect. Hyde and colleagues (2009) showed that fMRI-measured activation in the right Heschl's gyrus was greater in children who were trained on an instrument for approximately a year and a half when compared to untrained controls, and that this increase in activation correlated with improvements in behavioral performance on auditory measures. Additionally, using diffusion tensor imaging, Imfeld, Oechslin, Meyer, Loenneker, and Jancke (2009) noticed white matter differences that were also dependent on the number of years of training in musicians relative to controls.

The logistics of implementing formal musical training as a (C)APD treatment will vary somewhat with the resources available to the patient. There is no evidence to date that one particular style of teaching music is better than another when it comes to treating (C)APD. It is important that the child is able to produce different pitches on the instrument, as is the case with most string, brass, and woodwind instruments. Additionally, the child's instructor should be educated about the nature of (C)APD and advised to gauge the difficulty of sessions to the child's ability. If sessions are initially made too difficult, there is a chance that the student would become frustrated, potentially decreasing motivation.

SELECTING THE APPROPRIATE TREATMENT PLAN

The structure of a successful (C)APD treatment plan will vary considerably with the circumstances surrounding each child. Most approaches will encompass a three-tiered plan, in which auditory training at school, auditory training at home, and classroom modifications will all be incorporated to some extent. Auditory training at school is generally process-specific, targeting the auditory process on which the child shows the greatest difficulty during CAP assessment. Informal strategies are utilized in this environment, as discussed previously in this chapter. Although there is no existing research to indicate that targeting the affected auditory process benefits the child more than

using a more general training paradigm, targeting the affected process would seem to have greater face validity as it attempts to improve an auditory skill by having the child use that skill. It is generally recommended that the child participate in this activity for approximately a half-hour, three to four times a week.

Unlike direct services received at school, training at home follows a more structured protocol and often utilizes computer-based training. These computer-based auditory training products are recommended to parents, with special consideration given to the type of operating system and availability of computer hardware. The recommended schedule for this computer-based task is generally a half hour, four times a week. Parents are reminded that, although the computer games may initially start out easy, they will become progressively more difficult over time as the child's level of ability is determined by the software. Although this computer-based approach does not necessarily target the CAP most affected by the disorder, it does attempt to strengthen general auditory processing and supramodal factors related to these skills. Depending on the interest level of the child, formal musical training may also be selected as part of the home training plan. If music training is chosen, then the amount of recommended time that the child spends on computer-based methods is typically reduced.

Modifications to the child's classroom situation are highly specific to the child's history and environment. For this reason, during the initial interview, it is important to determine specific detrimental factors in the child's classroom that hinder communication. Any number of classroom modifications, teacher communication strategies, or listening enhancement techniques on the part of the child can be used to provide a better learning environment. These types of recommendations are typically made for all children diagnosed with (C)APD and can yield considerable benefit with only a small degree of individualization required.

The decision to add hearing assistance technology or a personal amplification device is also specific to the individual student and family, and is often limited by financial considerations. Classroom modifications, such as preferential seating, can frequently accomplish the goal of these amplification devices without having the child wear any visual accessory and without the associated costs.

Age is also a consideration when selecting therapy options, especially as children approach their teenage years. If the personal amplification system or hearing aid is unlikely to be used due to a perceived stigma, then there may be little benefit to actually having the parents or school purchase a device. If it is determined that hearing assistance technology should be used by the child, then all involved parties must remember that the device is a short-term solution to the processing issue and continued use may only create a dependency on the system when listening in noise. For long-term solutions, it is likely that auditory training needs to be incorporated into the treatment plan as well.

As the overall treatment plan is being finalized, several additional limiting factors must be taken into consideration. The first of these factors is the importance of generating the management plan within the context of the other professionals working with the child. Among these professionals may be the school psychologist and/or SLP, both of whom may also have made recommendations for remediation. The CAP management plan should be explained to these other professionals, and the primacy, or lack thereof, of the CAP issue should be identified within the context of other developmental issues. The overall goal of this collaboration is to provide the child with an appropriate treatment plan that covers all diagnosed deficits, but does not overwhelm him. As stated earlier, the effectiveness of therapies tend to be dependent on the degree of motivation exhibited by the child. In this way, a few carefully selected exercises may be more beneficial in the long run than providing an abundance of suggestions that may not be incorporated.

In normal hearing individuals, informal auditory training effects are generally noted relatively quickly; that is, within a period of less than 2 months (Alonso & Schochat, 2009; Moore et al, 2009; Schochat, Musiek, Alonso, & Ogata, 2010). Monitoring of treatment effectiveness is generally desirable, although not always possible given the limitations of insurance coverage and patient finances. If benefits are not noted during the first several months of therapy, the treatment plan should be modified or intensified, depending on the degree of the deficit witnessed. Given that CAP ability is subject to maturational effects (Ivone & Schochat, 2005; Ponton, Eggermont, Khosla, Kwong, & Don, 2002), it is likely that performance on (C)APD measures will improve over time even in the absence of effective treatment. However, the initiation of an effective treatment plan prior to complete maturation can help children with (C)APD compensate for their deficits and may help them obtain academic results more consistent with their true abilities.

REFERENCES

Agnew, J., Dorn, C., & Eden, G. (2004). Effect of intensive training on auditory processing and reading skills. *Brain and Language, 88*, 21–25.

Akeroyd, M. A. (2006). The psychoacoustics of binaural hearing. *International Journal of Audiology, 45* (Suppl. 1), S25–S33.

Alonso, R., & Schochat, E. (2009). The efficacy of formal auditory training in children with (central) auditory processing disorder: Behavioral and electrophysiological evaluation. *Brazilian Journal of Otorhinolaryngology, 75*(5), 726–732.

American Academy of Audiology. (2010). American Academy of Audiology clinical practice guidelines: Diagnosis, treatment, and management of children and adults with central auditory processing disorder. Retrieved from http://www.audiology.org/resources/documentlibrary/Documents/CAPD%20Guidelines%208-2010.pdf .

American Speech-Language-Hearing Association. (2005). *(Central) auditory processing disorders* [Technical report]. Available from http://www.asha.org/policy .

Amitay, S., Irwin, A., & Moore, D. R. (2006). Discrimination learning induced by training with identical stimuli. *Nature Neuroscience, 9*(11), 1446–1448.

Amos, N. E., & Humes, L. E. (1998). SCAN test-retest reliability for first- and third-grade children. *Journal of Speech Language Hearing Research, 41*(4), 834–845.

Anderson, S., Skoe, E., Chandrasekaran, B., & Kraus, N. (2010). Neural timing is linked to speech perception in noise. *Journal of Neuroscience, 30*(14), 4922–4926.

Arehole, S., Augustine, L., & Simhadri, R. (1995). Middle latency response in children with learning disabilities: Preliminary findings. *Journal of Communication Disorders, 28*, 21–38.

Arnold, P., & Canning, D. (1999). Does classroom amplification aid comprehension? *British Journal of Audiology, 33*(3), 171–178.

Atcherson, S., Gould, H., Mendel, M., & Ethington, C. (2009). Auditory N1 component to gaps in continuous narrowband noises. *Ear and Hearing, 30*, 687–695.

Au, A., & Lovegrove, B. (2001). Temporal processing ability in above average and average readers. *Perception and Psychophysics, 63*(1), 148–155.

Bamiou, D., Campbell, N. G., Musiek, F. E., Taylor, R., Chong, W. K., Moore, A., . . . Luxon, L. M. (2007). Auditory and verbal working memory deficits in a child with congenital aniridia due to a PAX6 mutation. *International Journal of Audiology, 46*(4), 196–202.

Bamiou, D., Free, S. L., Sisodiya, S. M., Chong, W. K., Musiek, F., Williamson, K. A., . . . Luxon, L. M. (2007). Auditory interhemispheric transfer deficits, hearing difficulties, and brain magnetic resonance imaging abnormalities in children with congenital aniridia due to PAX6 mutations. *Archives of Pediatrics & Adolescent Medicine, 161*(5), 463–469.

Bamiou, D., Musiek, F. E., & Luxon, L. M. (2001). Aetiology and clinical presentations of auditory processing disorders—a review. *Archives of Disease in Childhood, 85*(5), 361–365.

Banai, K., Abrams, D., & Kraus, N. (2007). Sensory-based learning disability: Insights from brainstem processing of speech sounds. *International Journal of Audiology, 46*, 524–532.

Baran, J. (1998, November), *Classroom strategies*. Paper presented at the American Speech-Language-Hearing Association convention, San Antonio, TX.

Baran, J. A., Bothfeldt, R. W., & Musiek, F. E. (2004). Central auditory deficits associated with compromise of the primary auditory cortex. *Journal of the American Academy of Audiology, 15*(2), 106–116.

Benasich, A. A., & Tallal, P. (2002). Infant discrimination of rapid auditory cues predicts later language impairment. *Behavioural Brain Research, 136*(1), 31.

Billiet, C., & Bellis, T. (2011). The relationship between brainstem temporal processing and performance on tests of central auditory function in children with reading disorders. *Journal of Speech Language and Hearing Research. 54*, 228–242.

Boscariol, M., Garcia, V. L., Guimarães, C. A., Hage, S. R. V., Montenegro, M. A., Cendes, F., & Guerreiro, M. M. (2009). Auditory processing disorders in twins with perisylvian polymicrogyria. *Arquivos De Neuro-Psiquiatria, 67*(2B), 499–501.

Boscariol, M., Garcia, V. L., Guimaraes, C. A., Montenegro, M. A., Vasconcelos Hage, S. R., Cendes, F., & Guerreiro, M. M. (2010). Auditory processing disorders in perisylvian syndrome. *Brain and Development, 32*(4), 299–304.

Bradley, J. S., & Sato, H. (2008). The intelligibility of speech in elementary school classrooms. *Journal of the Acoustical Society of America, 123*(4), 2078–2086.

Cameron, S., & Dillon, H. (2008). The Listening In Spatialized Noise-Sentences Test (LISN-S): Comparison to the prototype LISN and results from children with either a suspected (central) auditory processing disorder or a confirmed language disorder. *Journal of the American Academy of Audiology, 19*(5), 377–391.

Chermak, G. D. (2002). Deciphering auditory processing disorders in children. *Otolaryngologic Clinics of North America, 35*(4), 733–749.

Chermak, G. D. (2010). Music and auditory training. *Hearing Journal, 63*(4), 57–58.

Chermak, G., & Musiek, F. (1997). *Central auditory processing disorders: New perspectives.* San Diego, CA: Singular.

Chermak, G., Somers, E., & Seikel, J. (1998). Behavioral signs of central auditory processing disorder and attention deficit hyperactivity disorder. *Journal of the American Academy of Audiology, 9*, 78–84.

Corriveau, K. H., Goswami, U., & Thomson, J. M. (2010). Auditory processing and early literacy skills in a preschool and kindergarten population. *Journal of Learning Disabilities, 43*(4), 369–382.

Dawes, P., Bishop, D. V. M., Sirimanna, T., & Bamiou, D.-E. (2008). Profile and aetiology of children diagnosed with auditory processing disorder (APD. *International Journal of Pediatric Otorhinolaryngology, 72*(4), 483–489.

Delhommeau, K., Micheyl, C., & Jouvent, R. (2005). Generalization of frequency discrimination learning across frequencies and ears: Implications for underlying neural mechanisms in humans. *Journal of the Association for Research in Otolaryngology, 6*(2), 171–179.

Delhommeau, K., Micheyl, C., Jouvent, R., & Collet, L. (2002). Transfer of learning across durations and ears in auditory frequency discrimination. *Perception and Psychophysics, 64*(3), 426–436.

Elliot, L., Connors, S., Kille, E., Levin, S., Ball, K., & Katz, D. (1979). Children's understanding of monosyllabic nouns in quiet and in noise. *Journal of the Acoustical Society of America, 66*, 12–21.

Finitzo-Hieber, T., & Tillman, T. W. (1978). Room acoustics effects on monosyllabic word discrimination ability for normal and hearing-impaired children. *Journal of Speech and Hearing Research, 21*(3), 440–458.

Fisher, L. I. (1976). *Fisher Auditory Problem Checklist.* Cedar Rapids, IA: Grant Wood Area Educational Agency.

Forgeard, M., Winner, E., Norton, A., & Schlaug, G. (2008). Practicing a musical instrument in childhood is associated with enhanced verbal ability and nonverbal reasoning. *PLoS ONE, 3*(10), 1–8.

Foxton, J. M., Brown, A. C. B., Chambers, S., & Griffiths, T. D. (2004). Training improves acoustic pattern perception. *Current Biology, 14*(4), 322.

Friend, A., & Olson, R. K. (2008). Phonological spelling and reading deficits in children with spelling disabilities. *Scientific Studies of Reading, 12*(1), 90–105.

Fujioka, T., Ross, B., Kakigi, R., Pantev, C., & Trainor, L. J. (2006). One year of musical training affects development of auditory cortical-evoked fields in young children. *Brain, 129*(Pt. 10), 2593–2608.

Gilley, P. M., Sharma, A., Dorman, M., & Martin, K. (2006). Abnormalities in central auditory maturation in children with language-based learning problems. *Clinical Neurophysiology, 117*(9), 1949–1956.

Gravel, J. S., Wallace, I. F., & Ruben, R. J. (1996). Auditory consequences of early mild hearing loss associated with otitis media. *Acta Oto-Laryngologica, 116*(2), 219–221.

Hall, J. W., 3rd, & Grose, J. H. (1993). Short-term and long-term effects on the masking level difference following middle ear surgery. *Journal of the American Academy of Audiology, 4*(5), 307–312.

Hall, J. W., III, Grose, J. H., Dev, M. B., & Ghiassi, S. (1998). The effect of masker interaural time delay on the masking level difference in children with history of normal hearing or history of otitis media with effusion. *Ear and Hearing, 19*(6), 429–433.

Hall, J. W., III, Grose, J. H., & Pillsbury, H. C. (1995). Long-term effects of chronic otitis media on binaural hearing in children. *Archives of Otolaryngology-Head and Neck Surgery, 121*(8), 847–852.

Hannay, H. J., Walker, A., Dennis, M., Kramer, L., Blaser, S., & Fletcher, J. M. (2008). Auditory interhemispheric transfer in relation to patterns of partial agenesis and hypoplasia of the corpus callosum in spina bifida meningomyelocele. *Journal of the International Neuropsychological Society, 14*(5), 771–781.

Hill, P. R., Hogben, J. H., & Bishop, D. M. V. (2005). Auditory frequency discrimination in children with specific language impairment: A longitudinal study. *Journal of Speech, Language and Hearing Research, 48*(5), 1136–1146.

Hodgson, M., & Nosal, E. (2002). Effect of noise and occupancy on optimal reverberation times for speech intelligibility in classrooms. *Journal of the Acoustical Society of America, 111*, 931–939.

Hoffman-Lawless, K., Keith, R. W., & Cotton, R. T. (1981). Auditory processing abilities in children with previous middle ear effusion. *Annals of Otology, Rhinology, and Laryngology, 90*(6, Pt. 1), 543–545.

Hurley, R., & Musiek, F. (1997). Effectiveness of three central auditory processing (CAP) tests in identifying cerebral lesions. *Journal of the American Academy of Audiology, 8*, 257–262.

Hyde, K. L., Lerch, J., Norton, A., Forgeard, M., Winner, E., Evans, A. C., & Schlaug, G. (2009). Musical training shapes structural brain development. *Journal of Neuroscience, 29*(10), 3019–3025.

Hygge, S. (1993). A comparison between the impact of noise from aircraft, road traffic and trains on long-term recall and recognition of a text in children aged 12–14 years. *Schriftenreihe Des Vereins Für Wasser-, Boden- Und Lufthygiene, 88*, 416–427.

Iliadou, V., Bamiou, D., Kaprinis, S., Kandylis, D., Vlaikidis, N., Apalla, K., & St. Kaprinis, G. (2008). Auditory processing disorder and brain pathology in a preterm child with learning disabilities. *Journal of the American Academy of Audiology, 19*(7), 557–563.

Imfeld, A., Oechslin, M. S., Meyer, M., Loenneker, T., & Jancke, L. (2009). White matter plasticity in the corticospinal tract of musicians: A diffusion tensor imaging study. *NeuroImage, 46*(3), 600–607.

Ivone, F. N., & Schochat, E. (2005). Auditory processing maturation in children with and without learning difficulties. *Pró-Fono, 17*(3), 311–320.

Jäncke, L., Gaab, N., Wüstenberg, T., Scheich, H., & Heinze, H. J. (2001). Short-term functional plasticity in the human auditory cortex: An fMRI study. *Cognitive Brain Research, 12*(3), 479–485.

Jentschke, S., & Koelsch, S. (2009). Musical training modulates the development of syntax processing in children. *NeuroImage, 47*(2), 735–744.

Jerger, J., Chmiel, R., Tonini, R., Murphy, E., & Kent, M. (1999). Twin study of central auditory processing disorder. *Journal of the American Academy of Audiology, 10*, 521–528.

Jerger, S. (1987). Validation of the pediatric speech intelligibility test in children with central nervous system lesions. *Audiology, 26*(5), 298–311.

Jerger, S., Johnson, K., & Loiselle, L. (1988). Pediatric central auditory dysfunction. Comparison of children with confirmed lesions versus suspected processing disorders. *American Journal of Otology*, *9*(Suppl.), 63–71.

Johnson, K., Nicol, T., & Kraus, N. (2005). Brain stem response to speech: A biological marker of auditory processing. *Ear and Hearing*, *26*, 424–434.

Johnston, K. N., John, A. B., Kreisman, N. V., Hall, J. W., III, & Crandell, C. C. (2009). Multiple benefits of personal FM system use by children with auditory processing disorder (APD). *International Journal of Audiology*, *48*(6), 371–383.

Katz, J., & Tillery, K. (2005). Can central auditory processing tests resist supramodal influences? *American Journal of Audiology*, *14*, 124–127.

Keith, R. W. (2000). Development and standardization of SCAN-C Test for auditory processing disorders in children. *Journal of the American Academy of Audiology*, *11*(8), 438–445.

Keith, R. W., & Engineer, P. (1991). Effects of methylphenidate on the auditory processing abilities of children with attention deficit-hyperactivity disorder. *Journal of Learning Disabilities*, *24*(10), 630–636.

King, C., Warrier, C. M., Hayes, E., & Kraus, N. (2002). Deficits in auditory brainstem pathway encoding of speech sounds in children with learning problems. *Neuroscience Letters*, *319*(2), 111–115.

Knecht, H. A., Nelson, P. B., Whitelaw, G. M., & Feth, L. L. (2002). Background noise levels and reverberation times in unoccupied classrooms: Predictions and measurements. *American Journal of Audiology*, *11*(2), 65–71.

Kraus, N. (1999). Speech sound perception, neurophysiology, and plasticity. *International Journal of Pediatric Otorhinolaryngology*, *47*(2), 123–129.

Kraus, N., & Chandrasekaran, B. (2010). Music training for the development of auditory skills. *Nature Reviews Neuroscience*, *11*(8), 599–605.

Kraus, N., McGee, T., Carrell, T., & King, C. (1995). Central auditory system plasticity associated with speech discrimination

training. *Journal of Cognitive Neuroscience*, *7*, 25–32.

Kujala, T. (2000). Basic auditory dysfunction in dyslexia as demonstrated by brain activity measurements. *Psychophysiology*, *37*(2), 262–266.

Kujala, T., Karma, K., Ceponiene, R., Belitz, S., Turkkila, P., Tervaniemi, M., & Näätänen, R. (2001). Plastic neural changes and reading improvement caused by audiovisual training in reading-impaired children. *Proceedings of the National Academy of Sciences of the United States of America*, *98*(18), 10509–10514.

Kuk, F., Jackson, A., Keenan, D., & Lau, C. (2008). Personal amplification for school-age children with auditory processing disorders. *Journal of the American Academy of Audiology*, *19*, 465–480.

Larsen, J. B., & Blair, J. C. (2008). The effect of classroom amplification on the signal-to-noise ratio in classrooms while class is in session. *Language, Speech, and Hearing Services in Schools*, *39*(4), 451–460.

Lemos, I. C. C., Jacob, R. T. d. S., Gejão, M. G., Bevilacqua, M. C., Feniman, M. R., & Ferrari, D. V. (2009). Frequency modulation (FM) system in auditory processing disorder: An evidence-based practice? *Pró-Fono*, *21*(3), 243–248.

Loo, J. H. Y., Bamiou, D., Campbell, N., & Luxon, L. M. (2010). Computer-based auditory training (CBAT): Benefits for children with language- and reading-related learning difficulties. *Developmental Medicine and Child Neurology*, *52*(8), 708–717.

Marin, M. M. (2009). Effects of early musical training on musical and linguistic syntactic abilities. *Annals of the New York Academy of Sciences*, *1169*, 187–190.

Mengler, E. D., Hogben, J. H., Michie, P., & Bishop, D. V. M. (2005). Poor frequency discrimination is related to oral language disorder in children: A psychoacoustic study. *Dyslexia*, *11*(3), 155–173.

Merzenich, M., Jenkins, W., & Johnston, P. (1996). Temporal processing deficits of language-learning impaired children ameliorated by training. *Science*, *271*, 77–81.

Moncrieff, D., & Wertz , D. (2008). Auditory rehabilitation for interaural asymmetry: Preliminary evidence of improved dichotic listening performance following intensive training. *International Journal of Audiology, 47,* 84–97.

Moore, D. R., Halliday, L. F., & Amitay, S. (2009). Use of auditory learning to manage listening problems in children. *Philosophical Transactions of the Royal Society of London Biological Sciences, 364*(1515), 409–420.

Moore, D. R., Hutchings, M. E., & Meyer, S. E. (1991). Binaural masking level differences in children with a history of otitis media. *Audiology, 30*(2), 91–101.

Moore, D. R., Rosenberg, J. F., & Coleman, J. S. (2005). Discrimination training of phonemic contrasts enhances phonological processing in mainstream school children. *Brain and Language, 94*(1), 72–85.

Moreno, S., Marques, C., Santos, A., Santos, M., Castro, S. L., & Besson, M. (2009). Musical training influences linguistic abilities in 8-year-old children: More evidence for brain plasticity. *Cerebral Cortex, 19*(3), 712–723.

Musacchia, G., Sams, M., Skoe, E., & Kraus, N. (2007). Musicians have enhanced subcortical auditory and audiovisual processing of speech and music. *Proceedings of the National Academy of Sciences of the U.S.A., 104*(40), 15894.

Musacchia, G., Strait, D., & Kraus, N. (2008). Relationships between behavior, brainstem and cortical encoding of seen and heard speech in musicians and non-musicians. *Hearing Research, 241*(1–2), 34–42.

Musiek, F. (Unpublished data). *Dichotic interaural intensity difference training in children with (C)APD.*

Musiek, F. (1983a). Results of three dichotic speech tests on subjects with intracranial lesions. *Ear and Hearing, 4,* 318–323.

Musiek, F. (1983b). Assessment of central auditory dysfunction: The dichotic digit test revisited. *Ear and Hearing, 4,* 79–83.

Musiek, F. (2004). The DIID: A new treatment for APD. *Hearing Journal, 57,* 50.

Musiek, F. E., Baran, J. A., & Schochat, E. (1999). Selected management approaches to central auditory processing disorders. *Scandinavian Audiology Supplement, 28,* 63–76.

Musiek, F., Baran, J., & Shinn, J. (2004). Assessment and remediation of an auditory processing disorder associated with head trauma. *Journal of the American Academy of Audiology, 15,* 133–151.

Musiek, F., Chermak, G., & Weihing, J. (2007). Auditory training. In G. Chermak & F. Musiek (Eds.), *Handbook of (central) auditory processing disorder—comprehensive intervention.* San Diego, CA: Plural.

Musiek, F., & Lee, W. (1997). Conventional and maximum length sequences middle latency response in patients with central nervous system lesions. *Journal of the American Academy of Audiology, 8,* 173–180.

Musiek, F. E., & Pinheiro, M. L. (1987). Frequency patterns in cochlear, brainstem, and cerebral lesions. *Audiology, 26*(2), 79–88.

Musiek, F., & Schochat, E. (1998). Auditory training and central auditory processing disorders. *Seminars in Hearing, 9,* 357–366.

Musiek, F., Shinn, J., Jirsa, R., Bamiou, D., Baran, J., & Zaida, E. (2005). GIN (Gaps-In-Noise) test performance in subjects with confirmed central auditory nervous system involvement. *Ear and Hearing, 26,* 608–618.

Neuman, A. C., & Hochberg, I. (1983). Children's perception of speech in reverberation. *Journal of the Acoustical Society of America, 73*(6), 2145–2149.

Norrelgen, F., Lacerda, F., & Forssberg, H. (2001). Temporal resolution of auditory perception in relation to perception, memory, and language skills in typical children. *Journal of Learning Disabilities, 34*(4), 359–369.

Parbery-Clark, A., Skoe, E., & Kraus, N. (2009a). Musical experience limits the degradative effects of background noise on the neural processing of sound. *Journal of Neuroscience, 29,* 14100–14107.

Parbery-Clark, A., Skoe, E., Lam, C., & Kraus, N. (2009b). Musician enhancement for speech-in-noise. *Ear and Hearing, 30,* 653–661.

Parviainen, T., Helenius, P., Poskiparta, E., Niemi, P., & Salmelin, R. (2006). Cortical sequence of word perception in beginning readers. *Journal of Neuroscience, 26*(22), 6052–6061.

Pillsbury, H. C., Grose, J. H., & Hall, J. W., III. (1991). Otitis media with effusion in children. Binaural hearing before and after corrective surgery. *Archives of Otolaryngology-Head and Neck Surgery, 117*(7), 718–723.

Ponton, C., Eggermont, J. J., Khosla, D., Kwong, B., & Don, M. (2002). Maturation of human central auditory system activity: Separating auditory evoked potentials by dipole source modeling. *Clinical Neurophysiology, 113*(3), 407–420.

Purdy, S., Kelly, A., & Davies, M. (2002). Auditory brainstem response, middle latency response, and late cortical evoked potentials in children with learning disabilities. *Journal of the American Academy of Audiology, 13*, 367–382.

Riccio, C. A., Cohen, M. J., Hynd, G. W., & Keith, R. W. (1996). Validity of the auditory continuous performance test in differentiating central processing auditory disorders with and without ADHD. *Journal of Learning Disabilities, 29*(5), 561–566.

Richard, G., & Ferre, J. (2006). *Differential Screening Test for Processing*. East Moline, IL: LinguiSystems.

Richardson, U., Thomson, J. M., Scott, S. K., & Goswami, U. (2004). Auditory processing skills and phonological representation in dyslexic children. *Dyslexia, 10*(3), 215–233.

Schmithorst, V. J., Holland, S. K., & Plante, E. (2011). Diffusion tensor imaging reveals white matter microstructure correlations with auditory processing ability. *Ear and Hearing, 32*(2), 156–167.

Schochat, E., & Musiek, F. (2006). Maturation of outcomes of behavioral and electrophysiological tests of central auditory function. *Journal of Communication Disorders, 39*, 78–92.

Schochat, E., Musiek, F. E., Alonso, R., & Ogata, J. (2010). Effect of auditory training on the middle latency response in children with (central) auditory processing disorder.

Brazilian Journal of Medical and Biological Research, 43(8), 777–785.

Schon, D., Magne, C., & Besson, M. (2004). The music of speech: Music training facilitates pitch processing in both music and language. *Psychophysiology, 41*, 341–349.

Shapiro, L. R., Hurry, J., Masterson, J., Wydell, T. N., & Doctor, E. (2009). Classroom implications of recent research into literacy development: from predictors to assessment. *Dyslexia, 15*(1), 1–22.

Sharma, M., Purdy, S. C., & Kelly, A. S. (2009). Comorbidity of auditory processing, language, and reading disorders. *Journal of Speech, Language, and Hearing Research, 52*(3), 706–722.

Smoski, W., Brunt, M., & Tannahill, J. (1998). *Children's Auditory Performance Scale*. Tampa, FL: Educational Audiology Association.

Soncini, F., & Costa, M. J. (2006). The effect of musical practice on speech recognition in quiet and noisy situations. *Pró-Fono, 18*(2), 161–170.

Strait, D. L., Kraus, N., Parbery-Clark, A., & Ashley, R. (2010). Musical experience shapes top-down auditory mechanisms: Evidence from masking and auditory attention performance. *Hearing Research, 261*(1–2), 22–29.

Sussman, E., Stemschneider, M., Gumenyuk, V., Grushko, J., & Lawson, K. (2008). The maturation of human evoked brain potentials to sounds presented at different stimulus rates. *Hearing Research, 236*(1–2), 61–79.

Tallal, P. (1980). Auditory temporal perception, phonics, and reading disabilities in children. *Brain and Language, 9*(2), 182–198.

Tallal, P., Merzenich, M. M., Miller, S., & Jenkins, W. (1998). Language learning impairments: Integrating basic science, technology, and remediation. *Experimental Brain Research, Experimentelle Hirnforschung. Expérimentation Cérébrale, 123*(1–2), 210–219.

Tallal, P., Miller, S. L., Bedi, G., Byma, G., Wang, X., Nagarajan, S. S., . . . Merzenich, M. M. (1996). Language comprehension in language-learning impaired children improved with acoustically modified speech. *Science, 271*(5245), 81–84.

Tallal, P., Stark, R. E., & Mellits, D. (1985). The relationship between auditory temporal analysis and receptive language development: Evidence from studies of developmental language disorder. *Neuropsychologia, 23*(4), 527–534.

Temple, E., Deutsch, G. K., Poldrack, R. A., Miller, S. L., Tallal, P., Merzenich, M. M., & Gabrieli, J. D. E. (2003). Neural deficits in children with dyslexia ameliorated by behavioral remediation: evidence from functional MRI. *Proceedings of the National Academy of Sciences of the U.S.A., 100*(5), 2860–2865.

Tillman, T., & Carhart, R. (1966). *An expanded test for speech discrimination utilizing CNC monosyllabic words* (Northwestern University Auditory Test No. 6). [Technical report No. SAM-TR-66-55], USAF School of Aerospace Medicine, Brooks Air Force Base, Texas.

Trainor, L. J., Shahin, A., & Roberts, L. E. (2003). Effects of musical training on the auditory cortex in children. *Annals of the New York Academy of Sciences, 999*, 506.

Tremblay, K. L., & Kraus, N. (2002). Auditory training induces asymmetrical changes in cortical neural activity. *Journal of Speech-Language-Hearing Research, 45*(3), 564–572.

Tremblay, K., Kraus, N., Carrell, T. D., & McGee, T. (1997). Central auditory system plasticity: Generalization to novel stimuli following listening training. *Journal of the Acoustical Society of America, 102*(6), 3762–3773.

Tremblay, K., Kraus, N., & McGee, T. (1998). The time course of auditory perceptual learning: neurophysiological changes during speech-sound training. *NeuroReport, 9*(16), 3557–3560.

Tremblay, K., Kraus, N., McGee, T., Ponton, C., & Otis, B. (2001). Central auditory plasticity: Changes in the N1-P2 complex after speech-sound training. *Ear and Hearing, 22*(2), 79–90.

Walker, K. M. M., Hall, S. E., Klein, R. M., & Phillips, D. P. (2006). Development of perceptual correlates of reading performance. *Brain Research, 1124*, 126–141.

Wambacq, I. J. A., Koehnke, J., Shea-Miller, K. J., Besing, J., Toth, V., & Abubakr, A. (2007). Auditory evoked potentials in the detection of interaural intensity differences in children and adults. *Ear and Hearing, 28*(3), 320–331.

Wang, W., Staffaroni, L., Reid, E., Jr., Steinschneider, M., & Sussman, E. (2009). Effects of musical training on sound pattern processing in high-school students. *International Journal of Pediatric Otorhinolaryngology, 73*(5), 751–755.

Wayland, R. P., Eckhouse, E., Lombardino, L., & Roberts, R. (2010). Speech perception among school-aged skilled and less skilled readers. *Journal of Psycholinguistic Research, 39*(6), 465–484.

Wechsler, D. (2003). *Wechsler Intelligence Scale for Children* (4th ed.). San Antonio, TX: Psychological Corporation.

Weihing, J., & Musiek, F. (2007). Dichotic interaural intensity difference (DIID) training. In D. Geffner & D. Ross-Swain. *Auditory processing disorders*. San Diego, CA: Plural.

Willeford, J. (1976). Central auditory function in children with learning disabilities. *Audiology and Hearing Education, 2*, 12–20.

Willeford, J., & Burleigh, J. (1994). Sentence procedures in central testing. In J. Katz (Ed.), *Handbook of clinical audiology* (4th ed.). Baltimore, MD: Williams & Wilkins.

Wilson, R. H., Farmer, N. M., Gandhi, A., Shelburne, E., & Weaver, J. (2010). Normative data for the words-in-noise test for 6- to 12-year-old children. *Journal of Speech, Language and Hearing Research, 53*(5), 1111–1121.

Wilson, R. H., Zizz, C. A., & Sperry, J. L. (1994). Masking-level difference for spondaic words in 2000-msec bursts of broadband noise. *Journal of the American Academy of Audiology, 5*(4), 236–242.

Wilson, W. J., Jackson, A., Pender, A., Rose, C., Wilson, J., Heine, C., & Khan, A. (2011). The CHAPS, SIFTER, and TAPS-R as predictors of (C)AP Skills and (C)APD. *Journal of Speech, Language, and Hearing Research, 54*(1), 278–291.

Witton, C. (2010). Childhood auditory processing disorder as a developmental disorder: The case for a multi-professional approach to diagnosis and management. *International Journal of Audiology, 49*(2), 83–87.

Wood, F. B., Hill, D. F., Meyer, M. S., & Flowers, D. L. (2005). Predictive assessment of reading. *Annals of Dyslexia, 55*(2), 193–216.

Wright, B., Wilson, R., & Sabin, A. (2010). Generalization lags behind perception on an auditory perceptual task. *Journal of Neuroscience, 30,* 11635–11639.

Xu, H., Kotak, V. C., & Sanes, D. H. (2007). Conductive hearing loss disrupts synaptic and spike adaptation in developing auditory cortex. *Journal of Neuroscience, 27*(35), 9417–9426.

APPENDIX 13-A

Instructions for Three Informal Auditory Training Exercises

INFORMAL TEMPORAL SEQUENCING TRAINING (TST)

What Is Needed for TST?

The Milton Bradley game Simon®, a piano, or any other means for consistently generating a sequence of tones.

How Is the TST Administered?

For the purposes of this example, it is assumed that the Simon® game will be used, although an alternative device can be substituted with some minor modifications to the steps below:

- The student should initially play the "Game 1" setting of Simon® for about 15 minutes several times a week for 2 weeks. This will familiarize the student with the tones generated by the standard game.
- Following this period of orientation, the therapist should verbally label or define the four different Simon® sounds for the child. The lowest and highest pitches produced by Simon® can be labeled "low" and "high," respectively. The tone that is slightly higher in pitch than the low tone can be labeled "almost-low," and the tone that is slightly lower in pitch

than the high tone can be labeled "almost-high."
- To familiarize the student with these labels, she or he should be turned around while the therapist generates some Simon® tones. (Setting Simon® to "Game 2" will allow the therapist to play tones separately without actually engaging the traditional Simon® game.) The therapist should start by playing the two easiest tones: "low" and "high." The therapist should provide the student with assistance for labeling the tones, and once they are mastered, introduce the "almost-low" and "almost-high" tones. The student should be able to label the tones with relative ease before the therapist moves to the next step. This may take several sessions, although it can occur relatively quickly depending on the child.
- Although the Simon® game can be used to perform many different types of sequencing exercises, three are recommended here in order of increasing difficulty. The therapist must produce the tone sequences while the student, with his or her back to the Simon® game, performs the appropriate labeling tasks:
  1. The therapist should label one of the tones as a target tone and play it for the student. The

student should repeat the label for the tone heard. Next, the therapist should play a sequence of three tones for the student. The therapist should hold the Simon® button down for about one second, wait an additional second, and then play the next tone. The student should then verbally label the target tone when he or she hears it. At the end of the sequence, the student should tell the therapist if the target tone was at the beginning, middle, or end of the sequence.

2. The therapist should play a sequence of three tones, holding each tone for one second with a wait period of one second between each tone, as described in the first exercise. At the end of the sequence, the student should label the tones of the sequence in the order in which they were heard.

3. The therapist should give the student a three-tone target sequence prior to beginning the exercise. For instance, the student could be told that their target sequence is "high high low." Next, the therapist should perform the sequencing task described in Step 2. The student should label the sequence as in Step 2 *and* indicate when the target sequence has been presented.

4. If the Simon® tasks are too difficult, limit the sequence length to two tones. If the Simon® tasks are too easy, increase the number of tones in the sequence.

INFORMAL SPEECH-IN-NOISE DESENSITIZATION (SND) TRAINING

What Is Needed for SND Training?

A CD player (e.g., Walkman™) with standard "iPod" style earbuds (i.e., non-occluding), a book that is unfamiliar to the student, and a CD containing "speech babble" or "restaurant noise" that lasts for 5 minutes or more in duration.

How Is the SND Administered?

For the purposes of this example, it is assumed that a CD player, disc with speech babble, and an unfamiliar book will be used:

■ The therapist should start playing the disc containing speech babble in the CD player and set the volume to soft level. The student should be able to understand approximately 90% of what the therapist is saying while he or she listens to the disc play at this level. The therapist should then make a note of the volume setting on the CD player.

■ After the volume level is established, the therapist should have the student insert the earbuds into both ears and start the CD player. The therapist should then begin to read out loud to the student from a book for about 2 minutes. The therapist should speak at a conversational level approximately five feet from the student. (Note:

The student should not be allowed to view the therapist's face while reading.) At the end of this interval, the therapist should pause the CD player and ask the student questions about what he has just read, in order to assess recognition. The therapist should make the questions relatively challenging to maximize the student's attention to what is being read. The therapist and student should repeat this approximately 10 more times (i.e., for about half an hour). This will conclude the session.

■ At the next session, the therapist should slightly increase the volume level of the speech babble CD prior to beginning reading a book. It is important that an attempt be made to increase the level of the babble at every session. However, the level of the babble should never exceed a conversational level (i.e., the level at which the therapist is reading the book). If this conversational level is reached, the therapist should continue to train the student at this level throughout the duration of the therapy, but increase the complexity of the recognition questions.

INFORMAL DICHOTIC INTERAURAL INTENSITY DIFFERENCE (DIID) TRAINING

What Is Needed for DIID Training?

Two separate audio devices, such as a television, computer, or iPod, along with a set of headphones that can connect to each of the devices. Media (DVDs, CDs, etc.) that have a great deal of dialogue are also needed.

How Is the Informal DIID Administered?

For the purposes of this example, it is assumed that a CD player will be playing an audiobook and a laptop computer will be playing a DVD:

1. The therapist should place the earphone from the CD player into the "weaker" ear and the earphone from the laptop computer into the "stronger" ear.

2. The therapist should start the CD player and set the volume so that the dialogue is close to a conversational level and can easily be understood. After doing this, the therapist should pause the CD player.

3. The therapist should turn on the laptop computer and set the volume to a level at which the student reports sounds being "like a whisper." After doing this, the therapist should pause the computer.

4. The therapist should instruct the student that both of the recordings will start at the same time. The student should be instructed to ignore what is heard from the laptop and attend only to the CD player. The therapist should start both the laptop and the CD player.

5. After about a minute, the therapist should stop the devices and make an informal assessment of how much material the student heard in the *attended* ear. The therapist can do this in a variety of ways, including

asking the student specific questions about key points of the CD's content or asking the student to note how many times a preidentified key word occurred during the recording. (The goal is to have the student perform the DIID at a level at which he or she scores about 50% on the measure used to score performance.)

6. If the student appeared to score significantly above or below 50% score, increase or decrease the intensity level (volume) of the laptop computer accordingly. (*Note:* Never increase the volume to uncomfortable levels!) After making this change, the therapist should repeat Steps 4 through 5. If the student now appears to achieve approximately 50% performance, the therapist should make a note of the level of the CD player and computer, then continue to Step 7.

7. The therapist should instruct the student to attend to the CD player for about 15 minutes. Then the therapist should start both the CD player and laptop. After 15 minutes, a 5-minute break should be provided. Then the therapist should have the student train for an additional 15 minutes.

8. Repeat this exercise approximately three times a week for 2 weeks. After 2 weeks, increase the volume of the laptop computer slightly and repeat Steps 4 through 7.

Educational Audiology in the Real World

Kathryn Tonkovich, MS
Educational Audiologist
Utah Schools for the Deaf and Blind
Salt Lake City, Utah

I graduated with my master's degree in Audiology from the University of Utah in 2001. I have been employed as an audiologist at the Utah Schools for the Deaf and Blind (USDB) for the past nine years. I currently work part time at the Salt Lake City campus, where I routinely test hard of hearing, deaf, visually impaired, blind, and deafblind students in self-contained and consultant programs. I work with children in the Parent Infant Program, ages 0 to 3, as well as with students within the educational programs at USDB, ages 4 to 22 years.

The Utah School for the Deaf and Blind is the state school for children with sensory impairments and has multiple campuses within the state of Utah. The majority of the students who receive services from USDB are hard of hearing or deaf and are enrolled in the school's oral program; however, USDB offers methodology options for parents to choose for their children, including American Sign Language (ASL) and total communication (TC), in addition to the Auditory-Oral option.

There are currently six audiologists employed by the school who serve children in their assigned areas throughout the state. The audiologists perform comprehensive behavioral hearing evaluations, including behavioral observation audiometry (BOA), visual reinforcement audiometry (VRA), and conditioned play audiometry (CPA). Students' personal hearing aids are monitored and analyzed to ensure that they are providing appropriate benefit. USDB audiologists employ verification and validation measures to ensure amplification devices are fit appropriately. USDB also has a loaner hearing aid bank, and loaner hearing aids are routinely issued to children in need of amplification, to use on a trial basis. The audiologists at USDB also collaborate with districts, health clinics, and other professionals throughout the state to ensure that children with hearing impairments have access to appropriate services and support. USDB does not provide routine hearing screenings; however, they are a referral source for several districts around the state of Utah who do not have their own audiologists and need follow-up testing for children who fail their school's hearing screenings.

My other duties include traveling to an assigned area approximately 3 hours away, where I provide audiological testing and services to children in the outreach area. One of the more interesting aspects of my job at USDB involves driving the school's mobile testing unit to the more remote areas of the state that do not have testing facilities. The mobile testing unit is a sound booth contained within a 5th wheel trailer, which is pulled by a large truck.

I also troubleshoot and inspect FM systems, install soundfield FM and infrared systems in classrooms as needed, fit and provide verification of loaner hearing aids, and provide loaner personal FM equipment for children to use on a trial basis. I help provide professional development to teachers and other staff members by presenting in-service trainings on "hot topics," such as cochlear implants and auditory neuropathy. I also participate in regular staff meetings with other members of the IEP team, in order to discuss the needs of individual children. The other professionals include speech therapists, occupational and physical therapists, psychologists, orientation and mobility specialists, vision specialists, and nurses.

Because there are several children on my caseload with cochlear implants, I provide troubleshooting services and equipment checks for students with cochlear implants, as needed. I communicate regularly with the mapping audiologists on the state's cochlear implant team to discuss potential problems and to help ameliorate communication between the medical and educational realms.

I am also an adjunct professor for the University of Utah's Audiology Department and have served as a substitute clinical supervisor there. In my spare time, I volunteer as a board member for the local chapter of the Alexander Graham Bell Association. I became a pediatric/educational audiologist because I enjoy working with children, and I find my work to be incredibly rewarding.

SECTION V

Future Directions

14

School-Based Audiology in the Future

Donna F. Smiley and Cynthia M. Richburg

OBJECTIVES

By the end of this chapter, the reader will be able to:

1. Identify areas of potential advancement for the field of school-based audiology.
2. Identify areas of future challenge for the field of school-based audiology.

INTRODUCTION

The future of school-based audiology holds promise for great advancements, as well as potential challenges. Because no one can predict the future, these ideas and challenges are in no particular order, but are areas in which we see "winds of change." Here, we present some topics for the student of school-based audiology to consider.

EARLY IDENTIFICATION AND HEARING TECHNOLOGY: IMPACT ON STUDENT EDUCATION

The first recommendation for the development and implementation of a universal procedure for early identification and evaluation of hearing impairment came with the Babbidge Report (1965). (This report was also mentioned in Chapter 1 due to its other implications related to school-based audiology services.) The result of that recommendation was the use of a high-risk registry in newborn nurseries, and ultimately led to what we now term *universal newborn hearing screenings*. The goal of universal newborn hearing screenings has been to lower the age of identification of hearing loss in children. The ultimate goal of these screening programs is that all infants with hearing loss be identified before 3 months of age and receive intervention services initiated by 6 months of age (AAP, Joint Committee on Infant Hearing, 2007). This goal would lead to significant improvements over what had been occurring even up to the 1990s, when children born with hearing loss were not being identified until 2½ to 3 years of age (Hoffman & Beauchaine, 2007).

As of this date, all states in the United States have established Early Hearing Detection and Intervention (EHDI) programs, and 43 states have enacted legislation related to hearing screening (National Center for Hearing Assessment and Management, n.d; White, Forsman, Eickwald, & Munoz, 2010). However, the most recent data available from the Centers for Disease Control and Prevention (CDC) indicate that, of the children who were screened at birth and subsequently diagnosed with a permanent hearing loss, only 67% were enrolled in intervention by the age of 6 months (Centers for Disease Control, n.d.). Therefore, the goal of the Joint Committee on Infant Hearing (JCIH) has not yet been achieved, but improvements have been seen over the last 20 years in the early identification and intervention of hearing loss in children. In addition, projects, such as "Accelerating Evidence-Based Recommendations into Practice for the Benefit of Children with Early Hearing Loss" convened by the Agency for Healthcare Research and Quality, will continue to push for advancements in the EHDI systems around the United States (Russ, White, Dougherty, & Forsman, 2010). These continued advancements in the EHDI process, along with existing data that support the premise that children who are early-identified infants with hearing loss demonstrate significantly better language scores than later-identified peers (Calderon, 2000; Calderon & Naidu, 2000; Kennedy et al., 2006; Moeller, 2000; Yoshinaga-Itano, Sedey, Coulter, & Mehl, 1998), will change the profile of students who are d/hh as they enter kindergarten.

Students who are identified, amplified, and provided with appropriate intervention early in their lives potentially will enter kindergarten with language skills commensurate with their hearing peers (Yoshinaga-Itano et al., 1998). This will translate into an improved capacity to remain on target academically. In many cases, these students will not qualify for special education services. They will have a "disability" (i.e., hearing impairment), but it may not adversely affect their academic performance. However, these students will need the support of the school-based audiologist, especially for technical assistance with hearing technology. In addition, school staff will need assistance making appropriate accommodations for these students and using the hearing technology to maximize the student's access to the auditory information of the classroom.

Improvements in hearing technologies continue to make auditory information more accessible to the student who has a hearing loss. As the signal processing continues to improve in all forms of amplification, students' access to oral speech and language will increase exponentially. Better technology, coupled with earlier identification and treatment, promises to produce more and more students who are able to function in the regular education environment with only technical assistance from the school-based audiologist.

The possibility that more students with hearing impairment will come to school equipped to learn (i.e., with appropriate language skills) is both exciting and challenging to the school-based audiologist. Some school districts view school-based audiology as existing only to provide services to students who are served under the umbrella of special education. However, students using hearing aids, bone-anchored implants (osseointegrated devices), cochlear implants, and any other hearing assistance technology most likely will need the support and input of an audiologist. It will be incumbent on school-based audiologists to advocate for a broader definition and scope of school-based audiology services.

SCHOOL-BASED AUDIOLOGY SERVICES FOR ALL STUDENTS

School-based audiologists bring a wealth of knowledge to the school setting about how listening and learning are impacted by noise and classroom acoustics. In addition to serving students with hearing impairment and other documented auditory disorders (e.g., auditory processing disorders), school-based audiologists can provide valuable input for students who

have learning disabilities, reading/literacy difficulties, attention problems, and those learning English as a second language (EAA, 2009).

The goal for school-based audiologists should be that they are seen as a professional who serves *all* students, not just those with hearing impairments. Hearing conservation programs, hearing screening programs, and classroom acoustics are areas in which school-based audiologists can be involved that may allow them the opportunity to be seen outside their typical roles.

CHALLENGES IN THE EDUCATION OF THE DEAF

There have always been conflicting views on how to educate children with hearing loss. Should children who are hearing impaired use sign language or spoken language as their primary mode of communication? Should children who are hearing impaired be educated in public schools or segregated schools for the deaf? Should children who are hearing impaired have a cochlear implant or not? These issues will continue to be debated in the future, and the school-based audiologist will not be immune to them.

Even with advances in identification and amplification, we still have a long way to go to ensure that the language and communication needs of children who are hearing impaired are provided for adequately. Many students with hearing impairment continue to leave school without the necessary skills to be productive adults (Antia, Reed, & Kreimeyer, 2005; Karchmer & Mitchell, 2003). The reader is encouraged to study a report published in 2005 and referred to as the National Agenda (National Agenda Steering and Advisory Committees, 2005). The National Agenda established a set of priorities (stated as "goals") that were designed to instigate significant improvement in the quality and nature of educational services and programs for students who are hearing impaired. These goals were presented as an "agenda," or list of accomplishments, to close the achievement gap that currently exists for children who are hearing impaired. The eight major goal areas of the National Agenda are:

1. **Early Identification and Intervention.** The development of communication, language, social, and cognitive skills at the earliest possible age is fundamental to subsequent educational growth for students who are d/hh.
2. **Language and Communication Access.** All children who are d/hh deserve a quality, communication-driven program that allows children to be educated with peers of similar communication modality, age, and cognitive skills, as well as language proficient teachers and staff who communicate directly in the child's language.
3. **Collaborative Partnerships.** Partnerships that will influence education policies and practices to promote quality education for students who are d/hh must be explored.
4. **Accountability, High Stakes Testing, and Standards-Based Environments.** Instruction for students who are d/hh must be data-driven and focus on multiple measures of student performance.
5. **Placement, Programs, and Services.** The continuum of placement options must be made available to all students who are d/hh, with the recognition that natural and least restrictive environments are intricately tied to communication and language.
6. **Technology.** Accommodations, assistive and adaptive technologies, and emerging technologies must be maximized to improve learning for students who are d/hh.
7. **Professional Standards and Personnel Preparation.** New collaborations and initiatives among practitioners and training programs must address the serious shortage of qualified teachers and administrators.
8. **Research.** Federal and state dollars should be spent on effective, research-based programs and practices.

Several states have developed coalitions to address the deficits in deaf education within their state. You should check your state for initiatives of this kind. The National Deaf Education Project NOW Web site is a good place to start (http://www.ndepnow.org/).

FUNDING FOR SCHOOL-BASED AUDIOLOGY SERVICES

In 1991, Johnson reported the findings of a survey conducted by the Educational Audiology Association to determine the status of audiological services being provided to children with hearing impairments in educational settings. At that time, 11 states reported that third-party billing for audiological services was being used. Johnson (1991) concluded that third-party billing was evolving in many states and that it should be considered a viable source of supplemental funds for schools. She also suggested that schools consider interagency agreements to maximize resources and to eliminate duplication of services and equipment.

Richburg and Smiley (2009) conducted a follow-up survey in 2007 to determine a more current "state" of educational audiology service delivery in the United States. One of the survey questions asked whether or not school-based audiologists generated funds for their case loads. If a respondent indicated that audiologists generate funds within his or her state, the next survey question asked from where those funds came (e.g., Medicaid, insurance, etc.). Twenty-three respondents reported that audiologists in the schools within their states generate funds (AZ, CA, CO, GA, IA, KS, LA, ME, MD, MI, MO, MT, NM, NY, OK, OR, PA, SC, TX, UT, WV, WI, DC). Ten respondents reported that school-based audiologists in their states do not generate funds (AR, DE, FL, HI, IN, NE, OH, VT, VA, WY). Finally, 13 respondents indicated that they were unsure or did not know the answer to the question (AL, AK, IL, KY, MA, MN, NV, NJ, NC, ND, SD, TN, WA). For respondents who reported that funds are generated by school-based audiologists in their states, all 23 indicated that the funds came from the state Medicaid system (one respondent [ME] indicated that she also billed private insurance for audiology services provided in the school settings). Therefore, the findings of this 2007 study indicated an increase in third-party billing since the time of the Johnson (1991) report.

Districts and states continue to seek creative ways to fund services, such as school-based audiology services. Although they are considered to be a related service under IDEIA (2004), many school districts in the United States do not provide the services on site. Instead, they report that children with hearing impairments are managed by a clinical audiologist who will provide the guidance that is needed to educate the child. We would argue that management by a clinical audiologist alone is not sufficient for many students who are d/hh. School-based audiologists should possess a skill-set that includes information about and experience in educating students who are d/hh. These audiologists are the bridge between the student's medical provider and the educational setting.

The American Speech-Language-Hearing Association (ASHA) has a school finance committee that has been charged, in part, with developing strategies and initiatives to ensure appropriate coverage and reimbursement for audiology and speech-language pathology services to children in schools (see ASHA School Funding Advocacy Web site at http://www.asha.org/advocacy/schoolfundadv/). Check this Web site often for updates and issues that may affect funding for school-based audiology services. Currently, ASHA has an available issue brief regarding Early Intervening Services: Implications for Audiologists. Early Intervening Services (EIS) are funded under a new provision in IDEIA (2004), which allow up to 15% of Part B funds to be used for programs and services to nonidentified students who are struggling academically and/or behaviorally and who could benefit from added academic and behavioral support for success in the general education environment. This issue brief notes that, because audiology is a related service in IDEIA 2004, EIS can include audiological services that are designed to prevent problems that may lead to placement in special education.

In addition, ASHA recommends that audiologists consider school-based programs that prevent hearing impairment in children, due to the fact that prevention fits the intent of EIS. Also, under EIS funding, audiologists may be able to contribute their expertise about the importance of classroom acoustics for students who are at risk for academic success (ASHA, n.d.).

State and federal budgets are sure to impact school-based audiology services. Readers are encouraged to become informed of how school-based audiology services are delivered in their states and how those services are funded.

CONCLUSION

Because we do not have a crystal ball and are not capable of predicting the future, anyone's guess is as good as ours' regarding what the future of school-based audiology holds. However, there is one sure thing—change will occur. Whether that change is positive or negative depends largely on the audiologists who practice in school settings, or those who want to practice in school settings.

A concerted effort must be made to better educate school personnel, families of students who are d/hh, and policy makers at federal, state, and local levels. It is vital that school-based audiologists convey to these constituency groups that audiology services are *necessary* for students who are d/hh if benefit from educational efforts is going to be obtained. In addition, administrators and policy makers need to be informed that audiology services are not just for special education. Appropriate acoustical environments and knowledge of hearing loss prevention benefits all students, whether they have a hearing loss or not.

Departments of education, along with the Office of Special Education Programs (OSEP), need to be involved in enforcing a more uniform application of the provision of audiology services in the schools. Specifically for states where little to no school-based audiology services exist, it would seem that there is a need for intervention either at the state or federal level.

School-based audiology is a fulfilling and challenging profession, and it is our hope that the information contained in these chapters has conveyed both the highlights and pitfalls to practicing audiology within the educational system. We hope that these chapters, along with the real-world documentaries provided by educational audiologists across the United States and Canada, give the reader a clear idea of what life as a school-based audiologist is really like.

REFERENCES

American Academy of Pediatrics, Joint Committee on Infant Hearing. (2007). Year 2007 position statement: Principles and guidelines for Early Hearing Detection and Intervention programs. *Pediatrics, 120*(4), 898–921.

American Speech-Language-Hearing Association (ASHA). (n.d.). *Early Intervening Services: Implications for audiologists.* Retrieved from ASHA Web site: http://www.asha.org/uploadedFiles/advocacy/schoolfundadv/EarlyInterveningServicesAud.pdf

Antia, S. D., Reed, S., & Kreimeyer, K. H. (2005). Written language of deaf and hard-of-hearing students in public schools. *Journal of Deaf Studies and Deaf Education, 10*(3), 244–255.

Babbidge, H. (1965). *Education of the deaf: A report to the Secretary of Health, Education, and Welfare by his Advisory Committee of the Education of the Deaf.* Washington, DC: U.S. Department of Health, Education and Welfare.

Calderon, R., (2000). Parental involvement in deaf children's education programs as a predictor of child's language, early reading, and social-emotional development. *Journal of Deaf Studies and Deaf Education, 5*(2), 140–155.

Calderon, R., & Naidu, S. (2000). Further support for the benefits of early identification and intervention for children with hearing loss. *Volta Review, 100*(5), 53–84.

Centers for Disease Control and Prevention (CDC). (n.d.). *Summary of 2009 National CDC EHDI Data.* Retrieved from Centers for Disease Control and Prevention Web site: http://www.cdc.gov/ncbddd/hearingloss/2009-Data/2009_EHDI_HSFS_Summary-508-OK.pdf

Educational Audiology Association. (2009). *School-based audiology advocacy series: School-based audiology services.* Westminister, CO: Author.

Hoffman, J., & Beauchaine, K. (2007). Babies with hearing loss: Steps for effective intervention. *ASHA Leader, 12*(2), 8–9, 22–23.

Individuals with Disabilities Education Improvement Act of 2004. 20 U.S.C. §1400 et seq. (2004).

Johnson, C.D. (1991). The "state" of educational audiology: Survey results and goals for the future. *Educational Audiology Monograph, 2*(1), 71–80.

Karchmer, M., & Mitchell, R. E. (2003). Demographic and achievement characteristics of deaf and hard-of-hearing students. In M. Marschark & P. E. Spencer (Eds.), *Oxford handbook of deaf studies, language and education* (pp. 21–37). New York, NY: Oxford University Press.

Kennedy, C. R., McCann, D. C., Campbell, M. J, Law, C. M., Mullee, M., Petrou, S., Watkin, P., . . . Stephenson, J. (2006). Language ability after early detection of permanent childhood hearing impairment. *New England Journal of Medicine, 354*(20), 2131–2141.

Moeller, M. P. (2000). Early intervention and language development in children who are deaf and hard of hearing. *Pediatrics, 106,* E43.

National Agenda Steering and Advisory Committee. (2005). *The National Agenda: Moving forward on achieving educational equality for deaf and hard of hearing students.* Retrieved from National Agenda Web site: http://www.ndepnow.org/pdfs/national_agenda.pdf

National Center for Hearing Assessment and Management (NCHAM). (n.d.). *EHDI legislation.* Retrieved from NCHAM Web site: http://www.infanthearing.org/legislation/index.html

Richburg, C. M., & Smiley, D. F. (2009). The "state" of educational audiology revisited. *Journal of Educational Audiology, 15,* 63–73.

Russ, S. A., White, K., Dougherty, D., & Forsman, I. (2010). Preface: Newborn hearing screening in the United States: Historical perspective and future directions. *Pediatrics, 126*(S6), S2–S6.

White, K. R., Forsman, I., Eichwald, J., & Munoz, K. (2010). The evolution of Early Hearing Detection and Intervention programs in the United States. *Seminars in Perinatology, 34*(2), 170–179.

Yoshinaga-Itano, C., Sedey, A. L., Coulter, D. K., & Mehl, A. L. (1998). The language of early- and later-identified children with hearing loss. *Pediatrics 102*(5), 1161–1171.

Index